Explorations in African

Political Thought

Explorations in African

Political Thought

<IDENTITY, COMMUNITY, ETHICS>

EDITED BY

Teodros Kiros

WITH A PREFACE BY K. ANTHONY APPIAH

Routledge

NEW YORK   LONDON

Published in 2001 by
Routledge
29 West 35th St.
New York, NY 10001

Published in Great Britain by
Routledge
11 New Fetter Lane
London EC4P 4EE

Library of Congress Cataloging-in-Publication Data

Explorations in African political thought : identity, community, ethics /
[edited by] Teodros Kiros ; with a preface by K. Anthony Appiah.
        p. cm.
    Includes bibliographical references.
    ISBN 0-415-92766-8 (hbk.) — ISBN 0-415 92767-6 (pbk.)
    1. Political science—Africa. I. Kiros, Teodros.

JA84.A33 E96 2000
320'.01—dc21   00-032313

Acknowledgments ◄

I would like to acknowledge the following people for their invaluable help in completing this book: David Gullete for his editorial expertise, George Katsiaficas for his intellectual companionship, John Berg for all his advice in the preparation of the book, and Radhika Khanna for her editorial support. A special thanks to Professor Henry Louis Gates of Harvard University for providing the forum at the Du Bois Institute for the penetrating questions that the Du Bois fellows asked. My wife, May Farhat, an art historian, has helped me in the preparation of this manuscript. A special thanks to her.

Contents ◂

Preface ➤

When I first began teaching philosophy, as a teaching assistant at the University of Ghana at Legon in the mid-seventies, the materials on African philosophy of which I was aware consisted of four sorts of publications. There were journal articles, in journals like *Second Order;* there were a few books written by university-trained philosophers, including J. B. Banquah's *The Akan Doctrine of God* and Willie Abraham's classic *The Mind of Africa;* there were essays, in English, of political philosophy, by leaders such as Kaunda, Nyerere, and Nkrumah. If you included—as many were inclined to do—ethnographic materials on the conceptual worlds of various African peoples gathered in works in anthropology and religious studies, you could expand the resources further. (If you were disposed to go and talk to *nananom,* as we call the elders in Twi, you could gather more from the oral traditions recorded by the anthropologists, and these seemed mostly to be metaphilosophical musings on the question of the existence of "African philosophy.")

So it was with great pleasure that I greeted the publication, nearly twenty years ago, of Kwasi Wiredu's *Philosophy and an African Culture* and then, not long after, an English translation of Paulin Hountondji's *African Philosophy: Myth and Reality.* These books struck me as representing a new level of work in professional university-based philosophy: they assumed a conception of the subject that struck me as appealing. There were philosophers with first-rate training and, even more importantly, first-rate ideas, who were wanting to put these tools to work from their African situations while addressing anyone—African or not—who was willing to listen and listening to anyone—African or not—from whom they thought they might learn.

In the last fifteen years or so, this hopeful trickle has become a fast-flowing stream (if not yet a mighty flood) and African philosophy is now a rich project, contributed to from many directions by scholars with many conceptions of the task but with a shared conviction of the importance and the interest of an African presence in the global discourses of philosophy. In the recent *Routledge Encyclopedia of Philosophy* you can read articles on recent African philosophy in French and English and on work in Yoruba epistemology and Akan philosophical psychology. I could not have imagined, as

I read Wiredu's book for the first time, that within twenty years, at the turn of the new millennium, a book such as this would be possible. Teodros Kiros has gathered together many well-known scholars in what is now an established field and introduces us also to some newcomers whose work shows its vigor and vitality. The diversity of approaches and of questions reflects the same vigor. Together these essays offer material for fruitful reflection that should interest all those—wherever they make their home—who care to think philosophically about moral and political questions.

K. Anthony Appiah
Professor of Afro-American
Studies and Philosophy
Harvard University

African Philosophy:
A Critical/Moral Practice

Teodros Kiros

By African philosophy I understand a set of written texts, when available, as well as orally transmitted texts, that deal with the human condition in Africa on which Africans and non-Africans reflect. The human condition in Africa yearns for the attention of philosophers from all over the world. Philosophers are called upon to engage in thought with care, imagination, and critical commitment. These trying times in Africa require intervention by African philosophers.

Africans and non-Africans alike practice African philosophy, as well as Western philosophy, these days. Ethics, aesthetics, sociopolitical philosophy, and theories of knowledge are its most prominent subjects. So, given the range of subdisciplines, the variety of its practitioners, and the disparate theoretical vantage points, it seems unnecessary to locate a single static essence that might define a unique kind of philosophy. It is pointless to seek a totalizing narrative that captures the essential nature of African philosophy. Clearly, there may be certain entrenched habits and time-honored practices, but these can become oppressive and outmoded. These traditions are not the essences of any philosophy. They are merely important stages of people's self-understanding that sediment themselves in practices and habits. Crises in such traditions invite critical philosophical intervention. African philosophers should not shy away from taking positions on urgent moral and political matters that go beyond addressing the internal needs of the body (food, shelter, and clothing) which I discuss below. Ethnic cleansing in Rwanda, superfluous and expensive wars in Ethiopia and Eritrea, the menacing spread of AIDS throughout Africa—all should be severely critiqued by philosophers. Money is being squandered on unneeded commodities, pretentious skyscrapers are sprouting up in African capitals for the rising middle class, while millions of Africans are wasting away in huts and tin houses along unpaved, rocky streets. Children of all ages flood street corners, only to be whisked away like flies by the shamelessly well-off. In South Africa and elsewhere, AIDS-infected African bodies are being hidden from the international community, while healthy bodies are laboring away without protection and health benefits in the sweatshops of the African world. These deplorable conditions demand philosophical attention. They are insults to rationality. They need to be written about in public fora and discussed in classrooms.

The philosophers below have been chosen precisely because of their willingness to describe phenomenologically these entrenched practices, subject them to critical assessment, and, when necessary, displace them with better visions and research programs. The contributors to this book have already assigned themselves the task of interrogating and contesting the traditions of their own ethnic and linguistic communities. Some investigators have found on closer inspection that what appeared to be static traditions are in fact dynamic, open to critical revision—even transformation—by "new traditions" that promise to serve the people more fairly and humanely. Those values and norms that withstand and pass the severe scrutiny of reason can then be referred to as African philosophies. The contributors to this volume have also responded to the invitation to approach the realities of African thought with critical acumen. Ali Mazrui, Anthony Appiah, Kwasi Wiredu, Ajume Wingo, Ifeanyi Menkiti, and Dismas Masolo reconstruct our view of African traditions, viewing them as viable sources of consensual decision-making, capable of responding to demands for social justice, and of subjecting uncritical nationalism to the challenges of self-critical rationality. With an impressive speculative venture and an illuminating rigor, Anthony Appiah, an internationally admired philosopher of vast interests, tackles the enigmatic topic of ethnicity in Africa by focusing on his native Ghana, and compellingly argues that for the Asanti, ethnicity is a materially and psychologically useful political resource and not merely a part of civil society, immune from political intervention. I introduce Zara Yacob, a seventeenth-century Ethiopian philosopher, as the founder of modernity as rationality within the African experience. I argue that it is Zara Yacob who originally reconceptualized rationality as an amalgamation of reason and emotion, unlike his European counterparts, such as Descartes in France and Locke in England. The book proceeds further on with grand theorizing by the acclaimed Ali Mazrui, who has identified an analytic category called political culture, and insightfully shows how all African worldviews and traditions are marred by it. His sweeping generalities are at once informative and challenging. Mazrui displays his rigor by mapping out a reconstruction of African political thought under the typologies of tribalism, dignitarianism, sagism, and ideology. He sets the stage for professional philosophers to respond to his thoroughgoing and imaginative arguments. Claude Sumner,

George Katsiaficas, Gail Presbey, and Ajume Wingo, on the other hand, cel-ebrate a range of African traditions from which non-Africans can learn to interrogate their own traditions. Sumner achieves this by examining the world of oral wisdom embedded in proverbs, songs, and poems. Presbey per-forms her tasks by listening to the voices of tradition through the highly articulate dialogic interactions of sages. Wingo questions the false assump-tion that African indigenous traditions lack democratic values and structures of governance, suggesting instead that the notion of accountability, a central pillar of democracy, is in fact extant in indigenous traditions. Through a richly woven empirical tapestry, he provides a compelling study of the Nso' people of Cameroon, where individual citizens flourish by nurturing com-munal institutions.

Katsiaficas carefully explicates the seminal contributions of Ibn Khaldun as an African philosopher, defying the earlier racist attempts of some to exclude this peripatetic philosopher from identification with Africa. Katsi-aficas explodes these absurd ideological constructs, exposes Ibn Khaldun's limitations, and yet calls on us to celebrate his original theory of an Ethical Community. Modern communitarians will be stunned by Ibn Khaldun's rich insight into the tapestry of community.

As much as I admire the subtle analytic contributions of the philoso-phers in this volume, I feel compelled to point out that hunger, poverty, inequalities of wealth, and asymmetrical relationships of power are also top-ics that serious philosophy has not traditionally embraced. In my book *Moral Philosophy and Development,* I introduced two moral principles that should guide African philosophy as a moral activity:

> The first principle is the recognition of food, health, shelter, and clothing as inalienable human rights. African resources must be used in such a way that they can, with proper scientific aids, be channeled to eventually (a) eliminate the urgent human needs of poverty and hunger, and (b) address other attendant consequences of mental and physical health, hopelessness and under-motivation.
>
> The second principle is a demand for the absolutely necessary duty humans may have in the recognition of the importance of freedom for those who think and feel that they are unfree. When the basic human material needs of the poor are met, only then may the Africans be able to think about nonmaterial human needs, such as art and religion.[1]

Who should adopt these principles, and how should they guide every-day life?

In my view, they must be taught very early on in African schools, begin-ning in kindergarten and leading to universities. Schoolteachers and uni-versity lecturers must themselves take the lessons of philosophy seriously. The vision that philosophical consciousness must accompany everyday life should be taken to heart and be digested as a core value by those who teach our children at very impressionable ages. Unless the teachers themselves practice philosophy as a moral activity, those whom they teach cannot be expected to believe it. Philosophy becomes a material reality, as Marx taught us, only when it becomes a force—a moral force, I would like to stress.

Philosophy in the African cultural landscape is destined to be a practical/moral task, a task imposed by the tragedies of history: the brutalities of slavery; the exacting torture of colonialism; the menacing despotisms of the early phases of industrialization; the excesses of capitalist indifference to the plight of the poor; the impact of "progress" on the millions of Africans who have not seen or drunk milk or tasted meat for years; the widespread absence of technological facilities with which to combat disease and poverty; and, most acutely, the blindness of the African bourgeoisie to the condition of the poor in Africa. Intelligence, sympathetic imagination, and philosophy as a practical moral activity can overcome all these man-made obstacles.

How can African philosophy pretend to hide itself behind an abstract quest for knowledge and neglect the urgent practical needs of human beings? Do I have to know the epistemic status of hunger before I am reminded of my practical/moral task to participate responsibly as an existentially serious individual in the amelioration of the conditions that produce it?[2] I think not.

Responding to hunger calls only for the stimulation of my moral and practical imagination to act on behalf of the hungry. It need not be preceded by an abstract knowledge of hunger. Ending poverty requires of me only to curtail my selfishness and self-absorption. It does not require me to know what poverty is before I participate in projects ending the conditions that produce it. It is with these ends in mind that I argue that Africans need to verse themselves—as seriously as their American counterparts do—in the work of philosophers, particularly those who are attempting to influence policies made on behalf of citizens. Ironically, it is not the African poor but the self-absorbed African middle class who should be challenged by African philosophy's practical/moral task, and yet they are not. The question is why.

The two principles outlined above can be applicable in practical ways to the lives of the poor to inform the actions of a compassionate state and an active civil society, as Wiredu and Menkiti argue below with arresting illumination. Principles and moral passions might also function as limiting conditions in the lives of the rich, so that their selfish passions can be disciplined by scruples in places where the virtues of morality are absent.

Traditional African societies can be injected with the principles of practical reason and serve the governed via leadership assigned to the most upright individuals in various communities. These leaders must cultivate decentralized public spaces where African citizens who have hitherto been excluded from participating in politics will make their voices heard through electing socially just leaders, and indirectly by participating in collectively constructed institutions with checks and balances, as carefully described by Wiredu and Menkiti.

The first principle of justice commands categorically that food, shelter, and clothing must be available to all human beings in Africa, and the second principle defends freedom as a right to be extended to all Africans. The extension of democracy to all Africans is a possibility devoutly to be wished. Wiredu, Wingo, and Menkiti separately argue that there is a scarcity of democracy in Africa, although there is no scarcity of African traditions from which democratic institutions can be critically drawn. For Wiredu, democratic institutions seem to be absent only because Africa is still "conceptually colonized." Wiredu urges that Africans free themselves from conceptual colonization by returning to some rich African traditions. Traditions can be reconstructed critically to serve as potent sources of moral rejuvenation. A serious respect for Africa's communalistic societies constitutes a promising challenge for modern African thinkers. Africa's communalistic societies provide a sense of belonging, sympathy, and solidarity as alternatives to modernity's excessive individuality and insecurity. Communalism also provides instruments for building consensus through compromise and extended negotiations that come to an end when a working consensus is reached. Constructing consensus, argue Wiredu and Wingo, is not a mechanical process but a deliberative activity of reason, nor does it lead to the suppression of disagreements, as is often mythologized. Consensus building is always propelled by practical reason's attempt to persuade the dissenters. All participants can seek to persuade each other by the force of their wisdom, age, and eloquence, as Wiredu makes clear. In a masterful piece, Wingo demonstrates how democracy informs the everyday lives of decision-makers in his native Cameroon.

The nature of philosophical activity in Africa has been guided by both strict and broad orientations, as Sumner and Masolo argue. For Sumner, in the seventeenth century Zara Yacob exemplified the strict definition of philosophy; according to Masolo, Onyango Ayany is a twentieth-century model critical theorist of African enlightenment. Ayany participated in critiques of sacrosanct and self-enclosing African traditions. Exactly like Zara Yacob before him, he challenged the dead weight of tradition through the vehicle of self-originated principles of intelligence. Zara Yacob and Ayany are the articulate voices of reason in the discourse on modernity in African culture. Sumner and Presbey compellingly argue that orally transmitted folk wisdom and the insight of sages are philosophical interventions of high quality. After a series of seminal books on Zara Yacob, Sumner had promised the philosophical community a major work on the philosophical significance of orally transmitted wisdom. He has provided us with a penetrating analytic/hermeneutic examination of the proverbs, songs, and poems of the Oromo of Ethiopia. I hope readers will be amply rewarded by this long-awaited study with far-reaching impact on the status of all oral traditions as modes of philosophical reflection. This study belongs to what Presbey calls wisdom philosophy. Presbey takes Masolo to task for measuring the philosophical quality of sage philosophy by the severe measure of criticality and analytic acuity, the defining features of strict philosophy. Presbey is not convinced that Sumner's categories of strict and broad senses of philosophical styles are satisfactory devices for distinguishing between differing types of thought. I find these distinctions heuristic devices that can provide an economical framing of thought. In addition, Katsiaficas takes us to North Africa, which has for too long been associated with the Middle East. We are introduced to the theories of Ibn Khaldun as an original theorist of community, a community that fulfills the human yearning for belonging without depriving the individual of a sufficient sense of autonomy. Katsiaficas makes some telling points about the striking similarities between Ibn Khaldun and Hegel as theorists of ethical communities.

The contributions in this volume demonstrate the richness of African philosophy. These philosophers address perennial cultural, political, and ethical problems that plague the human condition in Africa. The authors seek to show that African philosophy can serve African people as a moral activity guided by the principles of practical reason in addressing the underlying problems of African social, political, and economic institutions. They examine the philosophical status of oral traditions in the proverbs, songs, and poems of the Oromo in Ethiopia; ethnicity is for the first time critically analyzed as a political resource; it is argued that governance is accountability; African traditions are revealed as sources of consensus building, an example of democratic, reflective deliberation; critiques of cultural traditions and uncritical rationalism in African philosophy are treated with great care; it is proposed that social justice can serve the African people as a potentially normative answer to Africa's current political malaise; Ibn Khaldun is compellingly presented as an African philosopher of a rational/ethical approach to community; and finally, Presbey provides an analytical exposition of the wisdom in oral traditions and in sagacity. Thus concludes this rich anthology of some of the best commentators on African reality, past and present.

The Wisdom of African Sages

Gail M. Presbey

WISDOM AND PHILOSOPHY: BACKGROUND OF THE SAGE PHILOSOPHY PROJECT

This paper will argue that there are many wise sages in Africa who merit further study by philosophers and others. H. Odera Oruka of the University of Nairobi was motivated to record the sages' wisdom, which had been passed down locally and orally, so that the larger philosophical community could become aware of them and benefit from their knowledge. In academic circles, Odera Oruka's project, called "sage philosophy," became embroiled in the larger controversy over whether there was philosophy in Africa. In fact, critics such as Dismas Masolo and Paulin Hountondji suggest that the entire sage philosophy project started off on the wrong foot insofar as it was a defensive reaction to European claims, as well as the claims of negritude thinkers like Senghor, that Africa was innocent of rational thought and philosophy.[1] Questions arise about the mixed motivation of the project—was it really to share the wisdom of the sages, or just to tell scoffers "you are wrong about Africa"? Several direct quotes from Odera Oruka himself show that the project started back in 1977 as a reaction to a challenge from skeptics. However, considering the sustained growth of the movement, it has surely survived and outgrown its initial external instigation.[2]

Embedded in this debate about the status of the rural sages is a larger question of the relationship of philosophy to wisdom. It is popularly considered to be the case that prior to philosophy in the "formal" sense there had flourished in several cultures wisdom literature concerned with the "art of living." Ancient Egyptian wisdom, such as the sayings of Ptahhotep in 2500 B.C., is described in such a manner. Often the works of ancient Chinese thinkers like Confucius and Mencius, as well as of ancient Hindu writers and Hebrew scripture writers, are described as wisdom literature because of their emphasis on maxims and counsels for the conduct of life. Insofar as rural African sages fit for the most part the paradigm of others considered "wisdom" thinkers, they become marginalized, as do the others, according to those upholding strict or narrow definitions. A debate has been raging regarding whether the marginalization of wisdom thinkers from what is now considered to be philosophy proper is justified or if it is, rather, another example of Europe choosing its own narrow conception as a standard by which all others should be measured.

The Western tradition of philosophy, however, has not always been so distant from the measure of the philosopher as someone who embodies wisdom. John Kekes in his book *Moral Wisdom and Good Lives* notes that the *Oxford English Dictionary* defines wisdom as "Capacity of judging rightly in matters relating to life and conduct."[3] The word "philosophy" itself, in its etymological origin, means "lover of wisdom," and the Pythagoreans who coined the word attempted to live in harmony with the cosmos. Odera Oruka argues that Pythagoras was being too humble in stating that no human can possess wisdom, that only the gods can, therefore humans can only love (or long for) wisdom. Odera Oruka argues that it is important not only to love wisdom, but also to possess and practice it. For him, a philosopher is one who has an intellectual concern for wisdom, and who has this concern not just occasionally, but as an integral part of life.[4]

Socrates saw both understanding virtue and living a virtuous life to be the goals of a philosopher. Stoic and Epicurean philosophers also had living a good life as the goal of their philosophizing. However, modern philosophy departed from that tradition, and now many philosophers produce works that have little or no bearing on practical life. As Brand Blanshard describes many notable modern philosophers, "their standing as purveyors or exemplars of wisdom bears no fixed relation to their eminence as philosophers. . . . Furthermore, by reason of unhappy temperament, some philosophers of name and influence, such as Rousseau, have been far from notable exemplars of wisdom in either controversy or conduct."[5] One could speculate that Socrates would be aghast if he knew that philosophers after him would see the search to live well and wisely as an optional, rather than necessary, part of philosophizing.

Odera Oruka himself praised the sages he had met for their wisdom and suggests that the best of them can be called sage-philosophers, since they use their wisdom (insight) for the ethical betterment of the community (sagacity). According to his terminology, Socrates is also a sage philosopher, and sage philosophers are to be valued over the "mere" technical philosophers, who have divorced philosophical speculation from the immediate questions of life.[6]

According to Blanshard, wisdom requires reflectiveness and judgment. Reflectiveness is "the habit of considering events and beliefs in the light of their grounds and consequences."[7] A wise, reflective person will have a broader view of grounds and consequences, causes and effects, than the average person. This means the wise person will more easily detect superstition and narrow-mindedness, and will have keener foresight than others. Judgment, Blanshard notes, seems to be intuitive; yet one should be cautious, for what seems intuitive could in reality be habit or prejudice. Experience can influence judgment, which is why age is often associated with wisdom. As Blanshard explains: "Experience, even when forgotten beyond recall, leaves its deposit, and where this is the deposit of long trial and error, of much reflection, and of wide exposure in fact or imagination to the human lot, the judgment based on it may be more significant than any or all of the reasons that the judge could adduce for it."[8] The sages demonstrate both qualities, reflection and judgment. Reflection is explicitly mentioned in their discernment process; that their judgments are respected is verified by the extent of their following and reputation.

WANJOHI AND MASOLO ON WISDOM AND PHILOSOPHY

Two former Kenyan colleagues of Odera Oruka, Gerald Wanjohi and Dismas Masolo, have both concerned themselves in their respective works with the definition of philosophy. They have also both been critical of Odera Oruka's sage philosophy project. Both seem to want to delimit philosophy's range, to exclude "wisdom" from philosophy proper. Wanjohi, in his study of Gikuyu proverbs, wants to sort out those that are merely "sapiential," or wise, from those that are philosophical. Wise proverbs either literally or symbolically state a universal truth or give practical counsel or advice. (Interestingly enough, he also lists Aristotle's wise sayings, to show that philosophers sometimes engage in wisdom.) A philosophical proverb, in contrast, is a well-known statement in a language, either literal or symbolic, that is easily amenable to further or deeper analysis. Wisdom is practical and technical, while philosophy is theoretical and speculative. Wanjohi admits that it is not a strict distinction, and it is good that he admits it, for if one were to look at his list of proverbs where he has sorted out the wise from the philosophical, one would not necessarily see the distinction easily.[9]

Wanjohi is perhaps getting his distinctions from Aristotle, who contrasted philosophical wisdom with practical wisdom (*sophia* and *phronesis*). Practical wisdom helps us improve human lives, both our own and those of others.[10] It is important to note that both forms of wisdom are valuable for all persons and specifically the philosopher. One should not draw the mistaken conclusion that *phronesis* is "merely" wisdom and not philosophical, or not a pursuit worthy of a philosopher. To think that philosophy is only about theory, not practice, would be to indulge in the worst stereotypes of philosophy as irrelevant ivory-towerism, as Kwame Gyekye warns against.[11] Gyekye insists that for Aristotle, the reason we want to know what virtue is, is so that we can become good. So practice cannot be divorced from the philosophical life.[12] Philosophers' study of the wisdom of proverbs, as well as the wisdom of sages, is therefore appropriate and needed.

As Jay van Hook insightfully states regarding several African philosophers' attempts to distinguish philosophy from nonphilosophy: "The preoccupation with disciplinary boundaries and disciplinary autonomy is a typically Western concern—one which is of doubtful credit to its inventors and perpetrators; and its self-evident usefulness to Africans is by no means clear."[13]

In a discussion of Placide Tempels in his 1994 work *African Philosophy in Search of Identity,* Masolo explains his own definition of philosophy. He states that there are two senses of philosophy: the ordinary sense, involving commitment to particular opinions, and the second sense, of commitment to investigation. The second sense aims at understanding principles, not just formulating them, and therefore necessarily becomes an academic study. Masolo thinks Tempels meant that Bantu-speaking people philosophized in the first sense, not the second. In other words, Bantu-speaking people had a worldview to which they were committed. But people thought Tempels meant Bantu-speaking people philosophized in the second sense, and so rallied to defend or denounce him. Masolo considers it ironic that Tempels was attacked by those who thought he had given away their monopoly on critical philosophy (when he hadn't), and was defended by those who thought he meant that Africans philosophized in this second sense (when he didn't).[14] Masolo's analysis regarding Tempels, his defenders, and his detractors is insightful. However, the passage shows that Masolo thinks that professional philosophers should be engaged in philosophy only in the second, "more important," academic sense, since the first or ordinary sense isn't even worth fighting over. But as we discussed earlier, to think so means that philosophy and the life of the philosopher are delineated much more narrowly than when the discipline began thousands of years ago. Should not one use critical inquiry to discern a set of opinions or a justified belief that leads to a good, wise, and just life? Another effect of his delineation is that the Bantu-speaking people are not considered philosophical (in the "important" second sense), moving the beginnings of African philosophy, therefore, to the last fifty years with the beginning of academic philosophy, giving Africa a very "late start" in the field.

Masolo himself notes that the idea of philosophy has changed throughout time. Tempels was influenced by existentialism and phenomenology, which were challenging the Vienna Circle that at the time dominated philosophical thought, and had a very narrow concept of philosophy as ratiocination. Tempels, like others, wanted a new conception of philosophy. Existentialists viewed philosophy as a practical enterprise growing from one's life and history rather than as a removed special discipline. Heidegger insisted that philosophical thinking is meditative, not calculative. "Questioning," "reflecting," and "meditating" became the new words to describe philosophizing. French-speaking intellectuals regarded the Bantu-speaking people as exemplary evidence of the existentialist subject, who is antiscientific but highly expressive, intuitive, and in touch with the richness and meaning of life—an expression of what Heidegger calls the unveiling of facticity, our experience of being before we have any reflection upon it.[15]

Although we may agree that it is an overstatement to call each Bantu-speaking person a natural, effortless philosopher in the Heideggerian sense (by virtue of their sharing a worldview), certainly it would not be far-fetched to say that certain persons in their community, who devote themselves consistently to reflections on the meaning of life and the search for wisdom, are philosophers. That is what the sage philosophy project claims. Therefore philosophy as questioning, reflective, meditative rather than "calculative," as Masolo describes Heidegger's ideas, is a helpful, fuller definition of philosophy and helps us to see more readily how the sages fit into the global tradition.

Masolo thinks there is a clear distinction between technical philosophy and deep wisdom. The question left unanswered is: Does Masolo think that the deep wisdom of Africa is worth learning? One gets the impression that he is devoted only to the second, academic sense of philosophy, which practices a considerable amount of detachment from any specific opinions, devoted to inquiry for inquiry's sake alone. This would mean that community-based, nonacademic Africans who are committed to opinions and the search for deep wisdom could be only subject matter for technical philosophy rather than philosophers themselves. In fact, from this position he repeatedly criticizes Odera Oruka's sage philosophy project, finding little proof that traditional rural Africans share his commitment, as an academic philosopher, to scrutinizing ideas.

Although Odera Oruka insists that philosophic sages hold only beliefs that satisfy rational scrutiny, Masolo charges that his examples do not live up to his claims. For example, Paul Mbuya throws out a mere commonsense metaphysical statement without much elaboration. To count as philosophic, Masolo wonders, is it enough for a statement to be nonmediocre or clever? He calls on Towett and Wiredu, who say that the difference between everyday thought and philosophy is that philosophy entails greater elaboration and sophistication of ideas. He agrees that the strength of philosophy lies in sustained explanation. Masolo concludes that "neither the form nor the content of traditional African wisdom is 'philosophical' in any exceptional way."[16]

But is Masolo's stance fair to the numberless reflective, wise thinkers, lost to us by name, whose wisdom lives on in Africa's oral tradition? As Gyekye and Segun Gbadegesin argue, African communal wisdom derives from ongoing critical debate and rational inquiry among individuals, which only later is popularly formulated and remembered, perhaps unquestioningly, as oral tradition. Thus they would argue that popular wisdom itself witnesses to earlier philosophic activity conforming to Masolo's second sense of philosophy.[17]

Such a position could be strengthened by reference to W. T. Jones. Jones explains that a philosophy of life attempts to provide answers about the ultimate value and meaning of life. He suggests that part of the criterion for showing that a philosophy is satisfactory is that a set of answers has satisfied a large number of people for a relatively long time. However, he further stipulates that endurance is not the sole criterion, for answers must satisfy a critical intelligence, must be accepted because they are reasoned, not based solely on the authority of the one posing them. He also notes that answers must be consistent with each other and with human experience.[18] This paper suggests that many sages put forward philosophies of life that are well respected by their communities, as is attested to by the fact that an informal consensus regarding the wisdom of the sages is formulated.

Gyekye also challenges the idea that academic philosophers do nothing but commit themselves to inquiry, pure and simple. There is room for belief in philosophy, which is shown by historical movements in philosophy. A glance at movements like "Platonism," "Cartesianism," and "Kantianism" would show that philosophy can in some sense be a "system of belief," a commitment to opinions that are judged to be sound by the philosopher, and part of a tradition larger than the mere individual.[19] To think of the philosopher as someone with no allegiances except to the method of critical, rational inquiry would perhaps be a case of Cartesianism—following Descartes's opinions.

Ochieng-Odhiambo suggests from his reading of Masolo's criticisms that it is not Masolo's intention to condemn all attempts at constructing a sage philosophy as futile or misguided. Rather, Masolo is waiting to be shown that there are sages that are deeply thoughtful in their reflections and rationally systematic in their insights into life. Short of such proof, Masolo will persist in his estimation of the sages as clever, insightful people who fall short of the title "philosopher," in which case Odera Oruka's claim to have found philosophers in rural Kenya will be taken to be unfounded.[20] In this spirit, we will explore the ideas of several sages to find the wisdom contained within. This paper will take up Masolo's challenge and show the sages to be wise philosophers, if only philosophy is considered in the wider sense of including both rational scrutiny and deep wisdom.

WHAT DID SOME SAGES SAY THAT WAS VALUABLE?

In the spirit of searching for the valuable wisdom of Africa, the rest of this paper will be devoted to expounding upon the wisdom of several rural Kenyan sages, on topics that were found to be close to the heart of many of them. The following sages were either part of Odera Oruka's original study, or others whom Odera Oruka's key project researchers, such as Chaungo Barasa, had identified in their area. When sages I interviewed were asked to explain what they see as their special role in society, and their general goal in their own lives, several reported, as Odera Oruka had noted, that their lives were devoted to the betterment of their communities, and their service to various individuals in that community. The common themes centered on the art of living in community happily. Two main aspects of that theme are:

1) The best life to live is the selfless one of helping others in need. Although prudential arguments are sometimes made in support of these actions (they will help *you* in the long run), it is often argued that one can find happiness in the act of giving. There is an emphasis on nurturing feelings of love and compassion for others.

2) All individuals in a community must learn to live a life where strong negative emotions are controlled. For example, jealousy is the cause of many contemporary problems. People who are angry out of jealousy need help and understanding, not condemnation. The surest way to avoid feeling jealous oneself is to have a proper understanding of one's own self-worth and to realize that riches and fame are of limited value.

THE SAGES

JONES LOZENJA MAKINDU was born in 1926 in Maragoli, Kenya. She sums up her philosophy by the exhortation to love others, and she suggests that loving others is wisdom in itself. If one did so, jealousy (which she considers to be the biggest obstacle to wisdom) would not arise.

Makindu states that wisdom is a gift from God to everyone, but only some put in the personal effort to develop that wisdom. Her own process of living and cultivating wisdom suffered setbacks from personal misfortunes (children dying, her husband paralyzed) and jealousy (of other women opposed to her development schemes). Yet the problems challenged her to further achievement. To pursue wisdom, she insists, is success in itself (even if it leads to trouble). In her own life she has lived out this philosophy of love in many instances, from the routine and recurrent work of reconciling battling spouses and family members to the more political situation of having Ugandan refugees accepted by her local chief and their needs accommodated within her community. Her work for women's empowerment has involved building a girls' secondary school.

Her reflections on her successes show that she has been a reflective and careful observer of human emotion and behavior. She knows how to get people to open up and tell her what's important to them, and she knows how to listen. Then she can find compassion in her heart to put forward the effort to help the person, no matter how unpleasant they are or how disliked by their community. As her friend Rose Mugandia, who says that she shares Makindu's philosophy of love, explains, one should never isolate the person who is feeling wrath or jealousy. Instead, one must approach such a person with love, and find out their problem.[21]

WANYONYI MANGULIECHI of Bungoma, Western Province, Kenya, often speaks at funerals, where he beseeches the relatives to continue to take care of each other as their forebears had always done. He is repeatedly called to comfort, console, and counsel the bereaved. Secondly, he is called to mediate in quarrels, where he reconciles the parties. Thirdly, he goes to schools where he teaches students "the ways of the world" or meets with other community leaders to chart out a "meaningful future." In his mediation work he emphasizes his need to reflect quietly after hearing all persons involved. He searches his mind for a relevant example from Bukusu oral history and rules so as to make his message clearer to others, but, as he explains, the tradition is broad and rich, with much leeway for alternative interpretations, so the applying of tradition to a contemporary context is not mechanical. In addition to being embroiled in the specifics of certain contexts, he speculates on the common causes of certain recurrent problems in the community. He explains:

> To do away with these societal conflicts, I always preach to people about the necessity of doing away with jealousy, envy, and bitterness and vengefulness against others, and I stress the need for unity as a prerequisite to social peace and progress, as envy and greed can only bring turmoil to all. I seek to reach all by arguing that we are the ones who bring evil to ourselves. For instance, if one is rained upon one ought not to blame the rain as it rains on him who sees. It is noteworthy that before it rains, clouds are formed and one who sees them should seek shelter. Just before it starts raining, it thunders for those with ears to hear also to seek shelter, if they had no eyes to see the clouds. In my counseling about the evils of society, I proceed along this symbolism.[22]

So we could say that Manguliechi's constant goal for himself is to challenge the members of his community to moral character development.

ALI MWITANI MASERO was born in 1939 at Emalaha, Utonga, Kakamega District.[23] As he explains, people come to him first and foremost because he is a unifier and he brings together those who have disagreed or have had mis-understandings. In addition to people seeking him out, he also involves him-self in conflicts that he witnesses. Masero is also a healer, so people come to him for both physical and emotional well-being.

Key to his ability to resolve issues is his knowing how to prod people in conversation to get at the heart of an issue instead of skirting the most important points. Masero defends his practice of giving people advice, for he explains that often what they think is best in the situation is wrong. Also aid-ing him is his caring nature. He explains that his desire to help others is something he gained from his father, who would take in destitutes and, with his mother's support, bring them up and even give them land. He himself has taken in a young girl named Habiba, whose mother died at childbirth. He expects that those who have been helped will later help others as well.[24]

NYANDO AYOO was ninety-two years old when he was interviewed in 1995. He has spent his life in the town he founded as a young man, Sega, in Ugenya, western Kenya. Odera Oruka has known this man since he was young, as they come from the same area. Ayoo describes his philosophy as one based on generosity. Inspired by the example of his father, who fed des-titute people during a famine, as a young boy he began bringing water to thirsty travelers who were going on foot between Kampala, Uganda, and Kisumu, Kenya. Later he set up a small hotel. As he explains, "Whenever I came across a sick person, or a mad person, then I would invite him/her home and give him/her water, food and a place in which to sleep. The fol-lowing day I would give the person some money to use in the course of the journey." As Odera Oruka reminisced about Ayoo's developing friendship with Turnbull, a missionary in the area, "they would stay here even at night over the fire, warming themselves. Occasionally, they would go to his rural home together with the Catholic sisters and he would give them either sheep or goats and bananas. And he just enjoyed doing such kind of things."

Ayoo is concerned about the present generation. He warns, "The people of today just like laughing at others." Compassion is gone. As Odera Oruka explained:

> He does not feel good with the spirit of this new generation because it is a spirit which is only for accusing others. It is a spirit which wants to be loved. But according to him, his spirit was not for him saying "I want to be more impor-tant than another person." He did not feel that when somebody is succeeding then that is putting him down. He always enjoyed and shared any success of his neighbor and he sympathized with his neighbor who met failures. He did not detach himself from others and believed that his success and happiness were not to be separated from those of others. Ayoo explains that just as God loves all equally, so he also tried to practice such love and compassion toward all. "Peo-ple should live in love," he insists.[25]

ANALYSIS

As John Kekes explains, "Moral wisdom is not merely disinterested knowledge of what is true or right; it requires also that the knowledge should actually be used for making good lives for ourselves."[26] Kekes calls moral wisdom a second-order virtue in that its goal is "the development of our character in a desirable direction by strengthening or weakening some of our dispositions."[27] But moral wisdom is concerned with ends as well as means, and so "it has among its tasks the critical scrutiny of the conception of a good life which motivates us to act according to moral wisdom."[28]

I suggest that the sages mentioned here have been practicing and articulating a moral wisdom, valuable both to their own communities as well as the larger global community. They are engaged in character formation by counseling love and control of fear, anger, and jealousy. They have explicated a conception of the good life that will motivate persons to follow a life of moral wisdom.

Although these themes may not be unique to Africa, and could be found in the wisdom of thinkers from many parts of the world, there is some uniqueness in each individual sage's way of communicating their message and living out their philosophy. One must be careful in balancing the uniqueness against the universality of the message. The sages have developed their philosophical opinions based on their own context, in rural western Kenya. But it would be mistaken to think that their insights, therefore, are limited in context. As Henrietta Moore explains:

> Anthropologists have always been happy to see local people as producers of local knowledge . . . but there was very little question of such knowledge being valorized outside the local domain. . . . The implicit assumption was therefore that the theories of non-Western peoples have no scope outside their context. . . . Anthropologists, for all their concern with local understanding and specificities, do not habitually view the people they work with as producers of social science theory as opposed to producers of local knowledge.[29]

This attitude resulted in what Moore calls "the parochialization of all theories other than those promoted by western science."[30] She is concerned that the deconstructive/postmodernist turn has ironically reinforced this idea that, since all knowledge can only be local, the ability for African ideas to challenge Western science or social science is limited or impossible. Moore suggests that "It is imperative that anthropology should recognize that local knowledge can be part of a set of knowledge properly pertaining to political economy and the social sciences, and can thus be comparative in scope, as well as international in outlook."[31]

It is on this topic of who produces knowledge for whom that Dismas Masolo has encouraging words for the sage philosophy approach. As he explains:

> sage philosophy addresses the crucial question of who produces knowledge in the modern hierarchised social formations. . . . The idea of sage philosophy suggests that professional philosophers ought to take sufficiently into account the problems posed by the sages in the course of their conversations, not just once but always. . . . By virtue of a proposal that seeks to narrow down the opposition between, on the one hand, the academy as the institutionalized production center and, on the other, the periphery as the location of pure consumers, Odera strips the academy of its colonial definition and status.[32]

There is much that Kenyan thinkers can teach those of us in other parts of the world.

The message of the sages goes beyond Kenya. Although the emphasis on giving, for example, happens in a unique context—an economy based on family obligations—and it would seem in a contemporary capitalist context to be mere foolishness to give away one's possessions, it is not necessarily so. Christmas gift buying and giving, as well as individual and corporate giving to charities, are known to be crucial to the functioning of the U.S. economy. Scenarios of "what if everyone gave?" would help the economy as much as ones where everyone spends on themselves. A generous social net of programs for needy children, the elderly, and the unemployed, whether run by government or private charity, would help the economy as much, or more than, military spending. All of these factors would have their influence even within the current capitalist framework. Such parallels aren't exact but hint that a spontaneous ethic of generosity could be a step in the right direction toward eradicating poverty and economic disparity in the United States. Nowadays there are Social Security and other forms of insurance to bureaucratically replace the act of one person giving to another. But has this justified a culture of not giving, of distancing oneself from those in need in the United States? Once budgets for social programs are cut due to citizen apathy, the circle of "not giving" is complete.

The sages' works of wisdom can be used to criticize our own society as well as their own. Traditions of giving can be perverted in contemporary Kenya. For example, "Harambee" community fund-raising has been used to generate money for medical emergencies, school fees, and other worthy causes; but now in some cases, people have been known to use such funds to buy themselves a new car. Practices of showing appreciation through the giving of gifts can be turned into governmental graft and corruption. Such discarding of moral values in pursuit of consumer luxuries in Kenya reflects its source in the consumerist values of the United States. As Christopher Lasch has pointed out, the Enlightenment ideal of progress has been perverted into a frantic consumer culture based on the ceaseless "transformation of luxuries into necessities." The culture has become obsessed with "making it." While many are willing to become successful careerists, most have neglected to follow a "calling," as Ayoo exemplifies, to do something special with their lives.[33]

Lasch explains in his most recent book that each generation must provide for its children, not just in the material sense, but more particularly by imparting to them a sense of value, thought, and feeling that would help them to find a meaningful life.[34] This is definitely the message of the above-quoted sages —they hope to impart a sense of value and meaning to the younger generation.

But where is this practice of sagacious wisdom to be located in regard to contemporary philosophy? Several academic philosophers have insisted that the gap be bridged between academic philosophy and wisdom. For example, Haig Khatchadourian complains of contemporary philosophy's "abdication of wisdom," noting in America the "profound impotence on the part of philosophy to influence the course of public affairs or even the private lives of this country's citizens."[35] He thinks that this impotence is linked to its abandonment of the theoretical quest for wisdom in both its current ordinary meaning as well as Socrates' understanding of it. While Socrates, Plato, and Aristotle took wisdom to be "knowledge of the highest things," everyday language usage describes the wise person as having "great insight into himself and other human beings, and into human nature and life in general; hence he is able to see life 'steadily and as a whole.' "[36] The wise person has "vision" in the sense of the exceptional ability to take the long or distanced view of things. In the twentieth century, humanity has neglected moral and existential self-knowledge, indulging in perfection of means while being confused in ends. Khatchadourian calls upon Western philosophers to help create a global consciousness by increasing mutual interaction and understanding by philosophers in Asia, Africa, the Middle East, and Latin America. Noting that philosophers cannot be spectators from the sidelines of life, he insists they must once again be seekers of wisdom.[37] Odera Oruka's sage philosophy project would easily and vitally be part of this proposed directive.

There are other champions of the movement to reassert wisdom's centrality to philosophy.[38] But such a movement is not unproblematic, and Kai Nielsen brings up several important criticisms. He suggests that it is not at all clear what we are searching for in searching for wisdom. Our societies do not have clear and incontestable paradigms of wisdom. Wisdom is hard to define; wisdom is a virtue, but a rare one compared to prudence, which

Nielsen calls a routine virtue widely possessed. Therefore the examples put forward by philosopher Patrick McKee's students, of wise acts being "asking for a ride home when you have been drinking, avoiding addictive drugs, staying in school, guarding your money from impulsive spending" could be called prudential, reasonable, or sensible rather than wise. Nielsen agrees with Godlovitch, who explains that wisdom is not a way of acting but a way of being; it is a state of mind rather than a readiness to act.[39]

The sharpest attack against wisdom, Nielsen explains, comes from the philosophers of modernity (like Hobbes and Hume) who think that there is no meaning of life to be discovered; therefore, what the wisdom philosophers like Socrates, Plato, Aristotle, the Stoics, Montaigne, Spinoza, and Schopenhauer seek is "nothing more than metaphysical incoherences generated by a longing to escape contingency and to gain an impossible objectivity and certainty."[40] Nielsen therefore concludes that what the wisdom philosophers want cannot be had; there can be no undying and objective truth about human life.

Despite his concerns, Nielsen clearly expresses the agreement that philosophy should be concerned with wisdom. While cautioning that wisdom is a matter of indifference or even disdain to many philosophers, and agreeing that it would be absurd and repellent for philosophers to set themselves up as sages,[41] he nevertheless argues that philosophers and sages should join forces to provide a guide for the perplexed.[42] Here is what he has in mind. What do sages or wisdom philosophers have to offer humanity? While many wise sayings are "platitudinous," sometimes seeming obvious and trivial, mundane or moldy, there is nevertheless a "way of viewing or responding to these truisms which yields conceptual space for a viable conception of wisdom." Kierkegaard notes how easily we can live in a forgetful or double-minded way, so that we are not mindful and do not take to heart the truth of truisms. As Godlovitch explains:

> Where the wise emerge amidst this apparent banality of content is in taking such knowledge seriously, recognizing how very stably true it is in the midst of passing deception so easily winning its victims.... The truisms of the wise gain respect not only because we are prone to accept their truth, but because the nature of that truth renders insignificant whatever screen of revealed illusions we have used to shield ourselves from it. The sayings of the wise are thus subtle provocations directed at our tendency to illusion.[43]

In the case of the Kenyan sages, whether it is Jones Makindu asserting that loving everyone is wisdom itself and would lead to the eradication of most social problems; Wanyonyi Manguliechi insisting that individuals should use foresight to avoid problems and suffering; Ali Mwitani Masero claiming that one should listen compassionately to all sides in a dispute; or Nyando Ayoo suggesting that each person be generous with others in need, the value of the statements isn't in their uniqueness. Indeed, one might complain that the sayings sound trite or banal, no matter how good the intentions behind them. But as Nielsen and Godlovitch point out, such sayings of the wise can challenge our own self-deception and illusions, since we repeatedly forget the truth in the truisms. Insofar as we think that love is dispensable, that scapegoats can be found for problems caused by ourselves, that understanding of others can be dispensed with as long as they can be forced to do things, that we are entitled to self-centeredness—all constant temptations in our present society, and all shortsighted—we will need the sages to say the obvious in a compelling and gripping way to get our attention and to spur us to pursuit of a wisdom that will help us live, individually and collectively.

The Proverb and Oral Society

Claude Sumner

INTRODUCTION

When, in December 1976, I convened in Addis Ababa the first Pan-African Seminar exclusively devoted to the topic of African philosophy, "The Existence and Nature of African Philosophy—Problématique d'une philosophie africaine," I presented to the participants gathered at Africa Hall the results of my research on the written philosophical literature of Ethiopia, a work that was far advanced at that time, but still incomplete. Yet even as far back as 1976 I announced publicly and to the whole community of Ethiopian/African scholars assembled on this occasion that no study on Ethiopian thought could be complete if it limited itself to its written formulation:

> In the expression "Ethiopian Philosophy" there are two terms and both need clarification. Modern Ethiopia can be the object of many distinctions: geographically, between the high plateaus and the lower plains with their deserts; linguistically, between the Semitic, Hamitic and Nilotic populations; religiously, between the Christians, the Moslems and the Jewish Falashas [not to mention the traditional beliefs, referred to in this present study]. In our research into the philosophy of Ethiopia, our methodological approach must be defined and delineated. Ethiopian philosophy is expressed in both oral and written language.
>
> Now, written texts offer great advantages: in them Ethiopians themselves present their own world view: there is less place for subjective interpretation and there are greater opportunities for a well-documented investigation. This does not mean that oral expressions of Ethiopian philosophy are discarded or denied. They are an integral part of the cultural heritage of Ethiopia; they are absolutely necessary in the elaboration of a total picture of Ethiopia's individuality, and it is the author's intention to begin such a research as soon as possible. But written documents already existed and it was felt that methodologically one should begin with them and then proceed from them to the unwritten traditions of Ethiopia. This methodological approach in the beginning limits one's investi-

gation, linguistically to the ancient Semitic language of geez usually referred to as "Ethiopic" and culturally to the Christian zones of influence on the high plateaus of Ethiopia.[1]

Consequently, once I had finished my research and publication project on the written philosophical literature of Ethiopia, I attempted to apply the same methodological approach to the oral expression of wisdom literature: proverbs, songs, folktales, gathering *all* the printed oral texts, translating them into English, placing on index cards each unit of oral literature, classifying these cards according to literary genres, and synthesizing the result of such a research. I have chosen the Cushitic Oromo people for the simple reason that, having no written literature or written language, they were an ideal group for a study based on oral literature.

At present I have written six books on the subject: not only a collection of proverbs (volume I), songs (volume II), and folktales (volume III), but also an analysis of the literary types in the light mostly of a structuralist approach, although the thematic and axiological elements are well represented. Two anthologies, in English and in French, follow the first three volumes: once again not only a collection of the most beautiful proverbs, songs, and folktales, but also the criteria for such an aesthetic type of selection. An illustrated album of folktales ends this series, as it attempts to reach out to a vast audience of children "from six to sixty years old!"

In this essay, I wish to move away somewhat from the specifically Oromo character of the proverbs in order to delve into the *problématique* of orality, of *all* orality. By *problématique* I mean not only the problem itself but elements of the problem, its "situation," and the context within which it arises and grows.

A society is constituted by the relations that unite its members. For a society of oral tradition, these relations are usually of the "face-to-face" type, and among all the factors that may convey them (exchange of material goods, of services, matrimonial exchanges), communication through the spoken word occupies a privileged position.

The spoken word functions through one who speaks and one who listens: there is a sender (S) and a receiver (R). In the special case of proverbs, the sender is the one who speaks in proverbs, the receiver is the one to whom one speaks in proverbs. Whereas the author of a written text entrusts his work to the public, ignoring what acceptance or rebuff he may receive from his readers, the sender and the receiver in oral communication must be present at the same time.

But both of them are fully aware of not being alone in the world: they perceive themselves as being part of a human group that has a common past and a certain type of adaptation to environment and human situation. This awareness of belonging to a tradition is extremely strong; an individual will hesitate to abandon the tradition of his fathers and mothers, which will tell him how to behave in actual situations.

Oral communication between individuals manifests this tradition. Everything takes place as if, to remedy the transitory nature of the oral discourse, tradition came along to support certain words, to underline them, to give them weight, and thereby to make of these landmarks in social experience.

These spoken words acquire the value of oral texts, exchanged between actual speakers, but loaded with a whole history. An oral text is therefore at the meeting point between two axes:

> —a horizontal axis, social in character, where the message passes from a sender to a receiver, whether the latter be one person or many persons;
> —a vertical axis, of cultural semantics, where the message starts from tradition and aims at an actual situation: even if this situation is reduced to the evocation of a fact of the past, it is in a certain way the fruit and the actualization of tradition.

For each major genre of oral text, we can define the particularities of the axis. For instance, the riddle does not qualify an actual situation, but it is a means of education for the handing down of images. For the song, a singer, with or without instruments, delivers a refrain that the group takes up again with or without making the cadence; a given situation is the occasion of formulating a well-adapted proverb that later on may be sung. The riddle brings together a sender and many receivers, the latter accepting and maintaining the communication in a well-determined way.

The proverb occupies a particular place at the intersection of these two axes. It is in the function of this position that we shall study its relations to society, in three points:

> —Study of the horizontal axis: the sender-receiver communication;
> —Study of the vertical axis: the relation between tradition and the actual situation;
> —The living unity of tradition and of the situations in which the sender and the receiver are involved.[2]

I. The horizontal axis sender-receiver

1. The conditions for communication

A certain number of conditions must be present in order that a proverb be formulated and understood.

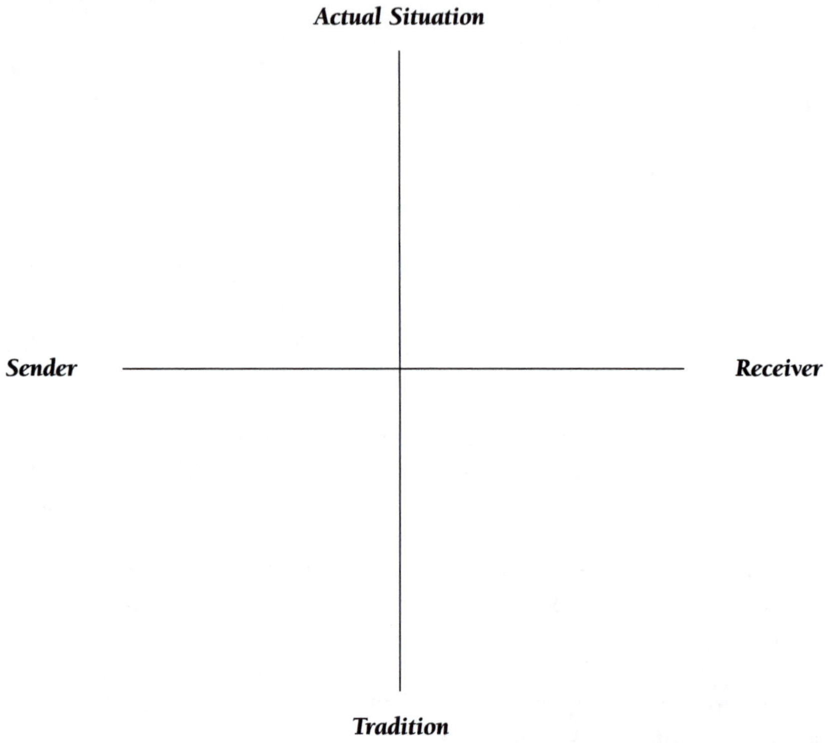

Actual Situation

Sender —————————————————————— *Receiver*

Tradition

Figure 1.

The communication must be established effectively between the sender and the receiver. There must be no considerable physical distance: a proverb cannot be shouted at a distance. A cultural unity must exist between the speakers; they share the same language, the same semantics, the same images, and the same values.

There are no social conditions for the usage of proverbs: everyone can utter them, young or old, men or women, at any time of day or night and whatever be the business of the moment.

But there are conditions arising from circumstances. The proverb is used in a concrete situation, which conditions its understanding. The sender and the receiver must somehow participate in this situation. The optimal condition is realized when the proverb definitively transforms the ambiguity of a situation and enlightens it, either for understanding or for action.

Here are two men quarreling about things that are beyond their control or means. A third man intervenes with a proverb:

Hawks fight one another on the ground for things that are in the sky.[3]

Everyone understands that there is no point in continuing the quarrel any longer; it is settled by the very awareness that it is impossible to settle it.

There is but one exception to these conditions: games of proverbs. One of the "opponents" utters a proverb, the other answers by another proverb. The first links up with a third proverb, and this process may last for a while.

The connection between one proverb and another can be a relation of similarity, opposition, or simply the suggestion evoked by a "hook-word" or an image. As a matter of fact, these games are rare and mean nothing. Their only purpose is to bring into the limelight the knowledge of one of the antagonists.[4]

2. *The sender*

The sender is a person who, in a given situation, says something concerning it. He expresses a "logical" truth of cognitive order, like the man mentioned above who intervenes during a quarrel. But he also expresses a "vital" truth: beyond the purely cognitive aspect, there is the involvement of the sender. The proverb translates his profound sentiment, his affective position approving or disapproving the experienced situation. "Excuse me," the man tells the wranglers, "but your quarrel cannot settle anything."

The sender, by appealing to a tradition-laden proverb, assumes the responsibility of what he is saying; he wants his words to carry a special weight. He knows he says a word that has a particular force as regards judgment or action.

The spreading of bean roots does not make yeast out of the bean.[5]

One does not have the real qualification for a job although apparently one introduces oneself very well.

The proverb is therefore the word of a man who is master of his thought and sentiments, and who considers that to the internal order that he lives, to the truth that he has an inkling of—at least as an ideal—there must correspond an external order, a truth experienced in society.

A drum sounds as loudly as it is beaten.[6]

Usually a proverb, a truth bequeathed by tradition is uttered by a mature man, in full possession of the lore of his people.[7]

3. The situation

The proverb appears when a fact, an event, a situation calls for a commentary. This commentary in proverbs is possible only because this fact and its circumstances are not absolutely clear for all: the sender needs to explain it to others, to draw their attention on one point, to express his opinion about it, or simply to link this fact to what he has learned from tradition. The proverb serves to enlighten the situation for those who have not understood it.

The dialectic between an experienced situation that was the occasion for uttering the proverb and the human spirit, which through the proverb gives it intelligibility, is one of the features proper to the proverb. The proverb cannot be studied as a mere linguistic fact cut off from reality: the latter is always present in the proverb.

She bought an [ele] when the previous one was broken; when the latter one was broken, she passed the night without eating her dinner.[8]

4. The receiver

Many Oromo proverbs are addressed to a group of individuals. This is the case of exhortatory proverbs, as for instance exhortation against ostentation or in favor of prudence. Most of them are couched in the negative: "Do not do such an action!" This type of wisdom in Ethiopia is common to both oral and written literature. In written sapiential literature, it is one of the most frequent didactic forms. It appears either as the saying of a father to his son, or more frequently still of a wise man speaking like a father to his son, or even without any mention of the person counseling or being counseled. The verbal form is the imperative; it positively enjoins a given action, or negatively cautions against a course of action.[9]

If you have nothing in exchange, do not borrow coffee.[10]

Do not dig a pit; perhaps you do not know if you may fall in it.[11]

Look at the mother, marry the daughter.[12]

Even when the imperative is not used, the meaning is one of counseling as if one were advising a group of young men or women: "Do not go beyond your capacity!"

One does not sing when grinding the grain one has begged.[13]

But most proverbs are couched in a general impersonal way, so that the receiver can be anyone, either an individual or a group, or an individual in the presence of a group that is taken as witness:

Butter is prepared in a bowl, but the one who enjoys it is the cup.[14]

The receiver of this proverb may be anyone according to the situation where it is uttered: for instance the lady of a house, if she expresses her contentment at receiving her guests and if one of these retorts that the enjoyment is rather for him or for the group of guests; or a group of students that manifests its satisfaction at the end of a public lecture that it has appreciated, or one of them who speaks up in the name of the group.

There is therefore a marked difference between the sender and the receiver. The sender knows what he means when he uses a proverb. The receiver must "receive" the proverb. This "reception" is made on two levels. He or she must first perceive that the statement just heard is a proverb, because the difference between an ordinary utterance and a proverbial utterance is very thin. Then he or she must understand what the sender meant by this statement. If, having recognized the utterance as a proverb, the receiver does not understand its meaning, he or she is supposed to have the will to search for this meaning and even to accept in advance affirmations that concern him or her. In order to discover the meaning of the proverb, he makes use of what he knows of the sender, of the experienced situation, or even of himself. If, in spite of his efforts, he does not succeed in understanding what was said, he may seek the advice of an elderly man or woman and ask him or her for explanations.

There are elderly people who willingly entrust their wisdom to youth, knowing that thereby tradition will continue after their death.

Finally, if the receiver has perceived and understood the proverb, it is left to him or her to express his or her own opinion. He or she judges the coherence between the proverb and the thought of the sender in relation to the experienced situation. Most of the time, the receiver accepts the proverb and either by word or by subsequent behavior, manifests agreement. However, the receiver may not accept the proverb entirely or even reject it. For the proverb is cast in a conversation, and in a conversation different viewpoints are expressed and mutually influence each other.[15]

5. Conclusion

On the axis that goes from the sender to the receiver, the proverb appears as a privileged factor of communication. It is situated, within the framework of conversation, as an interpersonal exchange. The sender purposes to say something and to manifest his or her thought concerning a given situation. In uttering the proverb, he or she addresses an individual or a group, but this utterance is not unidirectional. The receiver manifests his or her own opinion and, if he or she in turn utters a new proverb, the sender retorts with a new proverb and the conversation starts anew.

This exchange is not purely linguistic. The sender and the receiver share a particular situation; the proverb is enlightened by and sheds light on the situation where it is used.[16]

II. The transition from tradition to the actual situation

After considering the horizontal axis sender-receiver, we should study the vertical axis of cultural semantics: how can a proverb, transmitted by the elders, be adapted to an actual situation? In order to answer this question, we should investigate that which is transmitted (content, form), the organs of transmission, and their dependency on tradition.

1. The transmitted content

A speaker may always adorn his conversation with images: the only condition is that images be clear enough for his thought to be understood. But for whoever wants to utter proverbs (*makmaksa*), a second condition is added: he must draw his images from a culturally characterized stock.

A society experienced in the utilization of figurative language has selected through ages certain images that are considered as more typical. What are the typical images for the Oromo?

As I am about to delineate the profile of images transmitted by Oromo culture I am fully aware that I have already done such a study for each of the written works of Ethiopian written sapiential and philosophical literature.

1) The profile of images in Ethiopian written sapiential and philosophical literature. Images are very numerous in the whole of Ethiopian literature.

They appear under all forms: mostly metaphors and comparisons, but also typological emblems (*The Physiologue*), combinations of metaphor and comparison, parables, allegories, synechdoches, and metonymies.

The role of the image varies from one work to another. *The Physiologue* is essentially a typology, namely an emblem and a type. But if we penetrate into the interior of each chapter and if we try to see if it possesses some comparisons or metaphors different from the main emblem of the chapter or if the emblem is not resumed within the chapter and integrated within a new figure of style, we realize that we are in the midst of an exuberant forest of images. The number and variety of metaphors in particular, but also of comparisons and of combinations of both, are such that we must conclude that the image is the web and, except for a few sapiential and rhythmic types, nearly the entire literary tissue of *The Physiologue*. In principle these metaphors and comparisons appear in the hermeneutic section of each chapter, while in the naturalistic section vivid and kinetic descriptions abound.

The imagination that *The Book of the Philosophers* reveals is not that of the poet, but of the master of wisdom. The image is at the service of thought. Its end and content are didactic. It is not an addition coming from without; it is integrated into the web of the maxims. It manifests great sagacity and suppleness of intellectual life; an alert temperament whose sensibility is subtle and always in movement; a style that seeks less to develop the image for its own beauty than to persuade and to draw symbols from the simplest aspects of life and in particular from man himself.

In *Skəndəs,* and especially in the two series of maxims that prolong his biography, the quantity and quality of images transcend all the other works. Far from being subordinated to thought as in *The Book of the Philosophers*, the image in *The Book of Skəndəs* is treated for itself, for its own intrinsic poetic value. It often acquires the dimension of an intellectual thought pattern. It is a symbol.

The rationalist *Zara Yacob* shows economy of images (56 occurrences). Nearly all his images are limited to "heart" (22 occurrences), "light" (5), and "path" (4). Moreover, they are taken mostly from the Bible in general and from the Psalms in particular.

On the other hand his disciple *Wäldä əywåt* combines his master's rationalism with the traditional imagery of *The Book of the Philosophers*. He uses frequently and with finesse the comparison, the analogy of proportion, the metaphor, the metonymy, and the portrait. All these forms are characteristic of a sapiential, didactic, and pedagogical style and thought.

It is difficult to establish a precise statistical evaluation of the occurrences of images. When the same symbol, the "heart" for instance, comes back two or three times in the same context and with the same meaning, should one record the number of times the same word is repeated or retain as unit of image the ensemble where the same basic image occurs? I have preferred to use the unit of image as the criterion.

There are 1,611 such units: a very high figure when one compares it to the total number of sentences: 5,407, namely 30 percent. Let us now place these units in a logical frame, and distribute them according to the great categories of nature: man, animals, plants, inorganic things. One will immediately realize that a division must be made between artificial objects, the fruit of man's work, and things, like river, mountain, as they are found in nature independently of human work.

Onto a simple vertical line that goes progressively from A to D, namely in the ontological scale of entities from physical material things independent of humans to humans themselves, is now superimposed a pyramidal structure whose base is nature and whose summit is human beings. This is what I call, in the absence of a better term that I would have liked to borrow from the Ethiopian vocabulary, the "personalist" or "anthropocentric" profile of images. This mathematically verifiable "discovery" sheds a very penetrating light on Ethiopian written literature and culture.

All that remains for me to do now is to illustrate by a few quotations the conclusions I have just advanced. Nearly all the images (54.3 percent) are therefore of the following type: "The sun and the moon are those that have *explored* this world, and they *know* that great men do not remain."[17] The sun and the moon are physical entities; they exist in the objective order of nature—for the Ethiopian there is no doubt about this. Yet to material things typically human qualities are attributed: to explore, to know. In other words, human beings, the subject, are better known than nature, the object. It is in the function of human beings, of our bodies, of our organs and tissues, of our hearts, of our individuality, of our places in society, of the amplitude of our actions, that more than half the metaphors, comparisons, and other types of images are inspired and construed.

Units of Image

Categories of images	Occurrence	Percentage
D Humans	875	54.3%
C Plants and animals	196	12.2%
B Artificial objects	326	20.2%
A Physical material things	214	13.3%
Total	1,611	100%

The next group of images is intimately linked to the first, since it is composed of artificial objects made or determined by humans:

Clouds go like ships.[18]

Winds are like crowns surrounded with fruits, the delight of the earth.[19]

The ocean is the wall of the world.[20]

The heavens will be furled like paper.[21]

Once more, here are things that exist as such in the universe: clouds, winds, oceans, skies. To what are they compared? To the fruit of human work: ships, crowns, wall, paper. Humans are still present.

As to animals and plants, physical material things, they are undoubtedly known, but they rarely serve as axis of reference. Outside of humans and of what is made by them, the Ethiopian, as he is known to us by thirteen centuries of literary production, seems to lose interest.[22]

2) Typical images transmitted in Oromo culture. The typical images transmitted in Oromo culture do not in any way resemble the profile of images found in Ethiopian written sapiential and philosophical literature. If the latter is "anthropocentric" and "personalized," the former is "ecological." If in the latter, plants and animals represented only a small number of occurrences (196), in the former, animals constitute by far the most numerous category (303 proverbs out of 1,067). It is true that in both oral and written traditions of Ethiopia, food and beverage constitute the second most numerous category of images, but with a difference: for the latter the important viewpoint is the imprint of man's work on physical material things, for the former the family life, the social gathering (marriage, dance, burial) where eating and drinking play such a primordial role. Illness in the latter is but an aspect of man together with his health, his body, his organs and tissues, his heart, his individuality, his place in society, and the variety of his actions, in the former illness is, after animals, food, and beverage, an internal condition of human life. Water, as a material reality existing in nature, is one of the least-used images in Ethiopian written literature, but in oral literature, water (rainy season, flood, spring, lake, river, brook) is a characteristic feature of the green and fertile regions of Ethiopia where most of the Oromo live.

It is very clear that the typical images of Oromo oral literature are taken mostly from the life and work of a pastoralist and agriculturalist society, like "animals" and "farm life"; they are also taken from family life and social gathering, like "food and beverage," "social gatherings," and from the necessities and hazards of human life, like "clothing" and "illness."

Figure 2. *Typical Images (605)*

Subject(s) of proverbs		Total no. Category Occurrence	Image(s)
1. Animals		(303 proverbs with image of animals)	
	33	dog	1	33
	28	ass, donkey	1	28
	22	hyena	1	22
	17	goat	1	17
	16	horse	1	16
	13	cow	1	13
	10	calf; bull; snake, serpent, viper	3	30
	9	cat	1	9
	8	hide; sheep	2	16
	6	lion	1	6
	5	ant; beast; leopard; louse; monkey	5	25
	4	antelope; ape; cattle; cock; hawk; hen	6	24
	3	animal; bird; elephant; flea; rat	5	15
	2	bloodsucker, leech; buffalo; bug; butterfly; camel; chameleon; chicken; fumigation; heifer; moth; mule; quail; salt lick (for animals); tail; tapeworm; termite; wolf	17	34
	1	animal with no horn; anteater; bee; boar; cockroach; corral; crow; fly; francolin; frog; hippopotamus; lamb; [sik'o] locust; tortoise; vulture	15	15

If the speaker wants to speak in proverbs and not in simple images, he must have recourse to images recognized as inherited from tradition. But proverbs do not only transmit images; they also hand down norms to posterity: values, items of advice or warnings, orders or prohibitions that the sender makes his own, slightly modifying them sometimes, but without ever suppressing them.

Every proverb, with more or less force, is a carrier of the values of society: that is no doubt the reason why it was selected by tradition in order to become a constituent part of the common memory of a particular human group.

Through the image and the norm, the one who makes use of a proverb partly turns toward the past, or rather toward the social structure as a whole. The images transmitted by proverbs aim at representing a segment of the social order; a proverb conveys a part of the norms of the group, of its values. The force of tradition, the example of what the elders have accomplished, the image of the ideal society command the individual's attention throughout the proverb.

But the content of traditions is reactualized at each utterance of the proverb. Tradition exists only by this actualization. There is no kind of coexistence: tradition brings back to life and compels the adhesion to an anterior culture—the image as norm—into which the individual integrates himself in order to find himself adequate to social life. This content gives value to the present and inscribes him in the cultural tradition.[23]

2. The transmitter

The transmission of proverbs is quite different from that of stories. There are well-known storytellers whose celebrity is due to their personal value. They have learned stories at random on the occasion of evening gatherings and in time they have imposed themselves as specialists in storytelling.

Proverbs are much more current in the life of the people than stories that are told only on the occasion of certain social gatherings. Anybody can listen to or utter proverbs: there are no "depositaries" of proverbs. However, certain people are more gifted than others for the knowledge and utilization of proverbs, and although age may be helpful in increasing one's repertory, to speak in proverbs is not the privilege of the elders.

What are the qualities that concur in the making of a specialist in proverbs? One can underline three: (1) personal experience; (2) cultural experience; (3) training.

1) *Personal experience.* It is based on observation of nature and society. One must have observed the speed with which news spreads through end-

less plains and intricate forests, and have seen donkeys trotting along innumerable paths, to assemble the two images in a proverb:

Ears and donkeys go along the road.[24]

2) *Cultural experience.* A real transmitter of proverbs must know the images preferred by his culture and the realities his fellow citizens are sensitive to. Among animals the ass is characterized by its vulgarity;[25] so is the heifer;[26] the hyena by its voracity[27] and its pilfering, ferocious, filthy habits;[28] the goat is evil and the sheep is good;[29] the cow is peaceful;[30] the ant is known for its voracity and its fighting spirit;[31] the monkey for its ugliness,[32] its false appearance[33] and imitation of man.[34]

Within the category of food and beverage, butter is known as an aliment that needs to be prepared, while honey is ready-made;[35] lentils have two eyes;[36] *fandiʃa* is a high-quality sorghum, *k'ejila* a low-quality one;[37] cabbage is a poor man's food,[38] and seeds are eaten in time of scarcity.[39] As a cure against tapeworm, *het'o* is characterized by its repulsive taste.[40]

Certain traits are known only through this cultural experience: few Oromo peasants have seen the sea, and yet it is well known for its immensity:

Until they die, they are as great as the seas.[41]

3) *Training.* The third factor for the value of a transmitter is that he or she has heard numerous proverbs and that he or she has tried to utter a great number himself. Because he has a liking for figurative language, or because he desires to appear as a wise man, one speaks in proverbs more and more, as he has heard his predecessors do and as he would wish others to do after him. He thereby becomes a living center where tradition crystallizes. People come to him for the explanation of an utterance whose meaning is concealed, or for advice in a difficult situation. It will be for him the occasion to help others to understand the meaning of things and of society, to help in the transition from what is obvious to what is less known. In a society where the counsel is a central part in social relations, it will be for him the occasion to transmit a way of thinking and of living, of "cooling down what is hot and of warning up what is cold."[42]

3. The form transmitted

Tradition affects not only the images and the norm of proverbs. The form is also transmitted, but here the problem is more delicate because the form of proverbs is not frozen. The utterance of a proverb is transmitted with a certain suppleness.

I. "Good day! Good evening!" He knows how to say: but how he has passed the time, his father alone knows.[43]

II. The neighbor knows that someone has passed the night, but only this man himself is aware how he has passed it.[44]

III. You know that the sheep have passed the night but how they have passed it, only the master knows.[45]

The formulation of this proverb varies in order to adapt itself to the context of conversation, and to transmit images and norms with more or less force, by insisting on this or that aspect of the proverb. As a matter of fact, rather than in a literal repetition, the form transmitted is to be sought in a particular logical structure:

(1) the fact of passing the night
(2) the manner of passing the night
(3) the knowledge is of an intimate nature.

There is a link between each ring of the chain. The link between the first and the second rings is one of opposition: the fact and the manner; between the second and the third rings, the third and the fourth, the link is one of progressive depth and intimacy in knowledge.

Proverbs therefore are not always transmitted in the same terms. What is necessarily transmitted is the deposit of images and the grammatical structure. This transmission of proverb form eases memorization. When the beginning of a proverb is uttered, it is easy to remember its ending, for both the sender and the receiver.

Another frequent channel for the transmission of proverbs is the song. Indeed, many songs are proverbs that, during evenings of praise or work in the fields, the singer will address to this or that one in order to praise or encourage him.

Did the song give birth to the proverb? or vice versa? It is difficult to give an answer inasmuch as our study is necessarily synchronic. Two observations, however, impel us to affirm the anteriority of the proverb to the song and the story:

(1) From a grammatical viewpoint, proverbs always have a correct form, while songs easily suppress certain syllables, even for proverbial utterances. This is quite normal if we take into account rhythmic considerations; but in these conditions, it is easier to conceive a passage from the grammatically exact (the proverb) to the inexact (the song) than the opposite.

(2) From the viewpoint of the situation where it is employed, the proverb always designates a concrete situation experienced by the partici-pants. For songs and stories this relation with a designated situation is rather loose. It seems normal that a given situation has been the occasion to invent a proverb that later on could have been sung or included in a story. It is less probable that a song or a story not directly adapted to a situation could have given birth to a proverb that designates this situation.[46]

"This year it does not expand!" said the servant who pinch by pinch ended by eating the whole boiled corn.[47]

This proverb, "This year it does not expand!" is perfectly adapted to the experienced situation. The old servant in her hut is trying to keep the fire alive under the earthen pot with a narrow neck, (*tue*). In it boils the *mullu* for the master's table. She is hungry and, relying on the expanse of corn in its boiling, she plucks the *mullu* grain by grain, and eats the grains in secret in order to assuage the overpowering pangs of her hunger. Far from expand-ing, the earthen pot is half empty. This flares up the anger of the mistress. The poor servant, in order to find an excuse, accuses the times, exclaiming that the *mullu* of the year does not expand with boiling. The given situation has been the occasion to invent a proverb that later on will be included in its contextual narrative.[48]

Thus, according to Cerulli, the proverb:

He who has despised the poor man will not grow rich[49]

has been paraphrased in a 103-verse religious song where it occupies five verses:

Thou killest the kings, O Mary!
Thou makest rich the poor, O Mary!
Be propitious, O Mary!
The man who stoops, O Mary!
Gathers what he has sown, O Mary![50]

4. Tradition and creativity

If a speaker finds no convenient proverb to express his opinion in a given situation, may he create a new proverb?

A proverb in the strict sense must comprise a certain number of ele-ments. Its is possible to invent utterances that have all the peculiarities of a proverb: grammatical pattern, image, norm, rhythm, and so on. But they are not recognized as springing from tradition. A real proverb must be endorsed by the ancients.

We must therefore admit two apparently contrary affirmations: since proverbs exist and have been recognized by tradition, there was a time when they started to exist. But it is practically impossible to grasp a proverb in its nascent state, for as long as tradition has not recognized it, it is a figurative statement but not a proverb.

The sender, therefore, does not have the liberty to create new proverbs, nor even to employ proverbs in a sense contrary to social order. But when he speaks in proverbs, he does not simply repeat an ancient form or situation. Thanks to the choice of a particular proverb from the repertory and to the adaptation he makes of it in the conversation, the speaker awakens a latent form through which he situates anew a vital truth. The original image has been transcended: reasoning describes an actual situation with its peculiarities thanks to a past situation that has become typical; one creates with forms one has not invented. The manipulation of images permits one to find anew what was already known, and exhibits what is original in a situation.[51]

III. The living unity of tradition and of the actual situation

Through the proverb, the communication established between the sender and the receiver becomes a continual movement to and fro between tradition and the actual situation. We are dealing with a particular mode of knowledge and of communication that calls for a certain type of education and provokes a cultural consciousness.

1. A particular made of knowledge
The world of the phenomenon, the world of space and time, the world of social environment and of the event, that objective physical world as such is closed upon itself. It becomes intelligible thanks to the intervention of the human spirit, which discovers in the phenomenon that which gives it its internal unity, its signification. But the human spirit is not a pure intelligence, appearing suddenly from nowhere. It is modeled by tradition, by life in society, and by already experienced events. This human spirit perceives the intelligibility of a new situation by relating it to a situation known by itself or by tradition. This grasp of the real world by the human spirit is a kind of dialogue with truth: a truth already known by tradition but constructed in the present situation. It is a case of "hominization" of the world of the phenomenon, to use an expression coined by Pierre Teilhard de Chardin.

All figurative thought functions through relating a new situation to a known situation. But the proverb adds to this thought the guarantee of tradition and of the group, a kind of warrant of inherence. Those who speak perceive, understand, and experience situations as related to what they have received from tradition.[52]

2. The necessary education

The members of an oral society need to be educated from their childhood. This education is not by proverbs only, but by the ensemble of oral texts including riddles, puzzles, songs, stories, and so on.

This education is never the object of a magistral teaching: each situation, each conversation is the occasion of a dialectical movement between the weight of social thought and the freedom of the individual who can understand or not understand, who can accept or refute, who in any case is placed before his responsibilities: he may adhere or not! He is not forced . . . but usually he will not like to withdraw from the thought and the way of living recognized by his group and his culture.

This referring to a memory and a tradition that transcend the individual has important social consequence: the individual can acquire a high social status by his conformity to and identification with tradition. Even a poor man, a rich man, or a man of low extraction may find in the perfection with which he knows the tradition and wields proverbs the possibility of going up the social ladder without incurring jealousy.[53]

3. The function of the proverbial message

In its immediate range, the proverb has many functions: (1) cognitive, (2) expressive, (3) normative and educative, (4) discursive, (5) cultural.

1) *Cognitive function.* The first objective of the proverb is to give a form to reality. An experienced situation is not intelligible directly. It is the complex result of many factors: time, space, events, human liberty, and so on. To utter a proverb in this situation permits one to understand its signification, to discover its originality and pertinence, its dynamism and unity.

The clothes cry like the country itself.[54]

By saying this proverb, one shows someone else that he or she is not in conformity with local usages, with the *gada* system, for instance. This proverb has as its first function to render reality intelligible on a cognitive plane: lack of conformity of one's behavior to socially accepted customs.

2) *Expressive function.* In saying such a proverb, one does not remain only on a cognitive level. One expresses one's disapproval for such a lack of conformity.

3) *Normative and educative function.* Because it is embedded in a proverb, this expression transcends the simple objectivity of the sender. The

aim of the proverb is to recall the norms that impose themselves on the individual and to provoke a certain line of conduct: "Adapt yourself to the world in which you are!"

This constant recalling of the preferential behavior of the society is a real education: the proverbs train individuals and society.

4) *Discursive function.* The proverb always takes place in a discourse. It gives the discourse its force and can be its final point, for the receiver can hardly oppose himself to its power. In a conversation, proverbs represent the highest point, those upon which the sender intends not to come back: the proverbs are like the summits of the arc of thought.

5) *Cultural function.* When a proverb is said, the interlocutors are aware of belonging to the same human community. As soon as he recognizes it is a proverb, the receiver admits that he has with the sender a cultural past that carries with it images and norms that are anterior to both. The proverb is a dialogue with the Truth recognized in the group, in which sender, receiver, and the public participate. Its message goes beyond the individual and even the public that is listening. The latter appears as the actual witness of tradition, the representative of society. This "dialogue" of tradition speaking to tradition beyond individuals exhibits the force of the proverb. Even when it is humorous, it is a hieratic message. Of course its enunciation is contingent and colored by circumstances, but in any case it is a message that comes from beyond the individuals and reveals to them the possibility of transcending their limits in time and space.

IV. Conclusion: A society in its world

In order to show the connections between all these elements, we would like in conclusion to take over the diagram reproduced at the beginning of this chapter, in our explanation of its title: "The Proverb and Oral Society." In five diagrams, we shall set out visually the various relations that have been developed. In doing so we are following step by step the example of Jean Cauvin in his *L'Image, la langue et la pensée,*[55] but we are also, we hope, presenting in a pedagogical and easily accessible manner the main features of this chapter. Years of experience in university teaching and participation in international conferences have convinced me that a diagram immediately brings home even for an audience of experts and scholars the most relevant traits of one's research.

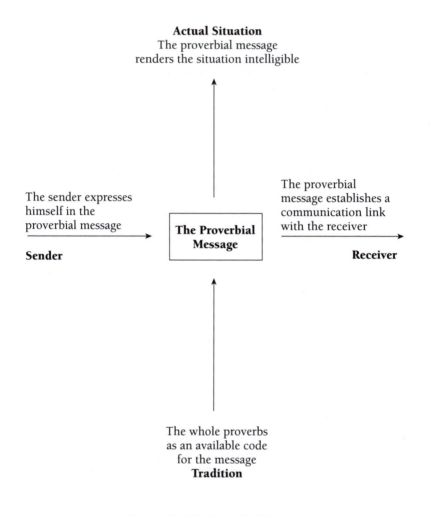

Actual Situation
The proverbial message
renders the situation intelligible

The sender expresses
himself in the
proverbial message

The proverbial
message establishes a
communication link
with the receiver

**The Proverbial
Message**

Sender

Receiver

The whole proverbs
as an available code
for the message
Tradition

Figure 3. The Proverbial Message

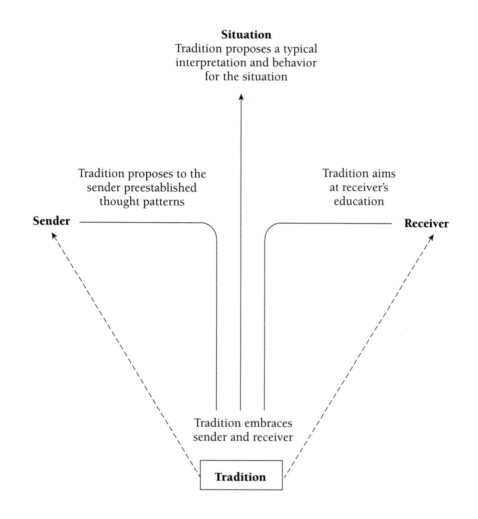

Figure 4. Tradition

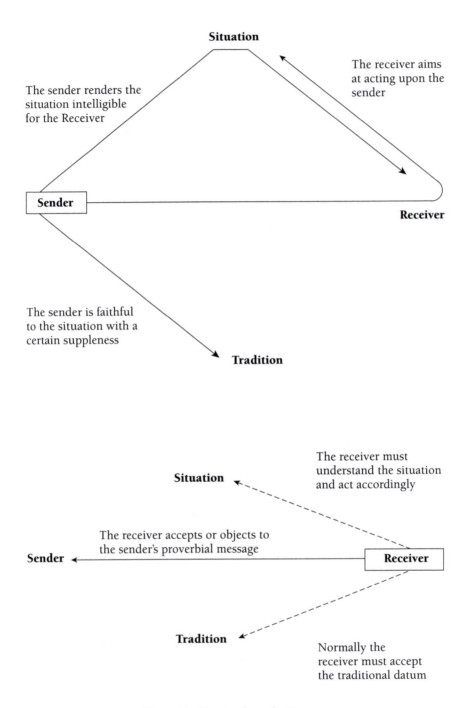

Situation

The receiver aims at acting upon the sender

The sender renders the situation intelligible for the Receiver

Sender

Receiver

The sender is faithful to the situation with a certain suppleness

Tradition

The receiver must understand the situation and act accordingly

Situation

The receiver accepts or objects to the sender's proverbial message

Sender

Receiver

Tradition

Normally the receiver must accept the traditional datum

Figure 5. The Sender—the Receiver

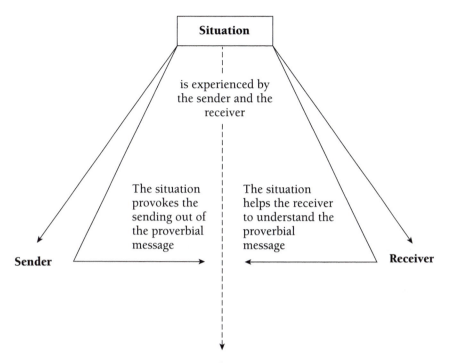

Figure 6. The Situation

Ethnic Identity as a
Political Resource

K. Anthony Appiah

In July 1999, for the second time in my lifetime, a king of Asante was installed on the Golden Stool in Kumasi. There was, as you would expect, much pageantry, much that was called "tradition," and a good deal (in the way, for example, of the sale of videotapes of the life of the previous king at the stadium on the day of the installation of the new one) that was decidedly new. As I sat in that stadium for many hours in the sun, awaiting the arrival of Nana Osei Tutu II (who brandished the musket with which he would acknowledge the Queen Mother and the paramount chiefs of the right and left wing of the battle order of the Asante army), I found myself sharply aware that nothing in the liberal political theory that I normally engage with seemed especially helpful in thinking about the relevance of this event and this institution to the politics of the contemporary republic of Ghana. The formal theory I normally endorse is democratic, deeply resistant to political hierarchies (except where associated with offices open, at least in principle, to all autonomous adults) and to social hierarchies—except some of those that reflect merit or achievement. It recognizes individual but no collective rights within the nation, and imposes most duties either on real persons, ideally in virtue of obligations freely undertaken, or on legal persons constituted by the voluntary association of real persons. (There are exceptions here, since, like most sensible people, I recognize duties owed to those—parents, caregivers, communities—who made us; and our relation to these people is not, on our own part, voluntary.) The political rights I recognize belong to people as citizens or as residents of towns and regions, not in terms of ascriptive or hereditary status. I celebrate individuality (even as I acknowledge the centrality of the social both in the constitution and in the self-appropriated ends of the individual). So my official theory seems to require that I treat Asante monarchy as, at best, an irrelevance, at worst, an embarrassment.

And yet, of course, our kingship matters profoundly and, far from being a source of embarrassment, it is, I find myself sheepishly confessing, a source of pride. The Asante monarchy is not just a quaint leftover of past glories: the symbolism of Asante monarchy, the paraphernalia that surround the Golden Stool, are potent because they engage with norms and ideals that are real and powerfully relevant today. But how, in our normative thinking about politics, should we engage with these ideals and norms and the institutions and people that embody them?

One possibility—articulated in President Museveni's understanding of the role of the reinstituted kingdom of Buganda—would be to define the sphere of the traditional monarchs as "cultural." What this means, except negatively—in terms of forbidding the mobilization of the symbolic and material resources of the institution in partisan politics—is not entirely clear. After all, either "culture" matters as a source of norms, a basis of solidarity, even perhaps as a set of traditions worth sustaining, or it doesn't.

If it *does* matter, won't people inevitably see the monarchy, whatever the explicit pronouncements of the monarch, as a guide to how to decide matters of social importance; won't they mobilize politically around social relations determined or, at any rate, shaped by their relations to those whose king he is; won't they think it worthwhile to spend resources—social resources—on sustaining the Kabaka or the Golden Stool? In short, won't it end up being political?

And if it doesn't matter, why on earth bother with it? To sustain it in this way looks like the equivalent of creating a vast state-subsidized twenty-four-hour-a-day opera, one that pleases (or, at worst, distracts) those who like the opera or claim a historic connection to it, but which fits into the public world only as a kind of entertainment, a permanent Ugandan or Ghanaian *Mikado*. "Panem et circenses," the Roman emperors offered their subjects: but this is a circus that doesn't even deliver the bread.

The "cultural" model doesn't seem the right way to go.

So can we do better? Ajume Wingo has suggested in his recent writings that there is a role for such traditional institutions, suitably mobilized, in shaping the public life of modern African nations. I think he is right. And he identifies one of the key ways in which they can operate positively: namely as theaters of civic pedagogy. This function is one that is often best performed in conjunction with more straightforward ends.

The Kabaka and the Asantehene can mobilize resources for public purposes—education, say, or health—that are unavailable to the national state, and they can, in so doing, express the value of the ends (and of social mobilization toward those ends) and, at the same time, contribute to their achievement. I am going to take it for granted (as the present Kabaka, the present Asantehene, and a host of other traditional rulers in Africa regularly do) that this is a function they can usefully perform.

The question I want to ask in this brief paper is how the norms that underlie liberal politics constrain or limit the extent to which traditional rulers can legitimately perform these functions within the framework of modern democratic republics. (So I am not interested in the roles of the monarchies in Swaziland, which has an executive monarchy, or Lesotho, which has a constitutional one . . . or of Morocco, which lies somewhere in between.)

One current way to understand this question—which I had myself originally been tempted by—was to treat traditional political institutions as no longer really political, in the sense of "part of the apparatus of the state," and see them instead as belonging to what is now called "civil society." Civil society is, roughly speaking, public life outside the state, away from formal political institutions, and apart from the economy. It is families, churches, temples and mosques, nongovernmental organizations, football clubs, and the like. This "and the like" draws attention to one of the great difficulties of the idea of civil society: it is hard to see the first members of the list as having anything very profound in common. And so, of course, there is little to stop us adding "chieftaincy" or "precolonial political institutions" to this list.

But there are two important reasons why it is not helpful, in my view, to see kingship and chieftaincy, as practiced in Asante-Ghana or Buganda-Uganda, as belonging in this sphere. The first is that even if neither Asante nor Buganda is a state today—in the sense of an autonomous sovereign political society—they both were states once and the institutions that remain were developed and structured for government and the exercise of sovereignty. It follows that we cannot understand such legitimacy as they have except on the model of state legitimacy, even if they may no longer use sanctioned secular force to obtain conformity to their commands. But their authority is not derived simply from consent, either. For at least some people, it derives from a source that we might call "religious": the spirits of the royal ancestors continue to be thought of as capable of producing effects. For others, it derives its power in part from the force of the idea that these are *our* customary ways of government whose logic we understand; and that, in this, they are rather different from modern state powers, whose behavior and logic often elude us. (And, of course, it is possible to have both thoughts at once.)

One reflection of the state-type logic of these ex-states is that adherence to these rulers is in a double way not a matter of voluntary association: loyalty is widely seen as required of Asante (and Buganda) and not required (in fact, perhaps even not desirable) on the part of non-Asante and non-Buganda. Not that this notion is enforced in law by the national state—far from it. From the Ghanaian state's point of view, all Ghanaians, whatever their ancestry, are free to withdraw fealty from traditional rulers.

But no one can simply ignore them in public life, because of the second, equally obvious, difficulty with the "civil society" picture, which is that these institutions are placed within a political order, located by a network of laws and constitutional practices and understandings that are profoundly interwoven with the exercise of modern state power. Let me focus here on Asante, which is the case I know best. Chiefs in Asante (as in Ghana generally) are chosen by processes that are governed by national law and subject to review by the courts. They have powers in relation to land law that are real and substantial, and that are reviewable by higher "traditional" authorities, including the Asantehene, and by the national Ghanaian High Court. You cannot ordinarily own land in Kumasi without a lease from the Asantehene. Powers like these are exercised under a customary law dispensation developed by the British in the colonial period, much of which has survived through various postcolonial constitutions and under military and civilian governments. Part of the social power of the chief or his queen mother comes, to be sure, from legitimation by processes and norms that are (or are thought to be) traditional; but part of it, too, comes from recognition by the modern state and reflects the powers that the state grants chiefs today.

At least in Asante, then, traditional rulers do not belong straightforwardly to civil society. They are clearly not simply private economic actors (even if there have been some who abuse their powers in ways that suggest that this is all they think they are!). But it would be quite misleading, as well, to see them simply as functionaries of the modern republic, charged with the management of certain forms of property. Not state, not economy, not civil society. We can be clear about what contemporary Asante kingship is not.

Of course, as I have already insisted, Asante kingship shares features with the state: its currency is, in some respects, political power. And it is in some respects like civil society: much of what surrounds it is sustained, like opera and soccer, by the voluntary support of those who value and participate in it. And, like soccer and opera, it clearly has economic dimensions: Asante kings inherit and manage farms and other properties *as kings*. But to see it as a hybrid institution in these terms is, I think, less helpful than trying to understand it as the institution that it is, created by its own history and the histories of the institutions among which it operates. And the key to understanding its persisting relevance, I think, is to understand that the currency in which it deals is neither power nor money, nor the solidarity of voluntary association but, as any Asante will tell you, a kind of symbolic legitimacy.

What is important, first and foremost, about the respect in which chiefs, up to and including the king, are held in Asante, is that it is not instrumentally grounded. Clearly people no longer fear kings because they have, as they had, the power of life or death (under the law). Nor do they treat them respectfully because they have economic benefits to distribute (even though they may). Indeed, if you asked most people in Kumasi why they respected the Golden Stool, and therefore owed respect to its incumbent, I think they would think this a strange question. For what the Asantehene still has residually is the kind of legitimacy that comes from having been properly appointed according to procedures that are (or are thought of as being) grounded in a rich tradition. (In case anyone outside Asante should affect to find this mysterious, I should point out that there are many examples in the world of this kind of legitimacy: many Americans who are perfectly solid in their republicanism are affected in this way by the British monarch.)

I do not propose an account of this form of legitimacy (and I don't think Weberian talk about charisma helps very much here). The point I want to insist on is that this form of legitimacy exists. Given that it exists, it can be mobilized, for good or ill. And I also want to insist that many people in Asante (and, I suspect, in Buganda) have an investment in the institution that means that they would not only regret but resist attempts to dismantle it once more (as Buganda was dismantled by Idi Amin and the Golden Stool was suspended by the British during the exile of Prempeh the First.) Given that this is the case, what is to be done with it?

The reason I insisted on not allowing these institutions to be seen as part of "civil society" is that that model answers too immediately the question of what should be done. If it were one of the voluntary associations of civil society, then the liberal answer would be that, provided it was freely sustained and everyone was currently free to enter and exit, it was none of the government's business. (Similarly, if it were a business enterprise, it could be constrained by reasonable laws regulating contract, competition, and negative externalities.)

But since we are not dealing with civil society or business—and since, on the other hand, though they are subject to state regulation and perform some regulatory functions (in the sphere of property) that seem properly to belong to the state, they cannot simply be identified with it—we cannot subsume these institutions under the usual rubrics.

To repeat the point: it is clear that the legitimacy of the Asante monarchy can be mobilized for public purposes in a positive way. The issue is whether these undoubted benefits outweigh the costs from the point of liberal political theory. But what are these costs? They seem to be of two kinds. On the one hand, recognition of Asante by the Ghanaian state offends certain liberal principles. Let me mention just two. First, the position of Asantehene is not a career open to talents. (Not that the Asantehene does not have to be talented: in our system we pick kings from eligible members of the royal lineage. But you *do* have to be descended from early royals in the right way.) Second, since Asante is not a private association, its principles of membership and exclusion distinguish among citizens in ways that might ordinarily be thought to be discriminatory. Not every resident of Kumasi or of Asante has the same sort of standing in relation to the Asantehene as does one of his "subjects."

On the other hand, the practice of monarchy lends symbolic support to and reinforces certain forms of social hierarchy that do not comport well with the liberal insistence on the equal dignity of all persons.

So our practice of monarchy both offends liberal principle and reinforces illiberal views. These objections have been made, of course, against modern monarchies elsewhere: in the recent debates about the monarchy in Australia, for example, or in British or Dutch republicanism. I think the only proper way to respond to them is to draw attention to the core liberal vision—of persons equal in dignity—and ask whether, despite these problems, our practice of monarchy contributes to more than it diminishes the flourishing of such persons.

I believe that in answering *that* question it is crucial to identify an element that is neglected in all the focus on the role of traditional rulers in development, the "public purposes" that I mentioned just a while ago. And that is the role of our monarchy in the constitution of the self-respect of Asante men and women.

It is a familiar idea in liberal theory since John Rawls that self-respect is an important good. "Self-respect" can sound like a remarkably individualistic end, so it is important that self-respect in many places is tied up with what we nowadays call "identity," and that a personal identity, in this sense, is constituted in part by what I will call its collective dimensions. These dimensions are important to the ways in which people feel pride (and shame) by virtue of their membership in social groups of many kinds. And feelings such as these are central to the phenomenology of self-respect.

It will help to have clearly before us what I mean by identity. The contemporary use of the concept to refer to such features of people as their race, ethnicity, nationality, gender, religion, or sexuality first achieved prominence (and perhaps had its origin) in the work of Erik Erikson. This use of the term identity reflects, of course, the conviction that each person's identity—in the older sense of who he or she truly is—is deeply inflected by such social features. And it is an undeniable fact of modern life that people have increasingly come to believe that this is so. In political and moral thinking nowadays it has become commonplace to suppose that a person's projects can reasonably be expected to be shaped by such features of their identity and that this is, if not morally required, then at least morally permissible. We understand the woman who organizes her life and her affiliations around her gender; or the Asante who sees his ethnicity as one thing that shapes the meaning of his life.

It seems likely that any adequate theory of identity will proceed by noting that each person's identity has at least two dimensions. There is a collective dimension, the intersection of the identities we have been discussing; but there is also what one might call a personal dimension, consisting of other socially important features of the person—intelligence, charm, wit, greed—that are not themselves the basis of forms of collective identity. Not every aspect of the collective dimension will have the general power of sex, gender, and sexuality or nationality, ethnicity, and religion. What the collective dimensions have in common is that they are what the philosopher Ian Hacking has dubbed "kinds of person": men, Ghanaians, Asante people, Catholics; but also lawyers, kings, and philosophers.

Hacking's key insight about "kinds of person" is that they are brought into being by the creation of names for them.[1] So he defends what he calls a "dynamic nominalism," arguing "that numerous kinds of human beings and human acts come into being hand in hand with our invention of the categories labeling them."[2]

Hacking begins from the philosophical truism, whose most influential formulation is in Elizabeth Anscombe's work on intention, that, in intentional action, people act "under descriptions"; that their actions are conceptually shaped. (What I do is dependent on what I think I am doing. To use a simple example, I have to have a wide range of concepts for my writing my name in a certain way to count as "signing a contract.") It follows that what I can do depends on what concepts I have available to me; and among the concepts that may shape my action is the concept of a certain kind of person and the behavior appropriate to a person of that kind.

Hacking offers as an example Sartre's brilliant evocation, in *Being and Nothingness,* of another kind of service professional, the *Parisian garçon de café*:

> His movement is quick and forward, a little too precise, a little too rapid. He comes towards the patrons with a step a little too quick. He bends forward a little too eagerly, his eyes express an interest too solicitous for the order of the customer.[3]

The idea of the *garçon de café* lacks the sort of theoretical commitments that are trailed by many of our social identities: black and white, gay and straight, man and woman. So it makes no sense to ask of someone who is employed as a *garçon de café* whether that is what they really are. Because we have expectations of the *garçon de café,* it is a recognizable identity. But those expectations are about the performance of the role; they depend on our assumption of intentional conformity to the expectations.

With other identities, however—and here the familiar collectives of race, ethnicity, nationality, gender, and the rest come back into view—the expectations we have are not based simply on the idea that those who have these identities are playing out a role. Rightly or wrongly, we do not normally think of the expectations we have of men or of women as being simply the result of the fact that there are conventions about how men and women behave.

Once labels are applied to people, ideas about people who fit the label come to have social and psychological effects. In particular, these ideas shape the ways people conceive of themselves and their projects. So the labels operate to mold what we may call "identification," the process through which individuals intentionally shape their projects—including their plans for their own lives and their conceptions of the good life—by reference to available labels, available identities. In identification, I shape my life by the thought that something is an appropriate aim or an appropriate way of acting for an Asante, an African, a philosopher. It seems right to call this "identification" because the label plays a role in shaping the way the agent takes decisions about how to conduct a life, in the process of the construction of one's identity.

Thus, as I have pointed out before, every collective identity seems to have the following sort of structure:[4] a label, "L," associated with *ascriptions* by most people (where ascription involves descriptive criteria for applying L) which lead to *expectations* about how Ls will behave; and *identifications* by Ls (where identification implies a shaping role for the label in the intentional acts of the possessors, so that they sometimes act *as an L*); and, finally, consequences in the way that people treat Ls (so that sometimes they are treated *as an L*.) These "as an L"s—acting as an L, being treated as an L—connect identities to conceptions of what Ls are or should be like.

In the case of the *garçon de café*, conventions of behavior associated with a role are explicitly central: the ascriptions are based on the simple idea that someone who works in cafés of a certain sort is expected to conform to certain expectations; the expectations are based on the conventions that govern the role of the *garçon de café*; because of those conventions, acting as a *garçon de café* means constructing the performance Sartre evokes; and people treat *garçons de café* better (they give them bigger tips, for example) if they perform the role well. But for some other identities—as an Asante, for example—there is more than convention.

The reason, of course, is that being Asante is, in part, a matter of being heir to certain traditions, and neither those traditions nor the fact that one inherits them is something that the Asante woman or man has chosen. You can choose whether or not to play a certain conventional role and, if all there is to an identity is a conventional set of behaviors, and you are capable of them, then you can choose whether to adopt the identity. But if the criteria for ascribing a certain identity include things over which you have no control—as is the case with ethnicity, gender, or race—then whether you identify with that identity (whether, for example, you think of yourself as Asante and act sometimes as an Asante) is not only up to you.

Now, the key to ethnicity as a source of self-respect depends on the fact, which I have mentioned already, that collective dimensions of identity form the bases of feelings of pride and shame. When I think of myself as an Asante, I can find myself proud of the collective achievements or the symbolic resources of Asanteman—the people of Asante—and I can also participate in a similar way in the achievements of particular other Asante people (as when a soccer player from Kumasi does well in the World Cup!). For many people in the world, this sort of symbolic participation, mediated by the thought of oneself *as an X*—where X is the name of some national or ethnic group—is, as a matter of psychosocial fact, one of the key bases of self-respect. It follows that where this is so, depriving someone of that thought by disestablishing the institutions that are the symbolic superstructure of that identity is depriving them of a good that liberal theory has insisted we should take seriously.

That, I believe, is one of the reasons why it seems wrong simply to go immediately from the way in which Asante kingship offends liberal principle to the conclusion that we should abolish it: in doing so we also ignore not only the material benefits whose provision may be coordinated by way of the Asantehene, we also ignore its significance for the central liberal value of self-respect.

Of course, in the long run we might feel that these feelings should be discouraged. Attaching oneself to an institution that offends liberal principle, and basing one's self-respect in part on its achievements, reflects an illiberal psychology, one might say. But for a liberal, I think, it will be important, if that is so, to set about persuading one's fellow citizens that it is so, so that they no longer need this basis of self-respect; one will not proceed to deprive them of it willy-nilly.

I have tried in this brief essay to explain—to myself as much as to you—why it is that I do not feel the urgency of republican sentiment in Asante. (Similar arguments make sense to me for Buganda and for chieftaincy and kingship in other places, including, for example, Holland, where it is a much more substantial element of the constitutional order.) I think that a substantial commitment to the present of Asante monarchy is consistent with the hope that, as time goes on, it will wither away because the needs that it meets today will be met by the institutions of the increasingly democratic society that Ghana will become. I hope that this commitment and this hope *are* consistent, because I feel them both today.

4 ✈

Ibn Khaldun: A Dialectical Philosopher for the New Millennium

George Katsiaficas

If we were asked to describe in a word the central concerns of Western philosophy, high on everyone's list of responses would be the individual. No doubt the formation of the autonomous individual is one of Europe's lasting contributions to world civilization. How then are we in the West to comprehend other forms in which the individual appeared in history? How should we read philosophers for whom the individual's place was foreshadowed by the group? The answer to both questions is: with difficulty. In this paper, I seek to synthesize philosophical first principles capable of orienting us in our rapidly changing world and guiding us in the future. In my view, it is imperative that we open our horizons to include thinkers like Ibn Khaldun. The dire effects of European individualism have been so great that we desperately need to rethink the categories of individual and group.

Any attempt to draw parallels between the philosophies of Europe and of Islam runs the risk of obscuring what is original in Islamic traditions, since we in the West are vastly more familiar with the former than the latter. Particularly in the case of Abu Zayd Abdel Rahman Ibn Khaldun, a fourteenth-century philosopher whose life was intricately interwoven with the great political and military dramas of his times, a veritable fountain of original thought could be dammed up by imposing the categories of European thought. Five centuries before Darwin discovered the specific features of evolution, Ibn Khaldun wrote that humans developed from "the world of the monkeys" through a widening process in which "species become more numerous."[1] Nearly half a millennium before Karl Marx sketched the systematic implications of the labor theory of value, Ibn Khaldun wrote that "labor is the real basis of profit."[2] Four hundred years before Auguste Comte's "invention" of sociology, Ibn Khaldun unveiled his "science of culture."[3]

Unlike scholars in the industrial West, where the division of labor marginalized them from the corridors of power, Ibn Khaldun served as chamberlain, secretary, ambassador, and adviser to various sultans, emirs, and princes in Andalusia (Spain) and throughout the Maghreb (the Arabic word for "Occident" that refers to Africa north of the Sahara—the "Island of the Sunset" from the perspective of Arabia proper). Wherever he went, revolutions, invasions, and political upheavals seemed to be the order of the day. Born in Tunis in 732 (1332 c.e.), he lived there much of his youth and was educated by some of the world's finest teachers in what was then one of the centers of learning in the world. Ibn Khaldun's life was thrown into turmoil by the plague (from which both his parents and nearly all his teachers died in 1349). He left Tunis and embarked upon a promising political career. Among his many interventions in history can be counted a meeting with Timur (also known as Tamerlane—the Chaghatai Turkish chieftain whose forces conquered much of the world). When Timur's cavalry surrounded Damascus, Ibn Khaldun was one of the notables who slipped out of the city to negotiate with him. Ibn Khaldun wrote a history of the Maghreb for the Mongol, and Timur showed his appreciation by sparing the lives of some of the city's elite when his men ravaged Damascus. He was the ambassador of the sultan of Granada to Pedro the Cruel, the Christian king of Castile, in 1363. Although once imprisoned for nearly two years, he was blessed with good luck and traveled extensively at a time when few people could find the means to do so. Soon after his entire family died in a shipwreck, he made the Hajj to Mecca. In 1377, in the short period of five months, he wrote the *Muqaddimah* (or *Prolegomena*) while secluded at a palace of Sultan Abu Hamu near Tujin.[4] Although he added to his work over the next five years, the whirlwinds of political change and courtly intrigue compelled him to set aside his *Prolegomena* and move to Cairo, where he became a noted professor, judge, and sheikh (manager) of Baybars, the greatest Sufi institution of that age. His final work, an autobiography, has yet to be translated into English.

Since Ibn Khaldun's life was so thoroughly connected to historical events, his theory organically links the realms of ideas and actions. Thus to pose the categories of his thought in the scholastic tradition of Western philosophy (particularly the idealism/materialism schism) completely fails to deal with the unity of these domains in Ibn Khaldun's system. The prevalence with which Europeans have compared Ibn Khaldun to Western scholars has led Franz Rosenthal, Ibn Khaldun's translator and one of the principal Arabist scholars in the United States, to coin the term "forerunner syndrome" to describe and simultaneously criticize this tendency.[5]

Praise, too, can be a means of obscuring the contributions of Ibn Khaldun. In his three-volume *Study of History*, Arnold Toynbee calls Ibn Khaldun's philosophy of history "the greatest work of its kind that has ever been created by any mind in any time or place."[6] For Toynbee, Ibn Khaldun was the "sole point of light" and "the one outstanding personality" of Islamic thought, absurd ideas that illustrate centuries of the West's utter disregard of the Islamic intellectual tradition. His cultural context incapacitated Toynbee, but his own system places Ibn Khaldun within the prevailing Western viewpoint that modern history begins with the Renaissance, an assumption that clearly transposes Western historical conditions onto world history. Toynbee fails to comprehend Ibn Khaldun's continuity with Hellenistic and Byzantine philosophy, or with Islamic historians who produced comprehensive world histories like that of Tabari (died in 923), Al Masudi (died in 945), and Idrisi's *Book of Roger* (written for the Norman king of Sicily in 1154). Early in his life, Ibn Khaldun became familiar with the philosophies of Farabi (died in 950), Avicenna (died in 1037), and Averroes (died in 1198), and much of his own work can be understood as a dialogue with these voices from the past.[7] Nor are Ibn Khaldun's contemporaries counted by Toynbee, thinkers like Rashid-a-din Fadlallah (died 1318) who published a *General History*, the Iberian Ibn al-Khatib, and the Persian Muhammed (born Ibrahim al Iji), whose treatise on historical methods appeared in 1381. Toynbee's ignorance of this tradition is curious since its importance is immediately apparent to any reader of Ibn Khaldun because of his reliance on dozens of thinkers from Aristotle to the seminal minds that produced the many localized histories that he critically examined in the course of constructing his own system.[8]

During the same century that Ibn Khaldun lived, there was not one Christian Arabic scholar in Europe.[9] Long before Europeans became acquainted with Muslim thought, Turkish scholars delighted in the treasures they found accessible to them. Despite Europe's ignorance, Europeans "discovered" the importance of Ibn Khaldun in the nineteenth century, thereby elevating his status from just another "footnote to Islamic historiography. . . . As the foremost Muslim historian of Ibn Khaldun, M. Talbi, remarked, 'It was in Europe that Ibn Khaldun was discovered and the importance of his Mukaddima realized.' "[10] Once the thought of Ibn Khaldun became known in Europe, however, a growing list of admirers appeared, and fawning admiration and inclination toward the appropriation of Ibn Khaldun into a preexisting system of Eurocentric categories accelerated.

The first European biography of Ibn Khaldun was published in 1697 in French,[11] and excerpts from the *Muqaddimah* were first translated in 1806. In 1812, a German synopsis of Ibn Khaldun's theory of the decline of dynasties appeared, followed by another extract of the original.[12] Although de Stacy published a complete French translation in 1856, it was not until 1957 that a complete English translation of the *Prolegomena* was published.[13] Whether or not Vico, Hegel, and Marx read about Ibn Khaldun in summaries of Arab philosophies is unknown (although H. Simon speculates that Marx and Engels may even have seen the French translation of his *Prolegomena*).[14] It seems quite likely that Machiavelli knew of Ibn Khaldun, although Enan insists that Machiavelli "undoubtedly knew nothing about him."[15] Hegel was well aware of the contributions of Arab scholars in both medicine and philosophy, and in his brief synopsis of their thought he praised their "assistance" to Europe:

> Philosophy, like the arts and sciences, when through the rule of the Barbarians of Germany, they became dumb and lifeless, took refuge with the Arabians, and there attained a wonderful development; they were the first source from which the West obtained assistance.[16]

Hegel included little of Arabic philosophy in his three-volume *Lectures on the History of Philosophy*, and he paid even less attention to Byzantine thought, giving the entire history of Byzantium only two passing mentions in his *Philosophy of History*.

In these brief remarks on Ibn Khaldun, I pay particular attention to two facets of his philosophy: the role of the individual and the place of the group in history. I examine what he wrote explicitly in relation to these two dimensions of history, and I also seek to situate him in his cultural context, thereby affording some sense of the implicitly understood values of his day. By so analyzing Ibn Khaldun, the cultural background of his philosophical thinking moves to the foreground. In his own day he was a celebrated teacher and philosopher as well as a player in the political dramas of societies whose place in the trajectory of world civilization is not to be minimized. He was a dialectical thinker for whom spirit was a material force, a staunch advocate of justice (which indicated to him the need for strong government), and a partisan in the struggle to ennoble the human species. I seek to illuminate his contributions to the forging of a contemporary understanding that is both spiritual and historical. While universalizing themes of importance in his cultural tradition, I try not to diminish his shining contributions and originality. Following the lead established by Marshall Hodgson, I seek to locate Ibn Khaldun in the "Oikoumene"—the whole Afro-Eurasian historical complex from the beginnings of history to today.[17]

PHILOSOPHICAL FOUNDATIONS

The tension between religious orthodoxy and philosophical inquiry continues today to animate Islamic thinking, just as it has for generations. In the middle of the fourteenth century, Ibn Khaldun rejected all previous attempts to reconcile the natural order of worldly events and the divine character of the cosmos. The Ash'arite understanding posed religious principles that were dogmatically defended, a theological philosophy that bordered on the rejection of reason altogether.[18] Using the newly developed science of logic, more "modern" thinkers used metaphysical doctrines from Aristotle and the Greeks to refute the Ash'arites. While Ibn Khaldun, like nearly all Islamic philosophers, regarded Aristotle as the "first teacher," he parted company with the moderns and differentiated between the physical world and the divine world, insisting that philosophy could not comprehend divinity.[19] He clearly believed that logical thought could not completely grasp all facets of life.[20] In this fundamental precept, he upheld the traditional Islamic notion (one that marked a major point of divergence from the Western synthesis of divinity and humanity in the person of Jesus), which had been central to the philosophy of Avicenna. According to Ibn Khaldun:

> Man is composed of two parts. One is corporeal. The other is spiritual, and mixed with the former. Each one of these parts has its own perceptions, though the [part] that perceives is the same in both cases, namely the spiritual part. At times, it perceives spiritual perceptions. At other times, it perceives corporeal perceptions. However, it perceives the spiritual perceptions through its own essence without any intermediary, while it perceives the corporeal perceptions through the intermediary of organs of the body, such as the brain and the senses.[21]

In posing such a model of human beings, Ibn Khaldun distanced himself from what was in his day the most recent philosophical legacy within Islamic thought. Unlike more traditional Ash'arites, however, he insisted that logical abstraction of universals (not the application of dogma) could lead to an understanding of the essential nature of the physical world. In this way, he opened the door to his new science of human culture.

The problem of the relation of the actions of human beings to the divine world was not a simple one to resolve. Ibn Khaldun understood the realm of Spirit as prior to and influencing the world of the body:

> there is something that exercises an influence and is different than bodily substances. This is something spiritual. It is connected with the created things, because the various worlds must be connected in their existence. This spiritual thing is the soul, which has perception and causes motion. Above the soul . . . is the world of angels.[22]

For Ibn Khaldun, the soul had form and substance[23] since its existence materialized in the exchange of "potentiality for actuality with the help of the body and [bodily] conditions." After the soul had materialized in actuality, it had "two kinds of perception," one through the body and the other "through its own essence, without any intermediacy" when the "veil of the body was lifted." Soothsaying, dream visions, augury, and divination constituted parallel forms of consciousness alongside sensuous observation of empirical reality. In these forms as well as in everyday events like the transition from sleeping to waking or in certain Sufi exercises, he located the possibility of transcending the senses and opening the door to the realm of spiritual perception.[24]

Having established empirical reality as an important object of inquiry, Ibn Khaldun wrote the *Muqaddimah* as an exposition of the patterns of human relationships in connection with environment and history. In the fourteenth century, the Islamic world—particularly in North Africa—was in decline from its glorious past, and Ibn Khaldun attempted to understand the causes of the changes around him. In the Maghreb, various rulers rose and fell, while to the east, Baghdad had fallen to the Mongols in 1258. Ibn Khaldun undoubtedly heard of the European cultural revival (the Renaissance) under way in Italy. Although he had faith that one day Constantinople would be an Islamic city, his own experiences convinced him of the need to ground scientifically his analysis of human beings in order to transcend the particular histories of any one group. By 1377, his own failures in active political life had produced disgust with courtly intrigue and petty rivalries, and thus his *Prolegomena* is an attempt to produce a history at a universal level, one that would not be situated in the personal needs of any ruler or the narrative history of any particular group.

A central issue in Ibn Khaldun's philosophy of history was the possibility of human beings understanding forces beyond their control. He sketched a historical process that, in the final analysis, was not simply a history of external events but rather that of human beings becoming who they in essence are. As such, he offers valuable insights into the character and conduct of our species. Ibn Khaldun comprehended specific actions as existing within an internal and invisible rational structure through which external facts could be understood. Narrative history, that is, the recounting of specific events, was inferior to philosophical history through which the inner causes and remote origins of events could be understood.

THE NATURE OF HUMAN BEINGS

What then was Ibn Khaldun's view of human beings? In a phrase, he was unambiguously negative. "Man is ignorant by nature. . . ."[25] Royal authority, a "natural" quality of humans, was necessary to ensure proper behavior.[26] But what of a transforming process through which humans might elevate themselves? For Ibn Khaldun, the unchanged individual might ascend to angelicality, but he was never transformed into an angel (the equivalent of self-transformation in secular thought). Moreover, where history might have a direction, a telos, for Ibn Khaldun, a natural cycle of growth and decay operated, a natural cycle of three generations for dynasties. For him, the rigors of desert life compelled toughness and puritanical self-restraint, the opposite of "urban weaklings" amid the "stupid mass." As Muhsin Mahdi summarized Ibn Khaldun's view:

> Man is by nature a domineering being; and his desire to overcome [*qahr*] others, and subdue and coerce them, is the source of wars and of trespassing the properties of others. It moves those desiring victories to struggle for political supremacy and for establishing the state in which they intend to be leaders. Those who are conquered and enslaved, on the other hand, wither away, since to be enslaved is contrary to human nature and leads to the loss of hope.[27]

At best, Ibn Khaldun hoped governments would rule as uncorrupted representatives of the divine laws, a belief that earned him a reputation as a harsh puritan while he served as a judge in Cairo.[28] For Ibn Khaldun, authority was one of the four attributes that distinguish humans from animals (the others being thought, labor, and civilization), a view that flows from his perspective that individuals were "savage" and the mass "stupid."

Humans were so tragically stuck in their God-given status that imagination in Ibn Khaldun's schema could not be a source of transformative behavior that might uplift individuals. Rather it gave familiar molds to inspired forms of knowledge. Imagination linked the spiritual and the secular.[29] In his understanding of the mind, Ibn Khaldun differentiated external sense perception and inward perception, the first type of which was common sense. In his schema, common sense transferred perceptions to the imagination, "the power that pictures an object of sensual perception in the soul, as it is, abstracted from all external matter."[30] Following Avicenna's psychology, imagination was then understood as leading to memory and the association of related abstract ideas, all of which culminate in thinking. In his typology of souls, there were three kinds: weak ones limited to the body, intermediate ones moving in the direction of angels, and ones like the prophets capable of attaining angelicality. Ibn Khaldun limited imagination to souls of the first kind. Intuition was characteristic of the second, revelation of the third.[31] Imagination was most strongly developed in soothsayers and augurs, persons whose "inferior" souls constrained their perfection but who nonetheless sought visions.[32] Imagination was an important resource for the common people since they were not capable of even glimpsing divine reality. Only prophets like Jesus and Mohammed could see God and the angels. As one analyst summarized:

the seeming naturalism of Ibn Khaldun's accounts does not proceed from appeals to a "nature" whose independent existence controls interpretation of it, nor to a "nature" capable of cultivation and refinement. His realism, better called tragic realism, invokes a conception of the mundane as a sad, fallen approximation of the sublime. Ibn Khaldun's man is not the child of nature nor the master of culture but the creature and creator of the mundane.[33]

In Ibn Khaldun's view, neither philosophers nor speculative theologians properly understand the character of imagined pictures constituted during dreams. The former "assume that imaginary pictures are transmitted by the imagination through the motion of thinking to the 'common sense' which constitutes the connecting link between external and inner sense perception."[34] The problem for Ibn Khaldun was that this view was incapable of distinguishing between divine and satanic inspiration. The theologians, on the other hand, understood imagined pictures (dreams) as "a kind of perception created by God in [the realm of] the senses." In this case, although we are unable to perceive how dreams take place, they provide evidence that sensual perception operates independently of the active senses—that is, on the level of the soul. In this fashion, Ibn Khaldun posed the theologians as correct, even to the point of urging that no attention be paid to the psychology of Avicenna.[35]

Unable to ground imagination in secular processes, Ibn Khaldun poses an ascension to the realm of angels rather than an elevation of human social organization as the direction for human perfection. For Ibn Khaldun, the power of thinking:

> wants to be free from the grip of power, and the human kind of preparedness. It wants to proceed to active intellection by assimilating itself to the highest spiritual power group (that of the angels), and to get into the first order of the *spiritualia* by perceiving them without the help of bodily organs. Therefore the soul is constantly moving in that direction. It exchanges all humanity and human spirituality for angelicality of the highest stage, without the help of any acquired faculty but by virtue of a primary natural disposition that God has placed in it.[36]

But in the real world of history, individual savagery and anarchy were continual dangers, all the more so since "People have no desire for virtue."[37] They have no special interest in virtuous people, and there is a general absence of individual virtue.[38] Ibn Khaldun was unafraid to state straightforwardly just how little regard he had for his fellow humans:

> One may compare the swarms of human beings with the swarms of dumb animals, and the crumbs from tables with the surplus of sustenance and luxury and the ease with which it can be given away by the people who have it, because as a rule they can do without it, since they have more of it.[39]

For Ibn Khaldun, the group, not the individual, was history's focal point and determining factor. Individuals seldom—if ever, unless they were divinely inspired—have more than a minor influence on the overwhelming forces of history. Indeed, the individual for Ibn Khaldun is practically neglected as a philosophical topic.[40]

INDIVIDUAL AND GROUP

Given the lack of virtue and low level of intelligence accorded to humans by Ibn Khaldun, how then could societies hold together? His answer was social solidarity, or *assabiyah* (translated as "group feeling" by Rosenthal). For Ibn Khaldun, those groups with a strong sense of *assabiyah* are destined to be strong and to rule—at least as long as they are able to maintain their sense of identity and solidarity. Thus, groups composed of blood relatives (as in the case of many Bedouin communities) have the strongest possible ties since they are based on kinship, while urban settings predispose any group to an eventual weakening of its group feelings. For Ibn Khaldun, *assabiyah* is the basis for political power and cultural hegemony, while unrestrained individualism was one source of the downfall of groups. He comprehended revolutions as consisting of the struggle for power between outsider groups struggling to overthrow insider groups whose "group feeling" was declining due to the comforts that ruling provided. (The outcome of revolutions often depended upon luck or astrological conditions.[41])

Having committed himself to an understanding of political power as resting upon group strength, Ibn Khaldun went on to portray groups in stereotypical fashion. He was enormously critical of the impact of nomadic Arabs on the civilizations they came to dominate. As examples of their destructive impulses, he gave their continual pulling out of foundation stones in buildings to make campfire circles, and their burning of finished roofs and other wood in the fires. Perhaps more than any of his contemporaries, he was extraordinarily critical of Arabs.[42] In Ibn Khaldun's words:

> because of their savagery, the Arabs are the least willing of nations to subordinate themselves to each other, as they are rude, proud, ambitious, and eager to be the leader. Their individual aspirations rarely coincide. But when there is religion among them, through prophecy or sainthood, then they have some restraining influence in themselves.[43]

He considered Arabs savage by "character and nature"—a "natural disposition that is the negation and antithesis of civilization." The transformation of these tough desert dwellers into "urban weaklings" is one explanation for the destruction of dynasties.[44] His criticisms of the Arabs can partially be understood here as a critique of the failure of any group to maintain a sense of inner solidarity.

Ibn Khaldun's *Prolegomena* also suffered from a stereotypical view of Africans:

> We have seen that Negroes are in general characterized by levity, excitability, and great emotionalism. They are found eager to dance whenever they hear a melody. They are everywhere described as stupid.[45]

Ibn Khaldun was a dialectician, but the nature of his dialectical method was limited to the first of two kinds of dialectic generally understood as comprising dialectical thought. It was external rather than immanent. (In the former, fixed assumptions and widely held propositions are made to totter by reasons external to them; in the latter, one delves into the object in question, discovering the black in its white and the white in its black. This second kind of dialectical thought is diametrically opposed to rigidly posed black/white categories.) Clearly Ibn Khaldun's notion of dialectic was limited to the first kind.[46]

Not only did he formulate his notion of the individual and the specific nature of groups in rigid categories, but the philosophical framework within which his notions of individual and group are contained precluded the transformation of either. As we have seen, individuals were tragically stuck in predetermined fates while groups' natures were statically formulated in hypercritical terms. The above examples of group stereotyping reflect a deeper problematic: the tendency of philosophers to pose rigid categories. Hegel, perhaps the greatest Western philosopher of history prior to industrialization, was an unabashed racialist:

> Negroes are to be regarded as a race of children who remain immersed in their state of uninterested *naivete*. They are sold, and let themselves be sold, without any reflection on the rights and wrongs of the matter. The Higher which they feel they do not hold fast to, it is only a fugitive thought. This higher they transfer to the first stone they come across, thus making it their fetish and they throw this fetish away if it fails to help them. Good-natured and harmless when at peace, they can become suddenly enraged and then commit the most frightful cruelties.[47]

For Hegel, the Caucasians' "infinite thirst for knowledge" was "alien to other races."[48] On the Teutonic nations, the world-spirit imposed the task of developing an embryo into the form of the thinking man.[49] What separated the Orient and Africa from the West was that for the former everything was explicit and so humans were "free," while the Europeans were in the midst of a process of making the implicit real—of realizing self-consciously determined Ideals. In his words:

> It is in the Caucasian race that mind first attains to absolute unity with itself. Here for the first time mind enters into complete opposition to the life of Nature, apprehends itself in its absolute self-dependence, wrests itself free from the fluctuation between one extreme and the other, achieves *self*-determination, self-development and in doing so creates world-history.[50]

It is to Ibn Khaldun's credit that, unlike Hegel and so many other philosophers, he did not elevate his own group above others and thereby succumb to ethnocentrism. To this day, the universalistic dimension of Islam, legendary from the transformation of Malcolm X because of his encounters with nonracist whites during his pilgrimage to Mecca, contributes to its status as the world's fastest-growing religion.

The group feeling of Muslims is surely one of Islam's noteworthy dimensions, but to return to an important issue: What is the status of the individual? Is there a relation between the Muslim prohibition of the human figure in art and Ibn Khaldun's understanding of the individual? Is *assabiyah* a mechanical negation of the savage individualism of which Ibn Khaldun was so critical, not its determinate sublation?

There has yet to be an adequate analysis of Ibn Khaldun's notion of the individual. It appears that his unwillingness to thematize rigorously his notion of the individual reflects the prevailing cultural values of the context in which he lived. The paramount significance of the group in both Arab and Islamic civilization appears to have blocked the emergence of the autonomous individual. Franz Rosenthal informs us that autobiography is "not highly developed" among Arabs.[51] Even the name by which Ibn Khaldun has become known in history is not his own but his father's. Arab patriarchy militates against the construction of autonomous individual identity today as much as six hundred years ago, at least if we judge by names derived from Abu (father) and Ibn (son). Within an elaborate web of (continually reproduced) familial identities, strict social conventions, and cultural obligations, individuals in Islamic societies remain bound by collective forms whose power has long since been diminished in the West. To be sure, an individual emerged in the Arab world, but it was a dependent individual confined in life options and social possibilities. We can observe this dynamic in many domains. Hodgson tells us that even in love poetry, "the realm of private sentiment, etiquette and courtesy reigned, and the poet's aim was to handle public images with grace and splendor."[52] (Of course, one consequence of poetry designed for public recitation—not private reading—is the forging of group solidarity and shared experience.) Other cultural links can be found: impersonality and collectivism are recurring features of Arab prose literature.[53] Arabic pedagogy is based on memorization and recitation, not individual creativity and thoughtfulness. Ibn Khaldun himself recommended memorization as the first step toward understanding the best of Arabic poetry and for acquiring literary taste.[54]

It appears that the Orientalist view of Arabs as "solitary, romantic men"[55] does not correspond to the inner reality of their group life. Indeed, the Orientalist view of unbridled Arab individualism appears to emerge from centuries-old European needs to defame Arabs and Islam in order to prepare for war against them:

> Ishmael had been driven into the desert. . . . Ishmael was a wild man whose hand was against every man's: could any better description of the Saracens be found than this?[56]

Even if we approach a contemporary example of what might be considered savage individualism, we find group feeling as the primary motivation. I refer to individuals who sacrifice themselves through actions like the "revolutionary suicide" of car bombers. As with Japanese kamikaze pilots, one result of such actions is the destruction of the individual who undertakes it. Such actions articulate an Eastern principle of the subordination of the individual to the group—in this case, in the struggle against an externally defined enemy.

No doubt, the tragic effects of Western savage individualism—the plundering of the planet for individual greed and the imperialist conquest of its peoples—should be mentioned at this juncture. In exploring the future potential of human freedom, however, it is important to distinguish between individuality and individualism. The former refers to a harmonious relation between the single human being's inward life and outward relationships to others while the latter denotes the individual as an isolated monad held in check by repressive groups (in which he/she may or may not claim membership). The determinate negation of the savage individualism of Western imperialism is not the mechanical imposition of group needs and identity but the metamorphosis of individualism into individuality and of collectivism into self-conscious collectivity (i.e., the transformation of groups through an immanent self-consciousness that they are part of the human family, not simply an identity defined in opposition to external Others). Ironically, the very scourge of the West—its savage individualism—may also contain within itself a noble contribution to global civilization. Finding the good in the bad, we might simultaneously locate the seeds of autonomous individuality in the West (understanding the role of the individual in history as forging rights and imagination) alongside the savage pursuit of wealth and power. Similarly, a contribution of Islamic civilization is the potential of a universal group feeling among human beings that transcends racial, ethnic, and even gender divisions. A dialectical sublation of Islamic group feelings synthesized with the determinate negation of Western individualism might result in an individuality that is simultaneously that of an autonomous thinking person and part of a species-cognizant group.[57]

CONCLUDING REMARKS

As the species develops a new self-consciousness from the global synthesis of cultural traditions at the end of the twentieth century, the role of philosophical reflection is paramount in solving some of the radically pressing problems humanity has posed for itself. As we destroy nature and our own natural identities, our problems increasingly demand the reformulation of first principles. The recent triumph of modern rationality and the continuing menace of savage individualism have diminished the significance of other cognitive forms. In this context, intuition becomes part of the subversive power of resistance. Ibn Khaldun's Aristotelian typology of altered states of consciousness (soothsaying, augury, divination, geomancy, etc.) provides one facet of the transcendence of materialistic sensuality and of consumer society. His attention to group feeling and spiritual values is one reason why his understanding of human beings is appropriate to a creative synthesis of tradition and modernity. It may well be that a New Age reading of his work may help produce waking dream visions that inspire action. Furthermore, his emphasis upon the group corresponds to the conditions of postmodernity, where the powers of the individual are diminished and those of groups enhanced. Today it is cultures and identities that are the subjects (and objects) of history; it is groups—not gods or individuals—that produce and situate our future.[58]

Despite the current fad of Fukuyama's "end of history," Ibn Khaldun provides a sense of the transitory nature of even the most entrenched social order. Unlike Fukuyama's flattened universe, one in which even its dialectical character is destroyed, the latent potentialities of the species mean reclaiming the thinking of Ibn Khaldun as part of the process of synthesizing philosophical first principles capable of reorienting and uplifting humankind.

Zara Yacob: A Seventeenth-Century Ethiopian Founder of Modernity in Africa

Teodros Kiros

INTRODUCTION

Zara Yacob introduces himself:

> I was born in the land of the priests of Aksum. But I am the son of a poor farmer
> in the district of Aksum; the day of my birth is 25th of Nahase 1592 A.D., the
> third year of the year of [King] Yaquob. By Christian baptism I was named Zara
> Yacob, but people called me Warqye. When I grew up, my father sent me to
> school in view of my instruction. And after I had read the psalms of David my
> teacher said to my father: "This young son of yours is clever and has the
> patience to learn; if you send him to a [higher] school, he will be a master and
> a doctor." After hearing this, my father sent me to study zema. But my voice was
> coarse and my throat was grating; so my schoolmaster used to laugh at me and
> to tease me. I stayed there for three months, until I overcame my sadness and
> went to another master who taught qane and sawsaw. God gave me the talent
> to learn faster than my companions and thus compensated me for my previous
> disappointment; I stayed there 4 years. During those days, God as it were
> snatched me from the claws of death, for as I was playing with my friends I fell
> into a ravine, and I do not know how I was saved except by a miracle from God.
> After I was saved I measured the depth of the ravine with a long rope and found
> it to be twenty-five fathoms and one palm [deep]. Thanking God for saving me,
> I went to the house of my master. After this I left for another school to study the
> interpretation of the Holy Scriptures. I remained ten years in this type of study;
> I learned the interpretations of the Frang [Europeans] and of our own scholars.
> Oftentimes their interpretation did not agree with my reason; but I withheld my
> opinion and hid in my heart all the thoughts of my mind. Having returned to
> my native Aksum, I taught for four years. But this period was not peaceful: for in
> the XIX of king Susanyos, while afons, a Frang, was Abuna, two years [after his

arrival] a great persecution spread over all Ethiopia. The king accepted the faith of the Frang, and from that time on persecuted all those who did not accept it.

The long paragraph above is a succinct and moving portrait of the Ethiopian philosopher's turbulent life. One immediately senses the presence of an independent, wise, and even shrewd mind. Beyond the self-portrait, there are a few remarks about Zara Yacob by Claude Sumner,[1] who was the first English-speaking scholar to introduce the thoughts of this philosopher to the philosophical world. The long debate over the authenticity of the authorship of the treatises of Zara Yacob has now been skillfully put to rest, and it is no longer doubted that Zara Yacob, and not Padre Urbino as Conti Rossini claimed, created the literary figure of Zara Yacob.[2] It was Sumner who undertook the arduous task of comparing Zara Yacob and Descartes on methods of thinking, for example, thereby establishing a solid place for him. Indeed for Claude Sumner, "Modern Philosophy, in the sense of a personal rationalistic critical investigation, began in Ethiopia with Zara Yacob at the same time as in England and in France."[3] Most recently, the philologist Mudimbe has also noted that Zara Yacob occupies a major place in the development of African philosophy.[4]

I will present Zara Yacob's thoughts on three perennial topics of philosophy:

(1) Methods of knowing God and the disclosure of truth;
(2) Human Nature;
(3) The obligations of humans.

I. METHODS OF KNOWING GOD

Zara Yacob's method could be roughly called a discursive subjection of faith, any faith, to a critical examination by intelligence or natural reason, which takes the form of honest searching or uncovering, called *Hasasa* or *Hatata*. Central to this project is the idea that reason itself is incomplete without God's guidance, yet reasonable human beings must subject their faith to critical self-examination before they believe. Faith in God must come after profound reasoning. All human perceptions, imaginations, judgments, and apprehensions should be carefully subjected to this discursive method. Nothing should be accepted without being tested by intelligence or natural reason. Unlike Kant, but like Descartes, for Zara Yacob faith is not superior to reason but can become so if it is first examined and passes the test of natural reason. To put matters in perspective, consider first the way Descartes expresses what Zara Yacob is asserting: "And therefore it seems to me that

I can already establish as a general principle that everything which we conceive very clearly and very distinctly is wholly true."[5] For Descartes, distinctness and clarity are the ideals of successful communication.

Similarly for Zara Yacob, truth is clearly revealed to whoever seeks it "with the pure intelligence set by the creator in the heart of each man."[6] Faith then is not an irrational form of giving oneself to an unknown external power called God. Not for Zara Yacob. Faith can become a rational and reasonable activity of the mind. It is an act of the intelligence that propels thoughtful and vigilant believers, like Descartes, to believe only after activating their intelligence to provide demonstratively the necessary and sufficient conditions for believing in an overwhelming power such as God. The proposition that "God exists" to Zara Yacob means, "I have proven to myself beyond doubt that the power called God definitely exists and that I now believe, and further, that from now onwards I will not subject God to doubt, since God has now become to me a clear object of rational faith. I now totally believe."

For Zara Yacob, a style of existence, such as marriage, is a legitimate practice, whereas monastic life is not. Marriage springs from the "law of the creator,"[7] monastic life does not. Put differently, by Zara Yacob's metaphysical yardstick, a practice such as marriage discloses a clear and distinct idea that originates in God's intention. When monastic life is measured against that yardstick, it proves to be inferior to married life. It does not pass the litmus test of reason. These claims could of course be unsettling to a nonbeliever. Even a believer may not be completely satisfied, in that one could be a devoted lover of God and still fail to accept marriage as the only way of life. Indeed, one need not agree with Moses to disapprove of marriage. But it is my belief that the argument in defense of marriage was not aimed at nonbelievers as much as members of the same religious convictions, most particularly at those ardent believers who consider marriage as the defilement of the body. He is challenging those "dogmatists" with the counterargument that the body was bestowed on humans not for repression or denial but for a moderate joy. The believers need not be deprived of joy. The body was given to us for a purpose, and that purpose is contained in the constancy of marriage. That is the first implicit argument, which I just fleshed out. There is a second argument.

The second argument was rather commonplace in the seventeenth century. It is an argument that Aristotle among others initiated. That is, it takes at least two to produce an offspring, and through it to populate the world. Without this act of propagation, strictly speaking, there will not be a world. Of course Aristotle was not so foolish as to think that everyone will have to marry in order to have a world. In his metaphysical/biological system, some would have to produce children, and others could be celibate.

Unlike Aristotle the pagan, Zara Yacob the religious thinker would not conceive of accepting children born outside the institution of marriage. To do so would be to put God on the defensive, in that in order for the children to be blessed, marriage, "the law of the creator, is a necessary and sufficient condition." Without that sufficient condition, marriage would have become an incoherent and indistinct norm.

Zara Yacob also has the following things to say about Mohammed:

> similarly, Mohammed said, 'the orders I pass to you are given to me by God'; and there was no lack of writers to record miracles proving Mohammed's mission, and [people] believed in him. But we know that the teachings of Mohammed could not have come from God; those who will be born both male and female are equal in number; if we count men and women living in an area, we find as many women as men; we do not find eight or ten women for every man; for the law of creation orders one man to marry one woman. If one man marries ten women, then nine men will be without wives.[8]

According to Zara Yacob, God does not order absurdities such as "Eat this, do not eat this; today eat, tomorrow do not eat, do not eat meat today, eat it tomorrow... neither did God say to the Muslims: 'eat during the night, but do not eat during the day.' "[9] For Zara Yacob, these are unreasonable laws created by human beings. God could not possibly stand behind them. These absurdities could not have emanated from human intelligence. God does not subject the human body to such traumatic deprivations. God loves his children too much to create cruel laws that disfigure the body, not to say the soul. God knows the power of necessity, and the difference between necessity and luxury. As Zara Yacob put the matter, "For God created man with the same necessity for food on each day and during each month. The Jews, the Christians and the Muslims did not understand the work of God when they instituted the law of fasting; they lie when they say that God imposed fasting upon us and forbade us to eat; for our creator gave us food that we supply ourselves by it, not that we abstain from it."[10] These absurd practices are guided not by truth revealed to human intelligence but by false faith, and false faith can be recognized, if one works at it and strives to know the truth. Zara Yacob introduces a method of recognizing false faith through the following procedure.

To begin with, he instructs, humans are all equal in the eyes of God. This equality is expressed by the fact that God created all humans with intelligence. And because humans are fated to die, they are equal. Death does not discriminate. It is the ultimate equalizer. The human body is not entitled to immortality. Also, all persons, given their intelligence, can understand God's doctrines through revelation. These revelations constitute the moments of truth. False faith is manifestly nontruth, and cannot be revealed to persons, who are fated to experience truth. Truth occurs only when all persons agree on a given matter or value; whereas it is possible for all to agree on truth, it is not possible for all to agree on falsity. Truth compels singular agreement, whereas falsity or false faith does not. For example, the fact of the existence of created things leads one to agree on a true proposition such as "Humans are created beings with a body and soul." The believer experiences the proposition as a true object of faith, whereas its opposite, "created things are because they created themselves," would not be true. More to the point, Zara Yacob argues that the love of others is a singularly true and compelling value that all humans can agree on, whereas hate, any form of hate, cannot be elevated to a value without serious resistance coming from human reason. The second is effectively an example of a false faith that cannot pass the test of reason guided by God's doctrine. It will be a failure of human intelligence, an abortion of reason, which is caused not by God's refusal to reveal a majestic truth that commands love, but rather by humans' notorious weakness, which prevents them from loving deeply and unconditionally. Zara Yacob put it thus: "the Christian faith as it was founded in the days of the Gospel was not evil, since it invites all men to love one another and to practice mercy toward all," but today my countrymen have set aside the love recommended by the Gospel (and turned away toward) hatred, violence, the poison of snakes; they teach things that are vain; they do things that are evil, so they are falsely called Christians."[11] In an attempt to address the question of why humans believe in falsities, of which false faith is a particular example, he develops the proposition that God has given reason to everyone, hoping that it will be used for the search of truth and the avoidance of falsehood. But human nature is too sluggish and weak to withstand the challenge. This leads me to a discussion of Zara Yacob's views of human nature.

II. HUMAN NATURE

Human beings are exceptional beings in that, should they exercise their willpower to its fullest capacity, they can decipher truth from falsehood and unfailingly choose the former over the latter. However, the nature of humans, when they resort to themselves only, is not sufficiently adequate to be enabling. Under their own direction, they cannot know the difference between truth and falsehood. God's direction, in the secular form of the possession of intelligence, is that power which enables individuals to judge and choose correctly. Note that the stress is less on blind faith and more on a faith that is guided by God's reason. Humans, when unaided by God's reason, are weak—so weak that they cannot choose truth over falsehood. The trappings of falsehood—wealth, status, power—easily lure them.

There are two kinds of laws, Zara Yacob contends: (1) the law of God, and (2) the law of humans. In order for humans to be self-governing in the realm of moral life, they must at all times consult the law of God. It is the law of God that completes the incomplete and deficient law of man. An exclusive use of (2) leads to falsehood; the use of (1), by contrast, enables humans, in a fashion that (2) does not, to recognize truth as truth, but also that truth itself is a semblance of falsity. It is only God who knows "the right way to act,"[12] and when persons want to act rightly, they ought to consult the law of God, which is in the heart of each person. It is crucial, Zara Yacob adds, that one knows the humbling fact that everything that is of and by humans is of limited use and duration, whereas that which comes from the original source, God's doctrine as such, is illuminated by a total intelligence. Ultimately truth cannot be reached by the affairs of humans only. Humans are liars, and that which comes from them is falsehood and false glory. True, the lies of humans do not affect the solid structure of the world in which they live. Lies are effective only in the defilement of human character. Thus, when we lie, it is our souls that we destroy. The world, created by the original source, remains the same, because "the order of God is stronger than the order of men."[13]

Humans are not merely liars. They are also are easy to tempt to errors and evil choices. It is God who sets up his children to the test of choosing evil over good. This test is God's way of separating the virtuous from the non-virtuous. In a manner reminiscent of Aristotle's *Nicomachean Ethics*, Zara Yacob argues that it is during the various agonizing moments of choice that we reveal to the observing world who we are. Evil choices are made not because we don't know what the good is, but because we choose evil even when we know that we should not. Human nature is revealed precisely at the crucial moment of choosing. Zara Yacob is here, on his own, landing upon a similar insight to Aristotle's, although there is no direct evidence that he has studied Aristotle as systematically as the Bible.

In a spiritually comforting passage, he observes that when we feel unjustly treated by God, we should not be tempted to give up our faith in him. For God has his own mystical way of judging. What one considers just when measured by human law is unjust according to God's law. We will be rewarded for it in the other life. We live in two worlds, the material one and the spiritual one; or as Kant would have it, the phenomenal and noumenal worlds. Two different laws govern these two worlds, and what is unjust in one is quite just in the other. As Zara Yacob put the matter,

> In this world complete justice is not achieved: wicked people are in possession of the goods of this world in a satisfying degree, the humble starve; some wicked men are happy, some good men are sad, some evil men exult with joy,

some righteous men weep. Therefore, after our death there must needs be another life and another justice, a perfect one, in which retribution will be made to all according to their needs and those who have fulfilled the will of the creator through the light of reason and have observed the law of their nature will be rewarded.[14]

III. ON OBLIGATIONS

The fundamental obligation of humans is toward God. That is the first wisdom, the beginning of all knowledge. God created humans and endowed them with superior intelligence with the hope that humans would use the endowment for the service of knowing God. As Zara Yacob put it, "God created us intelligent so that we may meditate on his greatness, praise him and pray to him in order to obtain the needs of our body and soul."[15] It is after we imbibe God, the symbol of reason, that we put ourselves in the condition of his willingness to be obligated toward all "others." Thus the first foundational obligation of human beings is to love others as you would yourself, and not to do to others what you would not do to yourself. It is reason, God's gift to us, that commands absolutely to love others as we love ourselves. Our obligations to ourselves are expressed in the secular form of meditations or the holy form of prayers.

Prayers are perhaps the deepest modalities of thinking (or if you like a fancier modernistic term, of philosophizing). The Ethiopian philosopher's prayers are deeply steeped in the mastery of David's psalms. It is via these intimate prayers that the relations among human beings are illuminated; it is out of these prayers that an original mode of African philosophy is born. The persecuted philosopher was very worried about the presence of other jealous and often vicious local religious competitors. He was intensely sensitive to the watchful eyes of the *Frang* [Europeans] with whom he was at odds. While he was self-exiled in the cave, he tells us, "I have learnt more while living alone in a cave than when I was living with scholars. What I wrote in this book is very little; but in my cave I have meditated on many other such things."[16] Zara Yacob's breakthroughs in the world of philosophy are chiefly his few powerful pages filled with the hermeneutic interrogation of the self via an entire surrendering to God, or Reason if you prefer. His meditations or prayers originated in solitude, away from the influence of derivative books. His only reference is the Bible. He meditated in a way that cannot be captured by formal language. His thoughts seemed to have been enraptured by feelings which demand a great deal of respect and attention from a resistant and arrogant modern reader. His meditations, like those of Descartes, were courageously radical. He used his intelligence to delve into the complexities, ambiguities, and plenitude of the meanings of the psalms. When the psalms of David did not agree with him, no fear of authority would detain his resolute mind from striking out on its own. In this medieval philosopher we sense the presence of a fiercely independent mind.

Consider, for example, some of his prayers:

> Save me from the violence of men . . .
> Do not withhold your kindness from me . . .
> May your love and faithfulness constantly preserve me . . .
> Do not let me be disgraced . . .
> Turn to me and pity me . . .
> Guide me and lead me . . .
> Rescue me from my persecutors.
> Let me hear your joy and exaltation . . .
> Do not take away my hope . . .
> Give me each day what I need to satisfy the necessities of life . . .
> Save me from the hands and tongue of men, from bodily sickness and sorrow of the soul.

After his two-year stay in the cave, Zara Yacob learned that the only everlasting value in the human world is the knowledge of God. Everything else is perishable, and human things are essentially vain and contemptible, inferior to the reason that the creator gave us so that we may: (a) know how and what to think and (b) guide ourselves to the knowledge of human nature and finally attain profound understanding of our obligations to ourselves and others. His greatest prayer reads, "I am little and poor in your sight, O Lord, make me understand what I should know about you, that I may admire your greatness and praise you every day with a new praise."[17]

CONCLUSION

Zara Yacob has not engendered as much secondary literature as his soul mate Descartes. This is hardly surprising. In spite of the seminal contributions that his short treatise makes to the field of religious thought in general, and moral philosophy in particular, I was disheartened to discover the nonexistence of major works on his meditations. Be that as it may, I now want to rethink his discussions of the nature of knowledge, human nature, and the moral obligations of human beings to one another.

What is truly outstanding about him is that contrary to the domestication of the rise of the Enlightenment solely to European cultural households and universities, here was a religious thinker who managed to arrive at one central motto of the Enlightenment—as Kant put it, "Have faith in your own Reason." Zara Yacob discovered this motto of reason's legislative power from the depth of his heart seasoned by a long and serious philosophic life in the imposing mountains of Ethiopia. He discovered the power of his mind to interrogate tradition, to examine the Gospels critically, to have faith only in God, whom he accepted as the symbol of reason and the creator of all human beings, when he dissociated himself from the influence of evil men, indifferent autocrats, and bad propagators of religious doctrines. He despised doctrines constructed by human beings. For him, the singularly effective doctrine is that of God, the most perfect, judicious, and wise observer of the human drama. When he criticized doctrines, he spared no one, neither the members of his own kind nor the *Frang*. The African is often portrayed by the Western gaze as hopelessly irrational, impervious to logic and reason. The Ethiopian philosopher's rational meditations conclusively disprove that. Indeed, Zara Yacob's consistent reference to intelligence, that peculiar gift to humans, often goes much further than the Enlightenment philosopher's similar reliance on reason as the ultimate arbitrator of humankind's infamous religious contestations. Even Kant, one of the greatest believers in reason, dissociated reason from faith and made God not the symbol of reason but rather the unknowable object of faith. For Kant, reason and faith are separable. Not so for Zara Yacob. For the Ethiopian thinker, God is embodied in absolute reasonableness. It was not only Hegel who corrected Kant, when Kant separated reason and faith. For Zara Yacob challenged the argument made by the local Ethiopian religious dogmatists as well as the European missionaries of his time that the Gospels are to be believed because they are only revealed by God. That is not enough. Not all the contents of the Testaments are believable. Some are less reasonable than others. Some merely reveal the incompetence and political agendas of the prophets, including Moses and Mohammed. As opposed to these methodological absurdities that either project foregone conclusions or tightly close the doors of interpretation, Yacob pushes the open argument that every intelligent human being has the inherent power with which to interpret the messages of the Bible, and that nothing is to be spared from critical interrogations by the mantle of reason.

For him, the rationalist, everything is subject to scrutiny and severe test of rationality. His reflections on human nature are equally original. He does not have many flattering things to say to us humans, himself included. He reminds us, rather pessimistically, that we are vain, indifferent, envious, and sometimes evil. As a corrective, contrary to the English rationalist Thomas Hobbes, who argued that life is nasty, brutish, and short, as are the human beings who live it, and that an absolute sovereign would have to be designated to silence men's insatiable passions for power, glory, and status, Zara Yacob instructs that it is only deep prayers and meditations that may redeem humans from their bestiality. God does not directly speak to men when they err, he reflects; rather it is the erring humans who must constantly inform their actions by God's guidance, and that God would listen to human agonies if he were consulted. Political life, then, has much to gain from God, if it trains its citizens to habituate themselves to silent prayers in the form of meditations. In the course of time, and rather invisibly, men and women might be transformed by these meditations into morally conscious citizens. Citizens who are morally and rationally formed need not be silenced and intimidated by an authoritarian or manipulative sovereign; they can be appealed to as human beings perpetually aware of the possibility of erring, of the unwanted grounding of their actions in evil. Zara Yacob places the tragic course of racial and class wars directly in the laps of a human nature that is wrongly habituated to indifference, envy, vanity, and self-absorbed glory.

Finally, the philosopher has quite a few challenges that he puts on human beings. The fundamental one is an absolute condemnation of ignorance as an excuse for not doing our duties. He holds men fully accountable for their actions. Similarly, Zara Yacob chastises his countrymen for imputing blame for deeds that they did not follow, wars that they could have avoided, greed and selfishness that motivated their actions, and the persecutions of all those whom they disgraced with their ways and doctrines.

For him, all these terrible actions are manifestly tragic exemplifications of the essence of a moral vision guided by the fear of God. Humans are simply fearful of what they should not fear, for example, death, and fearless of precisely those dreadful predilections which lure individuals to do the socially disgraceful: status, glory, fame, and wealth. The philosopher preaches that moderation and self-control are the cardinal virtues that a medieval Ethiopia, and through it the selfish and cruel world, desperately needs. And from what we know about the way he lived, he himself was a model of a moral hero, an ethical man, born to an unethical milieu. Finally, Zara Yacob makes great strides in the solution of a major question in moral philosophy, namely: When various individuals' images of God produce hostile doctrines that are eminently opposed to each other, what is to be done to avert cruel civil wars? His answers are challenging. First, for him there is only one incontestable doctrine, as far as believers are concerned. That he calls God's doctrine, which he sharply distinguishes from men's doctrine. God's doctrine is motivated by the search for truth, whereas human doctrine is tempted by falsehoods cloaked as truth. If one follows God's doctrine, one is invariably led to experience the disclosure of truth, through which one can develop appropriate sense of duties, of obligations to oneself and all those others with whom we share the world.

Through numerous reflections on methods of knowing, on human nature, and finally on the scope of moral obligations, each of which are guided by comprehensive reason filled with moral sensibilities, this solitary Ethiopian thinker, who lived in a cave for two years, managed to contribute to the founding of what I wish to call the African Enlightenment in the seventeenth century. It is he who indigenized reason and simultaneously gave it a regional and international color, for which his modern readers ought to be enormously grateful. Zara Yacob's indiginization of philosophy as a religious thinker was not flawless however. Consistent with the dominant prejudices of the age, his views of non-Christians, particularly Jews and Muslims, were not positive.[18] Indeed, his strong belief in the power of reason did not lead him to develop politically fair principles of toleration. Similarly, his insistence, like Aristotle before him, that marriage is part of the ontology of being would be shaken by tough challenges from feminists and postmodernists of the contemporary milieu. If we evaluate his program by the yardsticks of modernity, there is much in his vision of the good life that many persons would find quite oppressive and very intolerant. But still, in contemporary hermeneutics of discussions of reading the Bible, there is no substitute for the type of confidence and independence of mind, needed for interpretation, which Zara Yacob's philosophy solidly established. He provided a fecund philosophical foundation for a renewed interest in an expansive notion of rationality.

6

Critical Rationalism and Cultural Traditions in African Philosophy

D. A. Masolo

As the philosopher Charles Taylor has pointed out, human beings need to establish identity, an understanding of who they are—of their fundamental characteristics as human beings. And this identity will almost always include their membership in groups, communities supposedly distinguished by their moral and other forms of knowledge and practices. Since the end of World War II, concerns with sociocultural reconstruction have been at the center of African political movements, and the meaning of history and its impact on culture have been at the center of African intellectual practice in particular. Since then, African intellectuals' debates on history have either been spearheaded by philosophers or have incorporated clear philosophical arguments. But there have been differences in the power with which African philosophers and others have recast and rearticulated the conceptual ingredients of that history in the idioms and metaphors of the developmental theory. These concerns—with the relationship between the indigenous or "traditional" and the foreign or "modern"—have been all the more invigorated in the past decade by the emergence and use in African philosophical analysis of culture of "poststructuralist" and "postmodernist" literature in Europe and its quest for the "ordinary." Themselves often ambiguous in both their goals and conceptual use, these movements have not made things any easier for those who use their framework or "ideology" to analyze—in the hope of also reordering—the imagination and memory of social and cultural experiences in a historical context. The resulting picture is one that, at best, paints *modernism* as an ambiguous organizing concept

> at times celebrated and at times severely criticized. It places the 'machine' at the center of the modern age. On one hand, the machine can represent man's protean qualities, his creativity, his mastery of nature. On the other, it is demonic, sterile, representing technology as it reduces man to the status of victim. The 'ideology' of the 'machine' serves both as an expression of liberation from want and oppression and as an attack on the bourgeois ethos.[1]

The university has been a potent and revolutionary machine in the recent history of African cultures. Throughout the continent, the university has milled the ingredients of change in African societies. These ingredients, the intellectuals, technocrats, and their knowledge, became the agents for reshaping the structures and images of their respective indigenous communities in ways that eventually led to the debates on the meaning and nature of history. In this paper I will discuss the views on "traditions" of one Samuel Onyango Ayany, a well-known Kenyan educator and one of the pioneers of university education in East Africa as spearheaded by the then Makerere University College.

In the days when Onyango Ayany was a student at Makerere immediately after World War II, the East African Institute for Social Research at Makerere engaged students in conducting research into the customs and belief systems of their own communities. The resulting monographs were not only of admirably high quality in scholarship for undergraduates, they were also often highly analytically critical of the indigenous themes they analyzed. In East Africa, these monographs represent a significant stage in the early systematic discussions of local knowledges by a young and pioneer generation of African intellectuals. Viewed against the background of the political and cultural movements of the time, these critical monographs make up an interesting way of contrasting the fledgling critical rationalism with the rising cultural nationalism of the time. What emerged out of these monographs was a clear favoring of a selective approach to the valorization of what many of the young scholars, like Ayany, considered a "past." In the language of today's currency, they were already merged in the discourse of the opposition between "tradition" and "modernity." Mudimbe's recent autobiography, *Les Corps glorieux des mots et des êtres*,[2] captures the awareness of the idea and role of the university as an agent of change. It brings together the articulable and the visible (words and things, or statements and nondiscursive objects of institutions) that interrelate to form the rigid historical strata or epistemes that constitute the apparatus of knowledge, the archive.

Ayany Onyango's work, *Kar Chakruok mar Luo*, written in 1947 in the Luo vernacular, was originally a writing competition essay on local histories. After it won the first prize, he was urged by a local publisher to expand it to a small book length. It was subsequently published in 1952. With a penchant for controversy, Ayany intended his text to promote debate among his own community, which he believed to have a special liking for debate and learning. In the text, he asserted that history was all about ideas, and that he was aware of both good and wrong ideas which made up conflictual images of Luo society. His goal was to offer a radical solution. *Kar Chakruok mar Luo* is about a distinction between ideas that bring historical progress and those that are obstacles to history. One of these was what he perceived to be irrational clinging to traditional beliefs and customs even when reason dictated otherwise.[3]

Ayany's critique of some aspects of traditional beliefs and practices as rationally unjustifiable raises interesting questions within the philosophy of history. It finds its formal philosophical affinity and expression in the works of the famous Austrian-born philosopher Karl Popper. But African intellectuals have dealt with questions of history only in an indirect way. Rather than question directly and formally what history means, they have had to deal with the question by way of attempting to respond to the need to define matters of public policy such as modes of governance or by framing or critiquing what is offered as part of official ideology.

In Ayany's view, change generally, but especially in people's traditions and customs, occurs when people acquire better knowledge and when the claims of old beliefs lose their justifying suppositions—that is, when their supporting grounds are shown to be either faulty or nonconsequential. Reason, then, is the sole driver of history. By making these statements, Ayany joined many others of his generation who were the precursors of the current acolytes of poststructuralist discourse whose starting point is the exposure of the disjunctive moment in historical formations, the structural break, where a new subjectivity emerges. Like most philosophers of culture do, African thinkers also tend to focus primarily on the crisis (that is, barriers, boundaries, and limitations) effected by historical breaks, the transcending of which becomes the prime object.

Their focus has been on the breaks between epistemic fields and transformations. In other words, while they desperately want linkages between the present and historical traditions, their project is not a mere "sentimental and nostalgic longing for bucolic or romanticized virtues of preindustrial society." Nor is their project blindly intertwined with the subjectlessness of Foucault and Derrida, to whom some of them owe inspiration. Rather, their intellectual position is paradoxical. It reflects a form of reverse Eurocentrism that runs close to the position of Gilles Deleuze in seeking to give rise to positioned subjects who resist centralized forms of domination. Or, as the economist Samir Amin says, they seek by means of the very values and categories of Euro-tradition to establish an ambience that will "offer the new peripheries the possibility of escaping from their subordinate positions to become new centres."

Africans' cultural critiques reproduce the Popperian oppositional social-historical categories of "open" and "closed." And this opposition, in turn, raises the question of the degree of the autonomy of the subject from its (epistemic) field of operation. A distinctive contemporary generation of scholars has strongly argued that subjects and their epistemic fields influence each other in significant ways: that while subjects create new fields and objects as part of their location in history, these new fields and objects in turn constitute and transform the subject, who defines and asserts himself by claiming some of those very objects as his own. The subject influences the environment of his practice just as much as it influences his own subjectivity and practice. The subject is in this way only relatively and partially autonomous.[4]

Ayany's search for and appropriation of modernity is a significant historical signifier: it exposes what Charles Taylor calls the breakdown of the old orders, which allows the emergence of instrumental reason. "Once society no longer has a sacred structure, once social arrangements and modes of action are no longer grounded in the order of things or the will of God," Taylor says, "they are in a sense up for grabs. They can be redesigned with their consequences for the happiness and well-being of individuals as our goal."[5] But while for Taylor the individualism of modernity is also a form of its malaise, for Ayany, as for Popper, the autonomous subject is the key to liberation and freedom.

Samuel Onyango Ayany's cultural discourse on the idea of progress and, by implication, on the idea of history, clearly indicates that an important subjectivation has taken place in the postcolonial period and discourse. In both his confrontational character and (universalist) ideology, Onyango Ayany loved to defy what he considered unjustified beliefs. His text, by suggestion, could have opened with an epigraph from this Cartesian dictum: *We ought never to allow ourselves to be persuaded of the truth of anything unless on the evidence of our reason.* He considered many African cultural traditions and customs as types of unjustified collective belief. He thought that people stick to most of their customs and traditions for their sentimental rather than rational values and acceptability. As one philosopher of culture, Ernest Gellner, would put it, "It is this accumulation of complacent, confident conviction, and its acceptance, which leads men into error. There must be another and a better way."[6]

Ayany's text significantly reproduces the European Enlightenment rationality that is predicated on the acceptance as knowledge of only those (propositions) that are empirically justifiable. He believed that scientific reason, which is universal, must replace cultural sentimentalism. He believed that the young but enlightened African intellectuals had a mission: to liberate their folk from the damnation of the sentimental and misleading visions of their cultural knowledge. The text, translated and re-presented by Atieno Odhiambo here, leaves little doubt that Ayany envisioned himself as being in the Platonic role of leader from darkness to a state of enlightenment. Ayany champions historical modernity.

Ayany is not an epistemologist, yet he seems quite decided on the difference between two types of knowledge: that which incrementally brings quality and quantity to life, and that which either stagnates or draws back the quality of life for individuals and even for their whole communities. His premonition is against the latter: tribalism and other forms of social prejudice, ignorance resulting from lack of scientific knowledge, belief in magic and witchcraft, belief in the irrationality of taboo (*Chira*), the practice of polygamy and other economically and socially wasteful rituals, and taking pride in immoral qualities. Ayany's text is indeed also an exercise in the theory of cognitive modernity. (His argument about taboo, for example, anticipates a similar one made more than a decade later by Robin Horton,[7] complete with its fallacies. The argument—that African traditional religious explanations of causes and effects are the local approximations of Western scientific explanations of the same—assumes as identical what are actually different notions of "nature" and the relevant processes attributed to them.)

On political morality, Ayany insists on a new moral code for the sustenance of the institutions of state: loyalty to state authority, obedience of the law, meritocracy as sole criterion for the distribution of public goods and offices, respect for others and for their property reigning supreme above tribalism and other unjustifiable forms of public malaise. His text is a manifesto announcing the dawn of the nation-state as a new sociopolitical reality complete with its own (new) logic that transcends and replaces the traditional polity that was based on the promotion of kinship as a political value and goal. The new polity is to be erected upon the idea of the primacy of the individual, regardless of his or her ethnic and/or kinship origin, as the center of rights and of private property, and as the agent of change.

CULTURE, CHANGE, AND DEVELOPMENT: THINKING CULTURAL TRANSITIONS

Ayany's text raises fundamental questions about history, about how historical change occurs, and about how such change affects our understanding, appreciation, and practice of culture. He appears certain that change is both qualitatively and quantitatively measurable. His medium for articulating these ideas is, again, the usual comparison between the precolonial and postcolonial stages in the histories of African peoples. We have already referred to the diversity of theorizing the colonial as an explanatory and analytic concept in the study of African history and cultures. We shall now focus a little more on some of those ideas with reference to Ayany's text.

For Ayany, the colonial episode divides between two cultural realms that are historically and epistemologically disjunctive and discontinuous, one old and customary, the other new and modern. The former is superstitious, cognitively stagnant (because, as Popper also designates them, they are closed), often erroneous, and socially oppressive. By contrast, the latter is scientific or epistemically virtuous, materially rewarding, and socially liberating. While people can transit from one realm to the other, the two are otherwise formally and substantially separate. The disputes over how these two periods in African history relate to one another have produced, among other issues, two contrasting views of history. One is related to or inferable from Karl Popper's epistemological doctrine of falsificationism. The other, possibly the one shared by Ayany, has close affinity to the position widely attributed to Ernest Gellner. Carefully crafted out of the social theories of Marx, Weber, and Durkheim, it views every historical stage as substantively different from its predecessor. It claims that every historical stage is revolutionary.

In Ayany's view, modernity is first and foremost epitomized in the idea and reality of the state. The state, according to Ayany, enables people, as individuals and as communities, to engage in (largely economic) activities that bring them rapid and quantifiable "growth." Modern education (i.e. literacy) brings with it a better understanding of the law of causality, freedom of conscience, good and well-paying jobs that in turn may result in better housing, improved diet, better health management, and the ability to create and preserve one's wealth. But while the dictates of the logic of the state may have provided Ayany with some justification for his views on the past, he remained caught up in a particularly tormented breed of Western (same as in colonial?) rationalism, as the text poignantly refers to the simultaneously disturbing and comforting role that reason plays in cultural and historical transitions. Thus Ayany may well have been proposing two structurally related forms of rationality for the pragmatic approach to life in the postcolonial condition. One, which favors collective convictions and commitments, is designed to inform our knowledge of the state as a heterogeneous entity made up of social and geographical parts that are affected differently by historical peculiarities of their different peoples. Hence those who live and work within the idioms of state structure should be committed also to their social groups. But above this reigns another, "superior" and profoundly individualist form of reason whose justification is "evidence of reason." This superior reason reigns above custom, for while "that which is based only on custom is dubitable . . . that which is rational is not. Culture and Reason are antithetical."[8] In his own metaphor, while the move from homes (*mier* as the plural of *dala*, the cultural and cognitive center of the Luo universe) to mission compounds (as the geographical construction and metaphor of modernity) represented a qualitative leap to progress in cultural and cognitive representations, the reverse was a damning act of regress and self-abandon-ment. The following passage from Gellner's discussion of the place of Carte-sian reason in the transition to seventeenth- and eighteenth-century modernity will sum up Ayany's own similar culture defiance:

> It is the use of foundations laid by others which leads to error. The rational is the private, and perhaps the private is also the rational. . . .
>
> So individualism and rationalism are closely linked: that which is collec-tive and customary is non-rational, and the overcoming of unreason and of col-lective custom are one and the same process. Descartes wishes, cognitively speaking, to be a self-made man. He is the Samuel Smiles of cognitive enterprise. Error is to befound in culture; and culture is a kind of systematic, communally induced error. It is of the essence of error that it is communally induced and his-torically accumulated. It is through community and history that we sink into error, and it is through solitary design and plan that we escape it. Truth is acquired in a planned orderly manner by an individual, not slowly gathered up by a herd. Complete individual intellectual autarchy is, it would seem, feasible. It had better be, for it is our salvation.[9]

Ayany's obsession with legal suits against those he regarded as local (or cultural) historians reveals another quality of him that draws him close to yet another of the Cartesian values: classicist and bourgeois possessive indi-vidualism, in both its material and cognitive senses. In other words, moder-nity marks and coincides with the emergence of the sovereignty of the individual as much as it breaks with the practice of "choral support" for com-munal and cultural heroes and icons. Hence one of Ayany's important points is to subvert collective culture and popular custom, which, in his view, are endowed neither with the capacity to liberate people from ignorance and poverty, nor with the cognitive capacity to launch the process of transition to a historical condition that is both epistemologically and sociologically superior in its affirmation and protection of the individual. Has it not been said that "It is virtually a tautology [to assert] that the transition cannot be peaceful and smooth"? That "it must at some stage involve treason and vio-lence: for it must involve transfers of authority which cannot be validated, and which can scarcely be conceived, in terms of the concepts of the ancient order"? Modernity, for Ayany, is constituted both by the emergence of sci-entific reason and by the emergence of nationalism. As a result, he viewed the colonial dawn of this new social-political order as a ritual, a rite of pas-sage that ushers the individual into a radically different understanding and articulation of personhood.

The similarities between Ayany and Gellner are striking. Not only were their respective seminal works published about the same time—Ayany's in 1952 and Gellner's "Maxims" in 1951—their views on human history as structured into prescientific and scientific (for Gellner they were actually three, the premodern, the transition, and the modern), with accompanying disdain for the former or first stage, are also interestingly alike. Both saw literacy as a pivotal factor in effecting the transition from one stage of history to the next ("more advanced") one. Like Gellner, Ayany too appears to have believed that

> The manipulation of literacy by the clerisy—[the missionary enterprise for which the mission compound and Maseno as a mission–literacy complex stood as icons of historical change]—and the possibility, inherent in writing, of disembodied thought, make possible the emergence of scientific thought. [Gellner's] view of the decisive importance of the emergence of scientific thought has remained unchanged. In scientific thought we witness the birth of a new form of power, cognitive power, a development with immense social implications. Utterly new forms of social organization become possible, totally new demands for the improvement of life-chances are realistic.[10]

In Gellner's (and Ayany's) view(s), the old (epistemological) houses of tradition are not to be compared with the decisively better, permanent structures of modernity.

But there are at least some questions regarding this universalist assumption. The idea of the possibility of a historically and culturally unhindered reason has come under sharp scrutiny recently, first initialed by the skepticism of Michel Foucault[11] and fueled by work in structuralist anthropology set in motion by the seminal works of Claude Lévi-Strauss. According to Lévi-Strauss,[12] understanding is made possible only by the reducibility of surface data (such as language and concepts) to hidden universal strata of meaning, the unchanging collective properties of human culture. For him, "man" must be understood not as some isolated individual but as a collective mind that does not know at a conscious level how it has organized its world (of social culture) or by what laws it has effected such organization. And he thinks of this underlying stratum as the structural law of language itself. Foucault, on the other hand, while reasserting the structuralist notions, preferred the term "episteme" to "structure" for the hidden fields of knowledge that ultimately determine the ways in which we experience and perceive our role in society, and "archeology" for their scientific exploration.

This shift from the traditional focus on "what" knowable is to the *conditions* that render something knowable suggests what Gellner also observes as a tension in Cartesian epistemology. If our knowledge of the world is rendered possible only by the criteria provided by culture and which only culture can provide, how can we simultaneously make our knowledge free of culture? "Perhaps there can be no culture-free cognition," writes Gellner, "any more than there can be a genuine vindication of any world." He concludes:

> What may be possible is that mankind should attain a form of cognition which, though still culture-bound, is bound to a wholly new *kind* of culture (and one unwittingly heralded and exemplified by Descartes); and that this form of cognition is far more potent than any earlier forms of knowledge; and that, as part of the price of such power, it is obliged to shed the illusion that it can vindicate itself, and moreover, it will *not* be comfortable, and cannot ever recover comfort. Feeling securely at home in the world is something that will not be granted to it.[13]

Descartes, perhaps one of the best-known philosophers of radical transition, remains Gellner's best hero of freedom of thought—from politics, religion, or kinship. But alas, there are no immaculate processes, and so no immaculate conceptions either. Selves are pitifully social, at least as agents and participants of the cognitive world. They are encapsulations of traditions just as much as they are vehicles of their transitions. They create meanings, critically, through the dual acts of (cultural) memorizing and (philosophical) imagineering. Philosophy generally, and African philosophy particularly, can only be as polyphonic and ambiguous in character as the experience of culture itself; it is a cultural inquiry. The texts that constitute it go beyond the cognitive terrain in their examination of the complex and metaphysically mutant (unfixed) identities of persons. Fundamentally, they are predominantly about the nature of change, change in the identity of persons, in cognitive, material, and moral values, and in the forms of social and political constitutions that result from them; they are also (comparatively) about the relationship between these fields of change and the dynamics that effect and relate them; and finally, they are also about the role of social and cultural criticism in formulating and managing change.

There have been suggestions about how to manage cognitive change in ways that are different from the revolutionary purview of Descartes (and Gellner and, by extension, Ayany), at least in the domain of science. These suggestions comprise various shades of skepticism, notably the pragmatist theory of truth proposed by C. S. Peirce, and the falsificationism (sometimes also called fallibilism) of Karl Popper. Both Peirce and Popper were committed to the vindication of the scientific method, to the authority of experience, and to the skepticism regarding the (universal) validity of the inductive method. Both are strongly opposed to any form of dogmatic stand. Popper in particular claims that revolutions often have the tendency of bringing back the same old gods—of closed systems, which are a form of tribalism. But while Peirce sees truth as a social property of inquirers, that is, as a property of meaning, Popper's skepticism was based on what he called our ignorance of the totality of phenomena. Hence his position, against the rival principle of verificationism, was that propositional meaningfulness should describe those propositions that are falsifiable by counterevidence. Such propositions should be only tentatively accepted as true and regarded as corroborated until they are falsified. Every proposition, every view, is only held *pro tempore*. Nothing is unquestionable, both old and new alike.

Popper's epistemological position has won him a large following. A careful reading of Wiredu, for example, reveals an interestingly close if partial affinity between his position—which opposes the influence of anachronism, authoritarianism, and supernaturalism on intellectual and social-cultural values—and that of Popper,[14] with the exception of Wiredu's belief in induction and the openness of the "tribe." like Popper, Wiredu too believes that all knowledge, even "scientific knowledge, and the human rationality that produces it, are . . . always fallible, or subject to error." Weary of any form of dogmatism, whether of the traditional or of the rationalist brand, Wiredu has consistently applied Popper's critical rationalism as the only path for the advancement of knowledge and of human living conditions. Examples are his critiques of anachronism, authoritarianism, and supernaturalism as tendencies that hinder the replacement of the no-longer-suitable knowledge and practices by unjustifiably perpetuating the past.[15] And because critical rationalism asserts that when two positions on the same object conflict, one must be right and the other wrong, Wiredu also rejects recent brands of pragmatism that he suspects to be lenient towards such contradictions by supporting a kind of cognitive relativism.

Wiredu clearly rejects the tendency so identifiable with pragmatism, from Peirce to C. I. Lewis, of considering knowledge as built on systems of consensus within specific social and scientific communities. Often using the Akan as his point of reference, Wiredu has frequently tried to show that such consensus just doesn't exist even in the so-called traditional societies, which are frequently misrepresented as perfectly consensual in their beliefs. His papers contributed to *Person and Community* clearly show an eagerness and determination to counter the myth of consensual belief systems as a foundation for epistemological relativism.[16] It is this rejection of the idea of consensus as the prototypical character of African societies that differentiates Wiredu from Popper and makes him supportive of Odera Oruka's philosophic sage thesis—because it suggests that even within the various traditional contexts around Africa, there are those discrete thinkers who have broken from the popular positions of their groups by holding and defending individually crafted stances or views on a variety of theoretically significant issues. His argument appears to be that the discordant ideas which he expresses in his own work as a thinker who is also a member of the Akan-speaking community are no more critical than those that have always existed in the fabric of that society. The difference is that many of the earlier discords were much less known outside the Akan-speaking community than his own are.

According to Popper, tribal stands, by which he meant orthodox positions of any sort, but under which category he discusses mainly the historicist schools of philosophy, particularly in Germany, are irrationally closed and therefore incapable of change because they reject criticism. For him, tribal stands are a part of what he calls uncritical traditions. If Wiredu's position is that this view cannot be applicable generally to societies, he however shares Popper's view regarding the epistemological value of critical rationalism as the only means of overcoming the stagnation of "the *taboos* of a tradition."[17] Thus, in Wiredu's view, while the traditional societies incorporated some forms of critical thinking, the overwhelming anachronism, authoritarianism, and supernaturalism that come with many other aspects of any tradition must be replaced with the analytic and critical methods that allow for the regeneration of knowledge and betterment of human conditions.

Critical rationalism, either of Popper or of Wiredu (which, contrary to Popper's, allows for a totalizing, universal, or metahistorical truth), rejects all ideas of conceptual frameworks, at least that brand which, explicitly or by implication, condones relativism. For Popper and Wiredu, the truth value of a proposition is always a universal property. Charles Sanders Peirce, the acknowledged founder of pragmatism, shared this view of critical rationalism according to which the scientific method was the only valid means of acquiring sound knowledge. According to him[18] a proposition would be false if experience would refute it; implying, in the pragmatist fashion, that if experience would not refute a proposition, then the proposition is true. What Peirce meant, says Copleston is "not that a proposition is true if it is empirically verified, but that it is true if it would not be empirically falsified, supposing that such a testing were possible."[19] According to Hilary Putnam, "Peirce himself said that if he had to name his philosophy he would have called it 'fallibilism,' the idea that all truth worthy of the name is uncertain and subject to correction."[20]

What critical rationalism says of the idea of history is that as part of how people invent their identities by claiming the existence of an unchanging element about who or what they are over time, history is made up of diverse traditions, albeit constantly revised and updated. History is not made of absolute social systems dialectically succeeding one another—although such systems often claim and give appearance of such absoluteness. Civilizations have the reputation of being heterogeneous, ambiguous, or equivocal. Thus the destruction of even a single tradition can be the destruction of a civilization. "In other words," says Popper, "there is no earthly reason why a society whose traditional set of values has been destroyed should, of its own accord, become a better society—unless you believe in political miracles."[21] At the same time, however, there would be no reason for a society to continue believing in a set of values even when there is new and sufficient evidence that they are false. Popper's position, then, favors gradual and piecemeal reform as opposed to a holistic revolution. This reform is "controlled by a critical comparison between expected and achieved results." In other words, there is never at any given time an attained homogeneity of cultural form. Thus Popper states what anthropologists have always recognized as the nature of the field of their practice, that:

> In this way [i.e., by critically discussing and rejecting as erroneous old theories] we arrive at a fundamental new possibility: *our trials, our tentative hypotheses, may be critically eliminated by rational discussion, without eliminating ourselves.* This indeed is the purpose of rational critical discussion. The "carrier" of a hypothesis has an important function in these discussions: he has to defend the hypothesis against erroneous criticism, and he may perhaps try to modify it if in its original form it cannot be successfully defended. (Emphasis in original.)[21]

Clearly, Popper believes that much of what constitutes "history" resonates around the growth of knowledge, which he likewise believes to have some "plot"—the pursuit of truth. Thus, he asserts, history is interesting to the extent that it tries to solve interesting historical problems. And these are sometimes moral, sometimes epistemological, at other times economic, and so on. History is the dialectical relationship between conjectures and refutations. And, says Popper, "we criticize our conjectures from the point of view of their adequacy—that is to say, their truth, their significance, and their relevance. That we constantly have their truth and their relevance in mind is perfectly compatible with the fact that many conjectures that may appear to us to be true at one stage may be discovered at a later stage to be erroneous."[23] History, in other words, is selective, and its transitions gradual. Yet it is also true that while our ideas face the tribunal of experiential time, they "never face the tribunal alone and hence if they are convicted of crimes they may be convicted *en bloc* when in fact not all are responsible. Assigning responsibility may then become a major task in itself."[24]

CONCLUSION

How do we know that a transition is necessary at any given point in history, and in which aspect of a system? According to Popper and to Wiredu, it is when a criterion of error exists: when clashes arise within our knowledge or between our knowledge and the facts.[25] The point is that it is easier to recognize error than it is to affirm truth. And people can be in error without realizing they are. This is why criticism becomes important, not only for the growth of knowledge but also for the improvement of human living conditions and regeneration of traditions. And most of this is largely agreeable. Yet, like anyone else, philosophers make mistakes, just as do politicians, scientists, professionals of other fields, administrators, and even ordinary people. Certainly, some people have mistakenly thought that the process of industrialization must replace our civilizations, or that the influence of science and technology must eradicate, because they are discontinuous with, some judgments in our systems of thought that preceded or that continue to exist alongside them, or that the rise of modern capital is incompatible with our more affective social values.

But recent scholarship has reminded us of the truism that follows from the fact of human fallibility: that no one pontificates anything to anybody any more. Rather, workable theories and viable ideas are all products of a dialogical practice in the spirit of critical rationalism. Hence, we assert, *contra* those who have adopted the Platonic-Cartesian views against traditions, that while traditions are frequently false and/or unpleasant on a number of counts, they do not necessarily represent an epistemological fall from grace. Nor are those who trust and live their traditions sort of "epistemological sinners: hardhearted sinners who refuse to perceive the truth even when it is manifest before [their] eyes." This view, like that which sees only absolute perfection in one's own tradition, is overly uncritical and unrealistic. Our position is one that espouses neither empty revolution nor blind stagnation; rather, it calls upon all those who inquire into cultures that they "must not accept or refuse [anything] unthinkingly. We must *judge them critically*." That while some people strive "to understand in a general way what may be the function and significance of a tradition ... [there are also] those people who are ready to challenge and to criticize everything, including, [we] hope, their own tradition. They are ready to put question marks to anything, at least in their minds. They will not submit blindly to any tradition."[26]

Clearly, the dynamics that organize the process of change in scientific inquiry are different from those that organize cultural change generally. Post-Kuhnian work in the history and sociology of science has left us with the view that even scientific practice is not as perfect as Popper's *Conjectures and Refutations* had wanted it to look. We have learned from Kuhn that while science is crucially adversarial, it is not, as Mudimbe and Appiah point out, a free-for-all field devoid of limitations on the range of positions that will be entertained. Nor do scientists abandon their disciplines or projects simply because an experiment failed. Rather, as Kuhn (1962) has suggested, there is always a way in which old beliefs—and I think this depends on how strong they are or on how dear they are to our system—are often made to circumvent the wrath of new challenging evidence, assuming that there is *real* challenge.

Sufficient evidence shows that while elimination of error remains a goal even in ordinary history, it is by no means the only one by which change is effected, nor does the realization of the *falsity* of an old belief necessarily lead to its abandonment. There is a new term for what happens in such a case. At the end of the discussion ensuing from his rekindlement of the debate initiated by Evans-Pritchard's *Witchcraft, Oracles and Magic among the Azande* in the above Popperian terms, Robin Horton has suggested that old traditions can be "accommodating" to new rival ones. This makes it possible for different and even rival systems to coexist side by side. In the African cultural and cognitive landscape surveyed by Horton, this allows tradition to accommodate modernity without either disrupting the other. They significantly interface with each other.

An important observation is that while later Horton seems to have recognized, and I think rightly, that the realization of the falsity of an old belief does not necessarily lead to its abandonment, the concept of accommodation is built on the assumption that there is indeed real rivalry between general systems or between their specific beliefs when these are analyzed and contrasted. To constitute a condition of compatibility or otherwise, the exact content of contrasted propositions must be determined, something that is not exactly an easy task. It might be easy in cases limited to empirical propositions determinable by either experimentation or observation where these too are in turn determined to be the limited contents of such propositions. Anecdotally, ten years ago, while giving his famous evidence in the S. M. Otieno burial court case, the late Kenyan philosopher Odera Oruka was asked by the presiding judge if he, a person academically brought up in the analytic and empiricist traditions, believed in the existence of ghosts and their capability to haunt and kill living people. In response Oruka said: "Your Honour, I do not know of any analytic or empiricist ground upon which not to believe so."

Two things, possibly among others, which this response illustrates are, one, that analytic and empirical conditions—apparently of truth—are neither the whole range nor the sole determinants of what people believe; and two, that believing in two sets of propositions, one analytic/empirical, the other I-don't-know-what, does not constitute incompatibility unless the grounds thereof are clearly established. Horton's interesting and widely discussed comparison—of Western scientific theories and African traditional religious beliefs—appears to exhibit such an unwarranted categorical conflation. This is another way of saying that while the chances of older theories are obviously jeopardized when they fail to meet challenges posed by experiment or observation, perhaps more than just such failure results in their abandonment. Popper's rationalism may be a good reason why some beliefs should be abandoned, but it is certainly not sufficient.

On the other hand, people sometimes either cease to practice their old customs or replace them with others without obvious or evident reasons suggesting the superiority of the latest way. Unless they are confronted with situations where either open choice or theoretical comparison is called for, the old way could completely disappear as well, without any rational deliberation, giving the false impression that a critical judgment had indeed been used. At still other times, a pure political gesture may be good enough reason to practice what one may not necessarily consider the best "in itself." When confronted with relevant occasions, same individuals may deem it inconvenient or in other ways not a good idea to go back to "old" ways while not believing such ways to be less reasonable.

How, then, do we explain the revolutionary process by which older theories are rejected and replaced by incompatible new ones? The variables above indicate that neither the practice of culture nor the effecting of changes in it follow logical patterns, be it in Bourdieu's sense or in Popper's mode. Thus, while philosophers may indeed continue to reflect systematically on culture, those who create and live it will continue to do so for reasons not always in consonance with the dictates of the logic of philosophers.

Ideology and African Political Culture

Ali A. Mazrui

Throughout most of the twentieth century, under both colonial and post-colonial conditions, Africans have responded more to sociocultural ideologies than to socioeconomic ideologies. Sociocultural ideologies focus on issues of identity, ancestry, sacredness, and social values. Socioeconomic ideologies concentrate on solidarities of class, economic interest, and economic transformation.

In Africa's experience the most relevant sociocultural ideologies have been *ethnicity* and its belief system, *race* and its solidarities, *religion* and its value systems, and *nationalism* and the structure of its aspirations. This paper will address issues of ethnicity, race, and nationalism—but not of religion.

Socioeconomic ideologies that have been attempted in Africa have included labor movements, different varieties of African socialism, and Marxism-Leninism. Some of these socioeconomic ideologies captured political power and became the ideologies of the state—very similar to the sixteenth-century European doctrine *cuius regio, eius religio* (loosely translated as "the religion of the king becomes the religion of the state"). In postcolonial Africa the ideology of the president became the ideology of the state.

But when the grass roots have been able to express ideological preferences, it has been sociocultural ideologies that have exerted greater influence. Behind this phenomenon is the resilience of certain African values and cultural habits in spite of all the imperial disruptions of the twentieth century.

The study of African political thought has been excessively a prisoner of the categories of European thought and European ideologies. There has been excessive effort to make Africa's ideological experience conform to the European ideological categories of liberalism, conservatism, capitalism, socialism, Marxism, fascism, and the rest.

In the twentieth century there has of course been considerable overlap between African ideological orientations and Western categories. But just because two systems overlap need not mean that they are identical. Students of African thought should pause and reexamine the categories of their own subject matter.

African intellectuals have spent a lot of energy rejecting the concept of "tribe" for Africa. Why? Mainly because African intellectuals have known that most Europeans despised "tribes." Was that a good enough reason for rejecting the concept of "tribe"? Europeans have also often despised the black skin. Should we join them in the same prejudice?

If Africans joined Western contempt for "tribes," are Africans also joining Western contempt for Native Americans who classify themselves as "tribes"? Do we join the general arrogance toward indigenous peoples and tribal societies worldwide?

It may be time that the word "tribe" was saved from excessive political correctness. What is needed is not stopping the use of the word "tribe" for Africa but reviving its use for the European experience. Against the background of the primordial outbreaks of conflict in the former Yugoslavia, it is clear that "tribalism" can as easily wear a white face as a black one.

In this essay we use the more unusual word "tribality." We regard this concept as encompassing a set of beliefs and attitudes that, taken together, could be regarded as an ideological construct in its own right. For those who still insist on avoiding any reference to "tribe," we offer the alternative word of "ethnicism" for this ideological construct.

Behind it all is the simple preposition that European colonialism destroyed structures rather than attitudes, undermined traditional monarchs rather than traditional mores. Indigenous empires were annihilated, but tribality triumphed. What is the secret of the story?

This paper clings to the premise that while colonialism succeeded in destroying most of Africa's traditional political institutions, it fell considerably short of annihilating African traditional political values and ideas. In spite of British Indirect Rule, the organized indigenous instruments of authority and rule did atrophy in much of Africa. But normative African approaches to politics have revealed more resilience than might at first have been thought possible. One of the major problems confronting the imported institutions and Western-style systems in Africa is precisely this cultural lag. Colonialism came with the seeds of foreign institutions but did not succeed in changing the nature of the indigenous soil.[1] Where does tribality fit into this?

Clearly, such governmental organizations and instruments as the Western civil service, the cabinet system, the legislative council, and important aspects of the judicial system were essentially alien. But two or three millennia of African traditions and experience could not be eliminated by a single century of European intrusion into Africa. This substantial cultural resilience has both benefits and costs for the survival of some of the post-colonial institutions.

In an attempt to capture the essential elements of cultural continuity in African politics, we have grouped together a number of normative elements under different traditions. We propose to demonstrate that Africa's political experience in the postcolonial era is still being influenced by one or more of the following tribal or ethnicist traditions:

(i)   the elder tradition
(ii)   the warrior tradition
(iii) the sage tradition
(iv)   the monarchical tendency

Let us explore further the foundations of *continuity* before we examine the essence of *change*.

PRINCIPLES OF TRIBALITY AND ETHNICISM

There is a tendency in the study of African political thought to rely almost entirely on political ideas that have been captured in writing. A major underlying assumption is that thought is not thought unless it is also written. Because of this assumption there has been a relative disregard of the oral tradition in political thought, and an almost complete obsession with political *writers* and with the written speeches of *political leaders*. But there are three major sources for the student of political thought in Africa—the oral tradition, the written word, and the political behavior of Africans. We will call these the oral, written, and behavioral expressions of political ideas.

In this essay we investigate and interrogate six major traditions of political thought in Africa. First, there is the *tribal* tradition, with its emphasis on continuity rather than change. Second is the *dignitarian* tradition, responding to race. Third, there is the *nationalist* tradition, stressing collective solidarity and opposition to foreign rule and external control. Fourth is the *liberal capitalist* tradition, with its emphasis on property, production, and individualism. Fifth, there is the *socialist* tradition, sensitive to the morality of equality and opposed to class-based privileges. The sixth tradition is *democracy,* with its concern for accountability, participation, and openness. Can Africa afford democracy? Or is it too destabilizing?

In this section we begin with tribality in African political culture. Let us first identify some of its main characteristics as a conservative tradition before we relate it more directly to Africa's political experience.

An important initial premise of African tribality or ethnicism is the sacredness of one's ancestry. The tendency to treat ancestry with deference and deep respect is a characteristic of the conservative ethnicist turn of mind.[2]

Ancestry is taken so seriously by the tribal or ethnicist African partly because continuity is regarded as an important principle. Because continuity between the past and the present is important, continuity between the dead and the living is also important. Revering ancestors is a form of respect for the past. Kofi Busia's scholarly studies on the Asante of Ghana and Jomo Kenyatta's *Facing Mount Kenya* (1938) dealing with the Kikuyu of Kenya were works that validated and dignified ancestry.[3]

In that way, a conservative ethnicist might prefer continuity to change; he or she would not be opposed to all kinds of change.[4] Where change is necessary, all that a conservative ethnicist would insist upon is *gradualism*. A profound distrust of either *sudden* or *fundamental* change is part of the tribal tradition in any political culture. Busia and Kenyatta after independence belonged to that tradition.

A related characteristic of African tribality or ethnicism is a reliance on experience rather than rationalism or theory. This again is part of the logic of respecting the past. What has been tried out, and has seemingly withstood the test of time, is to be preferred to what is let out as a theoretical blueprint for social transformation. An understanding of history is regarded as a better guide to political action than is the knowledge of ideology.

Also arising out of this empirical emphasis is the tribal preference for the specific, for the concrete, as against the general and abstract. Rights and duties are often viewed as belonging to specific societies rather than in generalized terms such as human rights. An Anglo-Irish political philosopher of the conservative tradition, Edmund Burke, was sympathetic with the thirteen American colonies in their anticolonial rebellion against George III. But Burke felt that while the Americans had a good case, they worded it wrongly. Burke regarded the American founding fathers primarily as Englishmen. When they demanded the right of representation before they would obey the duty of taxation, they were demanding the rights of *Englishmen* rather than "the rights of man."[5] This Burkean approach was typically conservative and almost tribal, stressing specific rights that had developed out of the history of a specific society, rather than focusing on an abstract universal morality. Burkean philosophy later influenced the culturally relative British policy of Indirect Rule in Africa.[6]

Partly related to this aspect of social specificity, and partly because of the sacredness of ancestry, the tribal tradition takes kinship loyalties seriously, just as it idealizes family virtues. In Black Africa this ethnicism may take the form of "tribal" solidarity, both black and white. Among the Afrikaners of

South Africa "tribalism" may take the form of Afrikanerdom, the unity of the *volk*.[7] Sometimes kinship solidarity can be a metaphor for right-wing nationalism in Europe or Latin America. The sacredness of shared ancestry in Africa creates its own pull in favor of oneness on the basis of kith and kin.

Alongside this pull of kinship in the ethnicist tradition is the pull of religion. The conservative tribal tradition mistrusts "excessive" secularization and rationalization. Faith is often valued as a cardinal tribal virtue, emphasizing the links between the natural and the ultimate, between the secular and the sacred, between the mundane and the divine, between the temporal and the spiritual.[8] Partly for this reason, Léopold Sédar Senghor has described *atheism* as fundamentally alien to African culture.

Partially because of its link with the past, the tribal tradition in Africa is in many ways the most authentically indigenous of all the legacies of political thought. It concerns itself not just with the immediate colonial past but also with precolonial antiquity. The sacredness of ancestry is taken seriously—sometimes literally—to the mythical founding fathers of each particular "ethnic identity," be it Kintu for the Baganda, Gikuyu and Muumbi for the Kikuyu, or Gboro and Leme for the Lugbara.[9]

The principle of continuity includes the doctrine of shared loyalties between the living, the dead, and the unborn. The dead in turn in many African societies exist in two stages. The first stage is when they are still being remembered as specific individuals by those still alive, and the second stage is when the dead really do recede into oblivion. The Kenyan philosopher and writer on African religions John Mbiti has termed the stage when the dead are still being remembered by the living the *Sasa* stage, and the stage of complete oblivion the *Zamani* stage.[10] African interest in large families has sometimes been due to a desire to prolong the *Sasa* stage for parents. On the one hand, begetting many children is an insurance against the losses of infant mortality. But on the other hand, having many children who might remember their parents after they are dead and pass on that memory to their own children could be a passport to the immortality of the parents as they remain in the *Sasa* stage of death, maintaining contact with the living.

The manifestation of the tribal tradition in African political culture is either through the oral tradition or through the political behavior of African societies, in spite of alien postcolonial constitutions.

The preference for kinship solidarity as against theoretical ideology has manifested itself behaviorally in many African elections. The late chief Obafemi Awolowo in Nigeria was sometimes the most prominent voice of the left in his country. He articulated socialist rhetoric, trying to reach the disadvantaged of Nigeria regardless of ethnic origin. But whenever an election took place, and the chief looked to see who was following him, he discovered that his followers were almost invariably fellow Yoruba regardless of social class, rather than the disadvantaged of Nigeria, regardless of ethnic origin.[11]

In East Africa, Oginga Odinga was the Awolowo of Kenya. Again, he often articulated the rhetoric of the left in Kenya. But apart from a few intellectuals and academics, those who responded to Odinga's trumpet-call were not the disadvantaged of Kenya regardless of ethnic group but rather Oginga Odinga's ethnic compatriots, the Luo, regardless of social class.[12]

What this evidence reveals is the preference of the electorate in countries like Nigeria and Kenya for concrete kinship solidarity as against ideological theory, a preference for shared sacred ancestry as against commitment to radical change.[13] The conservative tradition in Africa is thus manifested and expressed behaviorally, rather than in written texts.[14]

To that extent, the ethnicist tradition in Africa tends to have invisible authors, a body of thought without attribution to specific individual thinkers. Ethnicism and tribality tend to be collective political culture rather than a theoretical masterpiece from one individual mind. Tribality is captured in the accumulation of specific attitudes across generations rather than in a specific text from a particular pen.

Because African tribal conservatism is captured cumulatively, it is almost by definition collectivist. It is a body of thought resting on a cumulative consensus, linking the past with the present and the future.

The behavioral resilience of tribal conservatism has emerged in related subtraditions. One is the *elder tradition* in African politics, conceding deference to age on the assumption that the older are wiser.[15] If experience is indeed the ultimate teacher, those who have lived longer have experienced more. Ernest Hemingway's statement that "experience is the name everyone gives to their mistakes" means that elders may guide the youngsters away from repeating the mistakes of their seniors. The elder tradition is at the pinnacle of this pyramid of analysis. Let us explore these cultural continuities more closely.

TRIBAL THEORIES OF LEADERSHIP IN POST-COLONIAL AFRICA

The elder tradition is a combination of patriarchal and gerontocratic elements. The patriarchal factor focuses attention on a single father figure commanding general allegiance and respect. Gerontocracy is a concession to age rather than to a single paternal symbol. Gerontocracy is, after all, an early form of government in many societies.[16] It used to be at one time a system in which the old men of the community were the rulers because of their presumed wisdom, special powers, and prestige.[17]

The elder tradition in Africa did indeed include this reverence for age. In postcolonial Africa, a particularly striking illustration of the elder tradition at work was the role of the late President Jomo Kenyatta after independence. His very affectionate national title, *Mzee* Kenyatta, meant "old gentleman Kenyatta" or "father-figure Kenyatta," or "Kenyatta the Elder." The late president Félix Houphouët-Boigny of Côte d'Ivoire and former president Ngwazi ("Conqueror") Hastings Kamuzu Banda of Malawi also qualified as elders in this special sense. Tunisia's former president Habib Bourguiba played the elder for so long that eventually he was forcefully retired when he became senile.[18]

The elder tradition can be either interventionist or permissive. When it is interventionist, the father figure demands almost constant scrutiny of the behavior and the performance of the other members of the society and seeks also to be almost constantly involved in decision-making.

But where a patriarch like Kenyatta is permissive, he may prefer to let the system make the most of what the patriarch regards as less fundamental decisions. He might withdraw behind a cloud of silent authority, commanding allegiance more by his presence than by utterance, compelling reverence more by what he is than by what he says.

It is possible in some situations to distinguish the elder tradition from the patriarchal tradition. Arguably the elder tradition should in fact be oligarchic rather than autocratic, involving a collectivity of aged wisdom rather than the authority of single person. As the saying goes: "The elders sat under a tree and talked until they agreed."[19]

But in this paper we merge together the patriarchal and the elder themes for ease of analysis in their implications for postcolonial African politics.

The elder tradition in places like Kenyatta's Kenya or Banda's Malawi does have characteristics that could make it difficult for a legislature to survive with vigor. The tradition puts a high premium on deference and reverence to the father guru. Politically, this often can translate itself into affirmations of loyalty. The elder tradition also puts a high premium on at least the appearance of consensus, "family unity," or "national solidarity."

The *warrior tradition,* on the other hand, prefers discipline to consensus, enforced agreement rather than a quest for compromise. The warrior tradition also prefers obedience to reverence, the salute of a soldier to the filial salutation of a child towards his parents. Obedience is a response to orders and instructions; reverence is a response to customary devotion and hallowed dignity and traditional respect. The warrior tradition also thinks of itself as action-oriented, seeking to achieve results by physical exertion or the threat of physical action.[20] Partly because the warrior tradition is heavily action-oriented, it tends to have a pronounced distrust of wordmongers—orators, politicians, and intellectuals. Wordmongers are the specialists in verbal gymnastics, putting a premium on verbiage as against valor, speech as against spear, wit as against war.

Clearly, the warrior tradition defined in these terms has all the makings of hostility toward a Western-style legislature. For what is a Western-style legislative assembly if it is not at its best an arena for wordmongers, for speech and wit, for argument and analysis as against armed bravery?

In Anglophone Africa a particularly intriguing—although transient and tyrannical—instance of the resurrection of the warrior tradition in African political cultures was the rise of Idi Amin Dada in Uganda in the 1970s. Amin symbolized the rugged, rustic warrior from the culture of the countryside, empowered suddenly with a modern army and with a state that was already a member of modern international organizations and a modern diplomatic system. Those aspects of the warrior tradition that were action-oriented, disciplinarian, anti-intellectual, distrustful of verbal skills based on analysis and argument, and partial to the skills of force and violent assertion played their part in sealing the fate of legislative and quasi-legislative institutions in Amin's Uganda.[21] Other African states under military rule suffered a similar fate.

The *sage tradition* conceptualizes political leadership not in terms of child and father, nor in terms of soldier and military commander, but in terms of student and teacher. The sage tradition gives political leaders the role of mentors in the skills and comprehension of politics, instructors to the general population about political virtue and political vice, guides to the nation through the intricacies of interpreting the present world and preparing for the national future.

If the warrior tradition is, at least ostensibly, distrustful of wordmongers, the sage tradition at its best often encourages a good deal of discussion and analysis, provided these are within the terms of the lessons given by their national teacher. At its best, the sage tradition not only avoids anti-intellectualism, it even attempts to promote general intellectual vigor. China under Mao Tse-tung was in part a case of the sage tradition. The debates which accompanied certain major modifications in the Chinese political orientation under the late Mao illustrated this partiality by the sage for vigorous argument and discussion.[22]

In Francophone Africa a particularly impressive sage was Léopold Sédar Senghor, poet and philosopher, as well as statesman. In East Africa, an interesting example was Julius K. Nyerere of Tanzania, himself long a great admirer of Mao Tse-tung. Nyerere continued to be referred to affectionately by his people as the *Mwalimu* (the teacher or mentor). His style as president had indeed included this inclination to transform the whole nation into a classroom. As for the texts that were to be used in this national classroom, some of these were provided by Nyerere himself, others in collaboration with his colleagues. In modern terms, the sage tradition has often gone alongside *documentary radicalism,* a desire on the part of political leaders to produce documents of reform or revolution. In Tanzania's experience, such documentary radicalism has ranged from the Arusha Declaration to the *Mwongozo,* from the terms of reference that led to the setting up of a one-party state to Nyerere's document *Education for Self-Reliance.*[23]

Another great sage was Gamal Abdel Nasser of Egypt, in power from 1952 until his death in office in 1970. In Nasser's Egypt, what was the impact of the sage tradition on the legislature? To some extent the legislature was indeed overshadowed by the great teacher of the nation. On the other hand, Egypt's political party, the Socialist Union, still enjoyed considerable rights of debate.[24] The sage tradition was not entirely distrustful of wordmongers but gave them new arenas of disputation and wordplay.

Modern forms of the sage tradition have recognized that the nation as a whole cannot conceivably be an alternative classroom without the necessary organizational structure to get the lessons across to the different parts of the country. As the modern version of the sage tradition gets radicalized, it finds it important to have a political party that can reach some of the remotest corners of the population. A radicalized sage tradition seeks to strengthen the party structure, partly to ensure that the nation is indeed an attentive classroom that can respond to guidance and direction, and partly to aid in unifying the artificial state, although not always successfully.[25]

Julius Nyerere tried to convert the old Tanganyika African National Union (TANU) into a viable party of national attentiveness and collective response. In 1976 TANU at last merged with the Afro-Shirazi Party of Zanzibar to make penetration across both parts of the United Republic of Tanzania easier through a single revolutionary party, Chama cha Mapinduzi (CCM).[26]

The *monarchical tendency* often characterizes all three traditions so far mentioned. The monarchical tendency in Africa need not be an independent tradition but could be a recurrent conditioning factor in the elder tradition, the warrior tradition, and the sage tradition. It is even arguable that the monarchical tendency is basically patriarchal and should be married to an analysis of patriarchal tendencies. In this interpretation one would therefore be inclined to remove patriarchy from the umbrella of the elder tradition and define it instead as a variant of the monarchical principle.

We define this monarchical tendency in terms of at least four elements of political styles. There is, first, the *quest for aristocratic effect.* In postcolonial Africa, this takes the form of social ostentation. More specifically, it means a partiality for splendid attire, for large, expensive cars, for palatial accommodation, and for other forms of conspicuous consumption. Ministers and Members of Parliament in African countries have been particularly prone to this kind of ostentation and are susceptible to corruption on a grand scale.[27]

Another factor that goes toward making a monarchical style of politics is the *personalization of authority*. On its own this factor could be just another type of personality cult. But when combined with the quest for aristocratic effect or with other elements of style, it takes a turn towards monarchism. Sometimes the personalization goes to the extent of inventing a special title for the leader—and occasionally the title is almost literally royal, though it can sometimes be "sacred" in another sense. Nkrumah's title, the *Osagyefo* ("Redeemer") was one such title. Hastings Banda, president of Malawi, has also adopted a neo-regal title, the *Ngwazi* ("Conqueror"). Bokassa took the monarchical tradition to its literal extreme—complete with an extravagant neo-Napoleonic coronation in the Central African Empire. And Idi Amin had a string of titles before and after his name as part of his official identity.[28]

This linkage between royalty and sacredness brings us to the third element in the monarchical political style—the *sacralization of authority*. As we indicated, this is sometimes linked to the process of personalizing authority but need not be. The glorification of a leader could be in nonreligious terms. On the other hand, what is being sacralized need not be a person but could be an office or an institution. The institutional form of sacred authority is, however, rare in new states precisely because those institutions are so recent and weak. Legitimacy for the office of the president or for a parliament was in most cases rather feeble. The fountain of legitimacy had not yet began to be politically sacralized.

The fourth factor in the politics of monarchism, especially in Africa, is the *quest for a royal historical identity*. This phenomenon arises out of a vague feeling that national dignity is incomplete without a splendid past. And the glory of the past is then conceived in terms of ancient, kingly achievement.[29]

As for literal monarchical systems in postcolonial Africa, those which have collapsed since the 1950s include the royal houses of Egypt, Rwanda, Burundi, Zanzibar, Buganda, and Ethiopia. The most resilient surviving monarchies include those of Ashanti, Morocco, and Swaziland.

ON RACE AND DIGNITARIANISM

That aspect of Africa's sociocultural preoccupation which is concerned with race might be called *dignitarianism*. This is a much more accurate term for it than the word "nationalism," although many authors (including this one) have often confused dignitarianism with nationalism.

Nationalism is concerned with either the defense of or the quest for nationhood and its sociocultural attributes. Digitarianism, on the other hand, is a defense of collective dignity in the face of a hostile or condescending environment.

The African people may not be the most brutalized people in modern history, but they are almost certainly the most humiliated. The most brutalized people in modern history include the indigenous peoples of the Americas and those of Australia, who were subjected to genocidal attacks by white invaders. Also among the most brutalized in more recent times were the Jews and the Gypsies in the Nazi Holocaust.

On the other hand, no other groups were subjected to such large-scale indignities of *enslavement* for several centuries in their millions as the Africans were. No other groups experienced to the same extent such indignities as *lynching,* systematic *segregation,* and well-planned *apartheid* as the Africans were.

It is against this background that Africa's dignitarian impulse was stimulated. A deep-seated African rebellion against humiliation was aroused. It has been a misnomer to call this rebellion "nationalism." This has not been an African quest for nationhood. At best nationhood has been just the means to an end. The real deep-seated African struggle has been a quest for dignity—human and racial.

Africans have been accused of being a people without a history of their own. This stereotype has denied Africans historical dignity. In the notorious words of the then Regius Professor of Modern History at Oxford University, Sir Hugh Trevor-Roper (1914–):

> Maybe in the future there will be African history, but at the moment there is none. There is only the history of the white man in Africa. The rest is darkness—and darkness is not a subject of history.[30]

Africa's dignitarian response has been partly rhetorical and partly in terms of concrete historical research. The rhetorical reply has been in terms of repudiating Trevor-Roper's argument with counterarguments. The response by research has resulted in more research by African historians themselves into the realities of the black experience across time. The eight volumes of the *Unesco General History of Africa* are part of the research answer to Trevor-Roper's breed of historical detractors of Africa.

It was out of dignitarianism that the earliest forms of Pan-Africanism were born. A sense of racial aspiration and cultural deprivation among blacks in the Diaspora led to the Pan-African Congresses, the most famous of which was the one held in Manchester, northwest England, in 1945. Future historical figures like Kwame Nkrumah, Jomo Kenyatta, and Hastings

Banda as well as W. E. B. Du Bois were among the participants at the Manchester Congress.

Subsequently, there evolved five different levels of Pan-Africanism. These levels were Trans-Atlantic, Trans-Saharan, Sub-Saharan, Western Hemispheric (or Trans-American), and Global.

Trans-Atlantic Pan-Africanism was a movement of solidarity among people of African descent in both Africa and the Western Hemisphere. It was this level of Pan-Africanism that gave birth to the Congress in 1945 and the preceding four Congresses, dominated by Diaspora Africans. The Trans-Atlantic version of Pan-Africanism was fundamentally dignitarian.

Also dignitarian was Western Hemispheric (or Trans-American) Pan-Africanism—a solidarity of blacks in North America, the Caribbean, and Latin America. Organizations that have fostered such Western Hemispheric solidarity have included the movement called the Caribbean African American Dialogue.

Also dignitarian are festivals like the African-American Kwanzaa, which is celebrated from December 26 to January 1 every year on the basis of seven principles (*nguzo*), which are expressed in the Swahili language. The principles are *umoja* (unity), *kujichagulia* (self-determination), *ujima* (collective work and shared responsibility), *ujamaa* (economic familyhood and cooperation), *nia* (purpose and will), *kuumba* (creativity), and *imani* (faith). These seven principles and the festival of Kwanzaa (meaning "first fruit") were first formulated by Maulana Karenga, an African-American scholar, in 1966.

Aesthetic dignitarianism has helped to sponsor Pan-African festivals of arts and culture that have been held in Lagos, Dakar, Accra, and in parts of the African Diaspora. These festivals have brought together black poets, singers, dancers, painters, orators, and writers from Brazil, the United States, the Caribbean, and Europe as well as Africa and elsewhere. To call such festivals "nationalistic" occasions would be a misnomer. They were in fact artistic expressions of African *dignity*. They were in that sense aesthetic manifestations of dignitarianism.

Global Pan-Africanism continues to be essentially inspired by this quest to reassert African or black dignity. This level of Pan-Africanism seeks to envelope not only Africans and the Diaspora in the Americas, but also black people in Europe, the Arab world, and even the Aborigines of Australia and the people of Papua New Guinea.

In no sense can these diverse peoples scattered across the world be searching for a sense of shared nationhood. The bonds that hold them together at festivals are not bonds of nationalism but ties of dignitarianism.

Sometimes dignitarian offense has been caused to these peoples by the school of thought that has portrayed Africans as a people without achievements in science and technology, without accomplishments in scholarship and philosophy. The African response has taken one of three forms—romantic primitivism, romantic gloriana, and the realist school of African historiography.

Romantic primitivism celebrates what is simple about Africa. It salutes the cattle-herder rather than the castle-builder. In the words of Aimé Césaire of Martinique:

> *Hooray for those who never invented anything*
> *Hooray for those who never discovered anything*
> *Hooray for joy! Hooray for love!*
> *Hooray for the pain of incarnate tears.*
>
> *My negritude is no tower and no cathedral,*
> *It delves into the deep red flesh of the soil.*

On the other hand, *romantic gloriana* celebrates Africa's more complex achievements. It salutes the pyramids of Egypt, the towering structures of Aksum, the sunken churches of Lalibela, the brooding majesty of Great Zimbabwe, the castles of Gondar. Romantic gloriana is a tribute to Africa's empires and kingdoms, Africa's inventors and discoverers, great Shaka Zulu rather than the unknown peasant.

Both forms of Pan-African cultural dignitarianism were a response to European imperialism and its cultural arrogance. Europeans said that Africans were simple and invented nothing. That was an alleged *fact*. Europeans also said that those who were simple and invented nothing were uncivilized. That was a *value* judgment.

Romantic primitivism accepted Europe's alleged facts about Africa (i.e., that Africa was simple and invented nothing) but rejected Europe's value judgment (that Africa was therefore uncivilized). Simplicity was one version of civilization, Romantic primitivism said:

> *Hooray for those who never invented anything*
> *Who never discovered anything . . .*

Romantic gloriana, on the other hand, rejected Europe's alleged facts about Africa (that Africa was simple and invented nothing) but seems to have accepted Europe's values (that civilization is to be measured by complexity and invention).

The same country in Africa can produce both types of Pan-African dignitarianists. Senegal's Léopold Senghor has been a major thinker and poet in the negritude school. Negritude is associated with romantic primitivism. Senghor's most hotly debated statement is:

Emotion is black ... Reason is Greek.

On the other hand, the late Cheikh Anta Diop, Senegal's Renaissance man who died in 1986, belonged more to the gloriana school. He spent much of his life demonstrating Africa's contributions to global civilization. And he was most emphatic that the civilization of pharaonic Egypt was a *black* civilization. This was all in the grand Pan-African tradition of romantic gloriana.

What about the *realist school of African historiography?* It is based on the reality of Africa. It recognizes a fusion of the simple and the complex, the cattle-herder and the castle-builder. It sees Africa as *more* than romantic primitivism and romantic gloriana. Future Pan-Africanism must in turn go beyond the quest for dignity and attempt to deal with Africa's other problems.

In the future Pan-Africanism of *economic* integration will be led by southern Africa with the new community that has added South Africa to the old SADC fraternity. The success of this economic subregional integration will be partly because one member of the new economic fraternity (Southern African Development Community—SADC) is more equal than the others—the Republic of South Africa. A pivotal state often helps to assure the success of regional integration. But a shared sense of Africanity will also be needed to sustain SADC.

The old European Economic Community (EEC), created in 1958, survived partly because some members were definitely more equal than others. The Franco-German axis was, under Charles de Gaulle, more "Franco" than German. But now German economic might has restored the balance in the new European Union (EU). However, a shared European culture was also needed all along to sustain unification.

Similarly, southern Africa has the advantage of having one member indisputably "the first among equals"—the Republic of South Africa. The pivotal power is the premise of regional survival. But a regional identity has to be culturally strengthened to sustain long-term unity.

Pan-Africanism of *lingocultural* integration will probably be led by East Africa with its good fortune of a regionwide indigenous language—the role of Kiswahili binding Tanzania, Kenya, to some extent Uganda, Somalia, and potentially Rwanda, Burundi, and eastern Zaire. Northern Mozambique and Malawi are also feeling Swahili influence.

Kiswahili is spoken by more people than any other indigenous language of Africa. It will hit its first 100 million people early in the twenty-first century if not sooner. Kiswahili is expanding more rapidly than any other lingua franca in the continent.

Pan-Africanism of *political* integration will probably be led by *North* Africa. There is already a kind of economic cooperation fraternity binding five countries—Libya, Tunisia, Algeria, Morocco, and Mauritania. The economic cooperation has been limping along. However, Egypt has now expressed an interest in joining this movement toward greater North African regional integration. The subregion is still a long way from political integration, but it is the best placed in Africa for such an adventure, since it shares a religion (Islam), a language (Arabic), a culture (Arabo-Berber), and a substantial shared history across centuries.

Part of the stimulus for North Africa's integration will be European integration. The economies of North Africa and southern Europe are to some extent competitive. The deeper integration of countries like Spain and Portugal and Greece into an enlarged European Union is ringing economic alarm bells in North Africa. This could help Pan-Africanism in Arab Africa.

Pan-Africanism of *military* integration is likely to be led by West Africa—with the precedent set by the Economic Community of West Africa's Monitoring Group (ECOMOG) under the Economic Community of West African States (ECOWAS). In spite of the difficulties and inconclusiveness of ECOMOG's attempted rescue operation in Liberia, the effort has been a major pioneering enterprise in the history of *Pax Africana*.[31]

Within Pan-Africanism, dignitarianism can link up not only with nationalism but also with nation-building and with the quest for development.

But distinct as dignitarianism has been in Africa's ideological history, it has not of course kept out nationalism proper from Africa's experience. On the contrary, African nationalism has sometimes evolved out of African dignitarianism. What had previously been a cry of rebellion against racial indignities developed into wider territorial or cultural forms of nationalism.

It is even arguable that nationalism in Africa developed from two very different parents—ethnicism on one side, and dignitarianism on the other. Ethnicism had contributed a tradition of collectivism and assertive solidarities rooted in indigenous culture. Dignitarianism had contributed race-conscious defensiveness and the new Pan-African solidarities.

Out of tribe-conscious ethnicism, race-conscious defensiveness, and the new Pan-African solidarity dignitarianism, modern forms of nationalism in Africa were born. Let us examine this force of nationalism more closely.

NATIONALISM: IDEOLOGY AND POLICY

But what is nationalism? We define it in this paper as a defensive or militant loyalty to one's nation, country, or culture, real or presumptive. The term is similar to the idea of patriotism except in degree of militancy. Nationalism is quite often a more militant form of patriotism.[32]

Nationalism can have a different focus depending upon circumstances. For example, it can focus on the issue of language. Language has an emotive and unifying political effect.[33] Among the peoples of Africa, the Somali are particularly nationalistic about their language, feeling a strong sense of loyalty and pride toward it. It is also a form of ethnicism. In Canada, the French-speaking Canadians have developed a form of nationalism with a linguistic focus, partly because many believe that French-speaking Canadians are disadvantaged in a country with an English-speaking majority that also borders the United States.[34] This is also a form of ethnicism.

But nationalism in other places can also be focused on *religion* rather than language. Jewish nationalism, or Zionism, for example, is primarily based on a cultural allegiance founded on religious ancestry. Loyalty to religion, especially when uniquely shared among a group of people, or perception of a threat to the religion, can have a powerful effect on nationalism.[35]

In the Sudan, the Mahdist revolt against foreign rule in the last quarter of the nineteenth century was partly inspired by a form of nationalism with an Islamic focus. The Sudanese religious and nationalist struggle continued until Britain reestablished control under the doctrine of the Anglo-Egyptian Condominium in 1899.[36] Militant ethnicism was also involved.

Likewise in 1899, a Mahdi (or Islamic reviver) was proclaimed among the Somali, who then organized raids on British and Italian Somaliland. From 1900 to 1904 there were four British expeditions against this new adversary, "the Mad Mullah," Seyyid Muhammad Abdilleh Hassan. Since then, Somali nationalism has continued to have a religious component as well as its traditional linguistic focus. Nationalistic and ethnicist Mahdist movements have also appeared in West Africa from time to time.

But Islam is not the only religion in Africa that has influenced the history of nationalism and ethnicism. Indigenous African religions have also played their part. Sometimes indigenous religious beliefs have been mobilized almost as weapons against the colonial order. The original primary resistance of African peoples against the incoming Europeans often invoked the support of supernatural forces against the white conquerors, sometimes with disastrous consequences. This is particularly true of such nationalistic and ethnicist resistance movements as the Maji Maji rebellion in Tanganyika against the Germans from 1905 to 1907. The African fighters believed in the protective power of suitably blessed water.[37] This belief was immediately put to the test. Would it protect African warriors from German bullets? Alas, the water was not enough of a shield. The warriors fell in the thousands. Nevertheless, the Maji rebellion is widely regarded in Tanzania as the fountainhead of modern nationalism in the country.

In addition to language and religion, nationalism can sometimes be based on *race* as a foundation. This is particularly widespread in Africa since World War II and is especially linked to dignitarianism. Racially conscious African nationalism is partly a response to the arrogance of white rulers and white settlers in colonial Africa. Because the rulers were so concerned with issues of racial differences, the colonial subjects in time became equally concerned about racial dignity. Out of this political defensive consciousness emerged a whole movement of dignitarian Pan-Africanism, especially that version which emphasized the solidarity of black peoples.[38]

In the first half of the century, the leadership of the dignitarian versions of the Pan-African movement was in fact held by people of African ancestry in the Western hemisphere; in Marcus Garvey of Jamaica, George Padmore of Trinidad, W. E. B. Du Bois of the United States—these were among the founding fathers of Pan-Africanism. As alluded to earlier, from 1900 on, there were Pan-African meetings to emphasize racial solidarity and organize for the struggle against discrimination and in pursuit of racial dignity for black peoples both in Africa and in the Western world.

It was not until 1945 that the leadership of the Pan-African movement passed from blacks of the Americas to blacks of Africa. This was the aforementioned fifth Pan-African Congress held in Manchester, England, in 1945. Some of those who participated later became founding fathers of the newly independent countries, such as Kwame Nkrumah of Ghana and Jomo Kenyatta of Kenya. The Africans at the conference were still slightly overshadowed by some of the giants of black nationalism from the Americas, but nevertheless 1945 signifies the re-Africanization of Pan-Africanism, the passing of the torch from Diaspora people of African ancestry abroad to citizens of African countries. Twelve years later Kwame Nkrumah headed the first government of independent Ghana, which was itself the first black African country to be liberated from European colonial rule.

But meanwhile a slightly different focus from race had entered the universe of Pan-Africanism. This was the focus of *territory*, of reestablishing control of the sovereignty of African lands. Dignitarianism was becoming nationalism. In a sense territory is a more prevalent focus for nationalism than language, religion, or race. In Africa, territorially based forms of nationalism in the last stages of colonial rule had at least two main levels—statewide and continentwide. African nationalism was concerned either with liberating each African country in turn or with the liberation of a whole region in Africa or the African continent as a whole. In our sense, regionally inspired nationalism goes beyond the focus of a single country and may encompass all of West Africa, all of East Africa, or all of North Africa. When it encompasses the African continent as a whole, both north and south of the Sahara, it becomes Trans-Saharan Pan-Africanism. While the Trans-Atlantic variety of Pan-Africanism emphasizes the solidarity of people with a black skin, the Trans-Saharan version of nationalism emphasizes the solidarity of the African countries, both black and Arab. The Organization of African Unity (OAU), established in May 1963, is primarily based on the principle of Trans-Saharan Pan-Africanism, urging a unity based on the mystique of the African continent.[39]

The fifth focus of nationalism (after language, religion, race, and territory) takes us back to *ethnicity* and *ethnicism*. In Africa this takes the form of what used to be called "tribal" solidarity. There is a good deal of debate as to whether the Mau Mau movement in Kenya from 1952 to 1960 was a nationally inspired Kenyan nationalist movement or whether it was an ethnically inspired movement led by Kikuyu. The movement was a struggle against land hunger among the peoples of central Kenya and against European monopoly of the best agricultural land in the country. Mau Mau was also a struggle for political and cultural liberation.[40]

Religious symbolism used by the African fighters in the war was borrowed primarily from the religious heritage of the Kikuyu and related ethnic groups. This heritage was used as a basis for oathing ceremonies to sanctify commitment to the movement and discourage treachery and subversion within the movement. The Mau Mau fighters were preponderantly drawn from Kikuyu, Meru, and Embu ethnic groups. Can such ethnicism be nationalism?

Both the fighters and the religious symbols of the movement were ethnic. But were the political goals of the movement *national* notwithstanding? If the answer to the second question is yes, then the Mau Mau movement was a war of liberation carried out by the Kikuyu and related small "ethnic groups" but on behalf of the wider African political community within Kenya.

Similarly, Mugabe's army in Rhodesia, the Zimbabwe African National Liberation Army (ZANLA) two decades later consisted mainly of Shona ethnic compatriots, but the goals of the movement made it a liberation struggle for Zimbabwe as a whole. In short, it is possible for the composition of a movement to be ethnic while its political goals are national or even transnational.

At the initial point of colonization the distinction between national and ethnic resistance did not in any case make much sense. The ethnic groups of Africa resisted as autonomous societies against encroaching European penetration. Until the Europeans drew the colonial boundaries and created new proto-nations, any fighting by the Shona and the Ndebele was in each case both national and ethnic. Similarly, the struggles of the Banyoro in Uganda or the Hausa-Fulani or Yoruba in Nigeria involved political communities where ethnic boundaries substantially coincided with ancient national boundaries. It was the colonial mapmaker who disrupted this congruence between "tribal" and "national" identities.[41] Following colonialism, nationalism and ethnicism were often at loggerheads.

CAPITALISM: IDEOLOGY AND POLICY

But political ideas are not only linked to culture and history. They are also profoundly affected by economics. Production and values are inseparable.

Most of the debates about African policy options fail to draw a simple distinction between restoring African economies to market forces and entrusting them to private ownership and private control. It is true that the liberal doctrine, at least since Adam Smith, has tended to assume that the market comes into relatively independent play when the pursuit of wealth is left to private initiative. What we now call *privatization* was deemed to be the only viable approach to the triumph of the market. Privatization was the means; *marketization* was the end.

But in reality an economy could be in private hands and not be subject to the free market because of factors downplayed or ignored by liberal thinkers. Or it could be under state ownership and still respond to market forces and to the laws of supply and demand.

The imperatives of restructuring African economies have all too often assumed that the only route to the free market is through privatization. Indeed, economic reformers concerned with Africa have equated privatization with marketization. Is it time to take another look?[42]

The free market in Africa can be constrained or inhibited by a number of factors that have very little to do with the state *per se*. A notorious inhibition of the free market in Africa is the simple fact that the whole market can be cornered or monopolized by an ethnic group. Africa has not yet discovered ethnic antitrust laws to prevent or break up "ethnic monopolies" in certain key industries. Nigeria underwent the trauma of a civil war partly because the Igbo had been perceived in the north as monopolizing certain economic areas of activity—and the nation had no "antitrust legislation" for dealing with ethnic specialization and monopoly.

Unfortunately, neither ethnic specialization nor counterethnic resentment ended in 1970 when large-scale fratricide came to a close in Nigeria. The civil war was concluded, but the precise cultural differences between the ethnic groups did not end. By the 1980s the Igbo were once again a little too visible for their own safety in the north of the country in certain areas of trade and industry.

We use the Igbo in this analysis purely as an illustration of ethnicity as a constraint on the market. In the 1980s in Nigeria there was more recognition of the need for ethnic "antitrust legislation" to prevent or to break up "tribal monopolies." Sometimes the euphemism for this description in favor of the disadvantaged is called "the federal character of Nigeria." This is Nigeria's nearest equivalent of the principle of affirmative action in the United States. But in both countries the restoration of ethnic balance is rather haphazard and sometimes in conflict with other democratic values.

Plateau State in Nigeria in the 1980s built what was reputed to be the largest marketing structure in black Africa. The head of state came to open it. Yet for a long time the building was left hauntingly empty in a desperate struggle to ensure that when it was indeed finally utilized, the majority of the owners of stalls and the merchants would be "indigenes" of Plateau State (and not "immigrants" from other parts of Nigeria). The precautions to prevent a "southern monopoly" of the market were successful at the beginning. But as so often happens, the process of a southern "takeover" through deepening penetration has since gotten under way.

But is not Igbo success in certain economic activities (or Yoruba success in others) a case of the free market finding its own equilibrium of efficiency? This would partly depend upon whether Igbo (or Yoruba) preponderance is due to the unencumbered free play of relevant market factors. But in reality there is devout ethnic solidarity and nepotism at play, and these ensure the success of some Nigerian entrepreneurs and severely handicap the efforts of others. The considerations of Igbo monopoly in the trade of car parts and other spare parts are not all rational elements of Igbo efficiency. Igbo success includes as one of its pillars Igbo nepotism. The same is true of Kikuyu success in Kenya in the late 1960s and 1970s. It is part of the reality of African *conservatism* in allegiance.

In addition to ethnic nepotism as a constraint on the market in spite of privatization, there is also the all-pervasive constraint of the *prestige motive* in Africa's economic behavior. Traditional Western liberal doctrine had often taken for granted the psychology of the *profit motive* (later identified as the maximization of returns). African economic behavior, on the other hand, is often inspired more by the pursuit of *prestige* than by the quest for profit. Precisely because African cultures are more collectivist, members of the society are more sensitive to the approval and disapproval of the collectivity.

On the positive side, the prestige motive serves as a device of income distribution. Those who are financially successful often desire renown for generosity. Obligations toward wider and wider circles of kinfolk are fulfilled. Word gets around to relatives far and wide—"Our son has killed an elephant. There is more than enough meat for us all to chop." Those who succeed share their rewards with many others. Here too is cultural continuity.

On the negative side, the prestige motive in African economic behavior encourages ostentatious *consumption* and self-indulgent "aristocratic" and "monarchical" exhibitionism. The Mercedes Benz has become the symbol of Africa's ostentatious indulgence—but in some places in Nigeria the expensive fleet of cars often goes with a palace or two, sometimes a private plane and a helicopter, and a loud way of life, all for a single family!

While the profit motive in classical economic theory was supposed to lean toward greater *production,* the prestige motive in contemporary African economic behavior leans towards greater *consumption.*

What is more, because they often have to be imported, the consumer products commanding the most prestige require foreign exchange. Privatization on its own does not make an African economy produce more. The prestige motive operates both privately and at the state level, eating ominously into the resources of the country.

When Westerners call upon African countries to privatize, they are expecting the profit motive to be given a free play. But in fact, *the problem in most of Africa is not simply how to liberate and activate the profit motive,* but also how to control and restrain the prestige motive. Arguably the latter crusade is even more urgent than the former.

Indeed, the ultimate crusade may well turn out to be how to tap the prestige motive in such a way that it serves the goals of production and not merely the appetites of consumption. Can we make creativity more prestigious than acquisition? Can we make production more prestigious than possession? Should we take a closer look at the problem of *incentives* in Africa? How can we be more precisely sensitized to the *African* equilibrium between prestige and profit?

A third major *private* constraint on the market (after ethnic nepotism and the prestige motive) is the general problem of bribery and corruption prevalent in postcolonial Africa. Corruption can clog up procedures and substantially paralyze production and distribution. Again, corruption can be both in the public sector and in the private; it can be bureaucratic or omnipresent. Privatization of the economy may simply mean the *privatization of corruption*—and sometimes this is more contagious in the wider society than the corruption of officials and bureaucrats.

Capitalism has come to Africa, but without the "Protestant ethic" of work and frugality. The white man in Africa himself set a dangerous example. He never washed his own clothes, or cooked his own food, or polished his own shoes, or made his own bed, or cleaned his own room, or washed his own dishes, or even poured his own gin and tonic! The luxurious aristocratic life of the white settler as he played master to the African servant was detrimental to the spirit of the capitalism that the white man had himself arrived with. Africa's own prestige motive—which had been sociable in its original indigenous versions—was now transformed by the aristocratic lifestyles imported by the white man. Africa's prestige motive was given the colonial incarnation of expensive European consumer culture complete with huge houses, domestic servants, and "garden boys."

If the ideology of entrepreneurship simply means acquisitiveness, this has now arrived in a big way in much of Africa. Indeed, those who do not take advantage of their opportunities to become wealthy, and to help their kinsfolk, are sometimes despised.

The challenge is partly about the means used to acquire wealth. Is the wealth *created* or simply obtained? Acquiring wealth from a prosperous farm is a creative process. Acquiring wealth as either a middleman on behalf of external interests or through corruption may not be creative at all. Can we transform the acquisitive instinct in Africa into something more directly productive?

But if the *means* of acquiring wealth need to be creative, the *ends* of acquiring wealth also need to be healthy. Ostentatious consumption is not usually among the healthier ends of economic success. In short, African ideology of entrepreneurship needs a fundamental reform of both the means and the ends of the pursuit of wealth in society.

Until that happens, privatization of African economies—far from being the best way of achieving a healthy and free market—may itself be detrimental to the marketplace. For those who are sufficiently attentive, the African experience demonstrates that privatization is not necessarily the best protection for the free market in all cultures.

But modern capitalism in Africa has often been almost inseparable from socialist aspirations and sentiment. It is to the complexities of Africa's socialist experience that we must now turn.

SOCIALISM: IDEOLOGY AND POLICY

As a generalization, we might say that the intellectual climate for socialism in Africa has been quite good, but the sociological and material soil has not been fertile enough. Let us explore this twin proposition more fully.

As to the reasons why the intellectual climate for socialism in Africa has been good, these include once again basic historical continuities and discontinuities. For one thing, many Africans both north and south of the Sahara have conceptually associated capitalism with imperialism. In reality, you can have socialism accompanied by imperialism. Indeed, the Chinese used to protest against "social imperialism" and "Soviet hegemony." It is also possible to be a capitalist country without being an imperialist country—Switzerland and Sweden might be considered by some as good illustrations of nonimperialist capitalism.

But in Africa's historical experience it is indeed true that modern capitalism came with imperialism. Kwame Nkrumah was very sensitive to this linkage.[43] The enemy of imperialism is nationalism; the enemy of capitalism is socialism. If there is indeed an alliance between capitalism and imperialism, why should there not be an alliance between African nationalism and socialism? Such a paradigm of intellectual and ideological convergence has been found attractive in many parts of Africa. Leaders like Sékou Touré and movements like the Front for the Liberation of Mozambique (FRELIMO) became socialist for *nationalistic* reasons.

A second consideration that has contributed to the favorable intellectual climate for socialism in Africa concerns the whole accumulation of frustrations with efforts to develop Africa through Western patterns of economic growth. Many Africans are seeking alternative strategies of social and economic improvement out of a sheer sense of desperation at the inadequacies of the first decades of independence. In reality, socialist experiments in postcolonial Africa so far have not yielded any greater improvement for the masses than other experiments. On the contrary, sometimes the social costs of socialism in Africa have indeed been rather high. It is arguable that while there were relatively successful petty capitalist experiments in countries including Kenya, Malawi, Tunisia, and the Côte d'Ivoire until the early 1980s, Africa as a whole has yet to produce a significant improvement in the material conditions for the masses. The nearest socialist success story until the 1980s was perhaps Algeria. But socialist Algeria needed to sell oil to the capitalist world to buttress socialism.

In spite of these contradictions, however, many Africans are so disenchanted with the first decades of capitalist independence that they would not mind experimenting with socialist approaches to social transformation.

The third factor that predisposes many Africans in favor of socialism is the rampant corruption among the immediate postcolonial rulers of the continent, all the way from Egypt to Zimbabwe within a few years of independence. Again, corruption is by no means a peculiarity of capitalism, as many of those who have traveled in socialist countries will testify. But there is no doubt that social discipline can at times be more difficult to uphold in conditions of laissez-faire economic behavior than in conditions of relatively centralized planning and supervision. On balance, it is indeed arguable that the socialist ethic in Robert Mugabe's own personal socialism is, almost by definition, more opposed to "kickbacks," "goodwill bribery," and even profit itself than is the ethic of acquisitive individualism in his own comrades.

The fourth factor that has contributed to the favorable intellectual climate for socialism in Africa is the widespread belief that traditional African culture was basically collectivist—and therefore socialist. There have been claims from quite early on by some African leaders, including Senghor, Nyerere, and Mboya, that the morality of sharing in traditional Africa, the ethic of responsibility for the young, for the old, and the disabled, is the imperative of a collective ethic akin to socialism.[44]

Because of this broadly favorable intellectual climate, most African governments soon after independence paid some kind of lip service to socialism. Even regimes like those of Jomo Kenyatta and Habib Bourguiba managed to adopt in the initial years of independence a partially socialist rhetoric.

Regimes that opted for the one-party state route were particularly tantalized by socialist symbolism. After all, the presumed centralizing tendencies of socialism could help justify a one-party monopoly of power. Prospects for socialism in the first decade of African independence did seem to be bright. Nasser, Nkrumah, Sékou Touré, Julius Nyerere, and Boumedienne were seen as architects of a new socialist Africa. From the 1970s, countries like Ethiopia, Angola, Congo, and Mozambique went all the way to Marxism-Leninism. In spite of the power of sociocultural solidarities, was a socioeconomic ideology taking root in Africa after all?

What went wrong? This is what brings us to the barrenness of the sociological soil for socialism, in spite of the favorableness of the intellectual climate. One obstinate sociological factor against socialism was simply the primacy of ethnicism in Africa as against class consciousness. Most Africans are members of their ethnic group first and members of a particular social class second. When the chips are down, Igbo peasants are more likely to identify with the Igbo bourgeoisie than they are with fellow peasants in Yorubaland. Socialism has been up against ethnicism.

On balance, it can be legitimately argued that whenever there has been a neat confrontation and competition between the forces of ethnicism on one side and the forces of class consciousness on the other side, ethnicism has almost invariably triumphed in Africa. This is one primary factor behind the infertility of the sociological soil for an ideology like socialism. Ethnicist conservatism is stronger than socialist theory. Sociocultural forces are still stronger *emotionally* than socioeconomic ones.

A related factor is the strength of cultural elites in Africa as against economic classes as such. The new elites especially have emerged out of the womb of Western imperial acculturation. It has not been the possession of wealth necessarily that opened the doors to influence and power, but initially the possession of Western education and verbal skills. To be sure, the initial political establishment of postcolonial Africa was disproportionately comprised of a Westernized and semi-Westernized core. This galaxy of Westernized stars has included names like Nkrumah, Nyerere, Senghor, Kaunda,

Ferhat Abbas, Obote, Houphouët-Boigny, Boutros-Ghali, Mandela, Banda, Bourguiba, Mugabe, Nkomo, Sadiq el-Mahdi, Machel, Neto, and others.

This created a basic sociological ambivalence on the African scene. On the one hand, it seemed that those most opposed to imperialism rhetorically, and the ones most likely to link it to capitalism, were precisely the elites produced by the West's cultural imperialism in Africa. Even when these elements became truly revolutionary, there was a basic contradiction. After all, Karl Marx had expected the most revolutionary class to be the least advantaged class in the most advanced societies. This was deemed to be the proletariat in industrial Western societies.

But when you look at the former revolutionary leaders in Angola, Tanzania, Guinea (Conakry), and Zimbabwe, and examine the Western credentials of the leaders, you may be inclined to conclude that the most revolutionary of all classes in those societies were the best advantaged. In other words, Westernized Third World bourgeois intellectuals were the most likely to produce the dream of socialist transformation. Therefore it is not the least advantaged social class in the most advantaged society (the proletariat in the West) but the best advantaged social group in the least advanced societies (the Westernized bourgeois intelligentsia in Third World countries) who have been the true agents of revolution in the last quarter of the twentieth century.

It is still a sociolinguistic impossibility for an African to become a sophisticated Marxist without being at the same time substantially Westernized. This is partly because the process of becoming a sophisticated Marxist requires considerable exposure to Marxist literature, both primary and secondary. Access to that literature for the time being is only minimally possible through indigenous African languages like Kiswahili, Yoruba, or Amharic. Even in Arabic, Marxist literature is relatively limited. An African who wants to read many of the works of Marx, Engels, and Lenin has to have been substantially initiated into the literary culture of the West.

Even Africans who go to Communist China or went to the former Soviet Union needed to have been previously Europeanized. Scholarships to China and the former Soviet Union were not normally offered to rural rustics untouched by Western schools or their equivalents. The nature of elite education in Africa can therefore be counted as an aspect of the uncongenial sociological soil that socialism has to confront in African conditions.

A third factor of this barrenness of the soil concerns Africa's organizational capabilities in the present historical phase. Many hastily assume that a tradition of collectivism in a traditional setting is a relevant preparation for organized collective efforts in a modern setting. Unfortunately, much of the evidence points the other way. Collective effort based on custom and tradition and kinship ties leaves Africa unprepared for the kind of organized collectivism that needs to be based on command rather than ritual. If socialism requires a rational, efficient command structure that is not based on custom, ethnic empathy, or ritual, the present stage of social change in the African experience is still inhospitable to socialist transformation.

The fourth aspect of the infertility of Africa's sociological soil for the socialist plant would take us back to issues of historical continuity. Many African economies have already been deeply integrated into a world economy dominated by the West. African countries that go socialist domestically find that they are still integrated in the world capitalist system. The rules of that system are overwhelmingly derived from principles evolved in the history of capitalism. In international trade, countries seek to maximize their returns. The rules of business and exchange at the international level, the banking system that underpins those exchanges, the actual currencies used in money markets and in meeting balance-of-payments are all products of the capitalist experience. Countries like Vietnam, Angola, and even Cuba discover soon enough that their best economic salvation is to gain international legitimacy by Western standards. Vietnam and Cuba may fail in gaining that complete legitimacy, but it is part of their ambition to begin receiving Western currency markets as well.

What all this once again means is that Third World countries can make their internal domestic arrangements socialist while at the same time remaining deeply integrated in the international capitalist system. It is even arguable that a country like Tanzania is today more dependent on the world capitalist system than it was before it inaugurated its neosocialist experiment under the Arusha Declaration in 1967.

Socialism in Africa suffered in the 1990s because of the collapse of communist governments in Europe, which had previously supported regimes like the self-declared Marxist ones of Angola, Ethiopia, Mozambique, and elsewhere. The sharp decline and disgrace of European communism was a blow to socialism in Africa.

This, then, is the configuration of factors that on one side reveals that intellectually, postcolonial Africa has been ready for socialism and, on the other side, warns us that the material conditions for genuine socialist experimentation in Africa are not yet at hand. The intellectual climate is promising; the sociological soil is forbidding. Once again a socioeconomic ideology has failed to take root in Africa.

Finally, let us turn to Africa's struggle to establish democracy without further loss of stability. We define democracy as a political system that makes rulers accountable, assures the citizens participation and choice in electing their rulers, guarantees openness in public affairs and civil liberties for the people, has checks against arbitrary use of power, and is committed to the pursuit of justice.

Can Africa approximate such a system without damaging even further its capacity to maintain basic stability? What is democracy up against in postcolonial Africa? Le us turn to this theme.

IN SEARCH OF DEMOCRATIC STABILITY

Every African government has continued to walk that tightrope between too much government and too little government. At some stage an excess of government becomes tyranny; at some other stage too little government becomes anarchy. Either trend can lead to the failed state. Indeed, either trend may lead to the collapse of the state, to death, and to large-scale displacement.

Somalia under Siad Barre was a case of *tyranny* finally leading to the collapse of the state; the Congo (Leopoldville), or what is now Zaire, in 1960 was a case of *anarchy* nearly destroying the new postcolonial state. It was saved by the United Nations' (until the 1990s) largest peacekeeping operation (ONUC).[45]

A major unresolved dilemma lies in civil-military relations. Perhaps in everybody's experience military rule often leads to too much government—almost by definition. On the other hand, civilian rule in countries like Nigeria and the Sudan has sometimes meant too little government, with politicians squabbling among themselves and sometimes plundering the nation's resources. If military regimes have too much power, and civilian regimes have too little control, countries like Nigeria and the Sudan have to find solutions for the future. Otherwise destruction and displacement loom threateningly.

Dr. Nnamdi Azikiwe, the first president of independent Nigeria, once proposed a constitutional sharing of power between the military and civilians. It was called *diarchy,* a kind of dual sovereignty. At the time that Dr. Azikiwe proposed the dual sovereignty idea (part military, part civilian) in 1972, he was roundly denounced, especially by intellectuals and academics who were against military rule. But the dilemma has still persisted in Dr. Azikiwe's own country, Nigeria, and elsewhere in Africa—how to bridge the gap between the ethic of representative government and the power of the military.

Has Egypt quietly evolved a diarchy since the 1952 revolution—a system of government of dual sovereignty between civilians and soldiers? Has Azikiwe's dream found fulfillment in Egypt, however imperfectly? Or is the Egyptian system still in the process of *becoming* a diarchy but has not yet arrived there? Starting as a military-led system in 1952, has it become increasingly *civilianized*—yet still in the process of change toward full power sharing?

Another dilemma concerning too much government versus too little hinges on the *party system*. There is little doubt that one-party states tend towards too much government. This has been the case in most of Africa.

On the other hand, multiparty systems in Africa have often degenerated into ethnic or sectarian rivalries resulting in too little control. This tendency was illustrated in the 1980s by Ghana under Hilla Limann, Nigeria under Shehu Shagari, and the Sudan under Sadiq el-Mahdi. The state was losing control in all three cases.

If one solution to the civil-military dilemma is diarchy (the dual sovereignty), what is the solution to the dilemma between the one-party state and the multiparty system?

Uganda is feeling its way toward one solution to the dilemma—a *no-party* state. Concerned that a multiparty system would only lead to a reactivation of Uganda's ethnic and sectarian rivalries, President Yoweri Museveni lent the weight of his name, office, and prestige to this principle of a Uganda without political parties for at least five years. In an election held in March 1994 to choose members of a Constituent Assembly, candidates in favor of a no-party Uganda seemed to have won a majority of the seats. The Constituent Assembly has yet to draw up the actual definitive provisions of Uganda's new constitution.

Under both Idi Amin (1971–1979) and the second administration of Milton Obote (1980–1985) Uganda experienced some of the worst excesses of both tyranny and anarchy at the same time. Although the state did not actually collapse, it lost control over a large part of the territory and was unable to perform many of its basic functions. Thousands of people were displaced or escaped into exile. Champions of a "Uganda without political parties" hope that their new partyless approach to politics may avert the type of situation that brought Idi Amin into power in the first place.

There are other possible solutions to the dilemma between multiparty anarchy and one-party tyranny. One possibility is a *no-party presidency* and a *multiparty parliament*. This could give a country a strong president with extensive constitutional powers, but one who is elected in a contest between *individuals* and not between party candidates. Parliament or the legislature, on the other hand, could remain multiparty. The president would not be allowed to belong to any political party.

A system of a presidency without a political party may indeed give undue advantage to Africa's millionaires or billionaires—the "black Ross Perots" or "other M.K.O. Abiolas." That may be the price to pay for a no-party presidency in a multiparty society.

All of the above are situations where the state succeeds or fails in relation to the nature of the political institutions (military or civilian, multiparty or one-party or other). But in reality a state succeeds or fails in relation to wider societal configurations as well. In postcolonial Africa ethnicity continues to be a major factor conditioning success or failure of the state.[46]

Yet here too Mother Africa presents its contradictions. The road to state collapse or state displacement could be through having either too many groups in the process—or, paradoxically, too few. Previous failures of the state in Uganda were partly due to the very ethnic richness of the society—the striking diversity of Bantu, Nilotic, Sudanic, and other groups, each of which was itself internally diverse. The political system was not yet ready to sustain the immense pressures of competing ethnocultural claims. Lives were lost, thousands were displaced.

Ethiopia under Mengistu Haile Mariam also drifted toward state failure partly because the system was unable to accommodate its rich cultural and ethnic diversity. Mengistu's tyranny did not foster free negotiations, or compromise, or coalition building among ethnic groups. Lives were lost, thousands were, again, displaced.

But how can a state fail or collapse because it has too *few* ethnic groups? At first glance it looks as if Somalia has been such a case.

George Bernard Shaw used to say that the British and the Americans were a people divided by the same language. It may be truer and more poignant to say that the Somali are a people divided by the same culture. The culture legitimizes the clans that are among the central bases of discord. The culture legitimizes a macho response to interclan stalemates. The culture legitimizes interclan feuds.

Interclan rivalries among the Somali would decline if the Somali themselves were confronting the competition of other ethnic groups within some kind of plural society. The Somali themselves would close ranks if they were facing the rivalry of the Amhara and the Tigre in a new plural society. It is in that sense that even a culturally homogeneous society can have major areas of schism if wise answers are not found for them.

In any case, Somalia even on its own could be studied as a *plural* society of many *clans* rather than of many "tribes." The single culture of the Somali people may be a misleading indicator. The pluralism of Somalia is at the level of *subethnicity* rather than ethnicity.

That disguised pluralism of Somalia was exploited by Siad Barre to play off one clan against another. Siad Barre's tyranny lasted from 1969 until 1990. It turned out to be the high road to the destruction of the Somali state. The Somali became more than nomads: they became refugees.

In Africa there is clear evidence that the people are tired of dictators. In one African country after another there have been riots and protests against dictators. There is genuine desire for democracy, but the capacity to democratize needs to be strengthened. The democratic spirit may be willing, but the political flesh is weak.

In the course of the 1990s much of Africa has continued to demonstrate this solid *desire* for democracy. What has yet to be tested fully is Africa's *capacity* to democratize. The desire for democracy has manifested itself in a variety of ways—from prodemocracy street demonstrations in Togo to the Muslim riots at the Kenya coast, from the political tug-of-war between soldiers and civilians in Nigeria to the electoral fall of Hastings Banda's tyranny in Malawi.

But are Africa's *will* and *capacity* to democratize strong enough? This capacity requires not only the urge to throw out one particular unpopular regime, but the determination to institutionalize legitimate political succession indefinitely. The will to democracy also requires readiness to permit an unpopular but legitimate government to govern without hindrance and complete its electoral term of office without being overthrown.

Ghana elected Kofi Busia in 1969, and the Ghanaian army overthrew him in 1972 before he completed his first electoral term. In 1979 the country elected Hilla Limann, and again the Ghanaian army overthrew him in 1981 before he completed his first term. What was even more astonishing, popular opinion in Ghana cheered both military coups. The Ghanaian will to democracy was not yet strong enough.

In 1992 a new situation arose. Flight Lieutenant Jerry Rawlings, formerly a military dictator, resigned his military commission and stood for election as a civilian. According to international observers, Rawlings won the 1992 election. Had he won it because the register of voters was unfairly incomplete? Or did he win because of actual vote-rigging during the election? Or were the opposition parties simply bad losers? Whichever of the above suppositions was the truth, it constituted evidence that Ghana's democracy was not fully consolidated. Will we see Jerry Rawlings, the *civilian,* allowed to complete his electoral term as president? The answer is in the womb of history. We need to help Ghana consolidate a democratic tradition.

The evidence that Jonas Savimbi and his National Union for the Total Independence of Angola (UNITA) are bad losers in Angola is probably clearer. Former United States protégé Savimbi was prepared to plunge the country into renewed civil war rather than accept even the first round of the presidential elections, which had gone against him. That Angola's will to democracy was weak was not surprising. The country had been ruled by one of the least democratic of all European colonial powers in Africa, Portugal. In the last decade of colonial rule, Angola was more accustomed to multi-*army* politics than to multiparty politics. The democratic tradition in Portuguese-speaking Africa had either been destroyed by the Portuguese domineering style or never arrived because Portugal ceased to be part of the European mainstream, and its colonies were ignored or brutalized as a result.

Mozambique suffered a comparable fate—more a multiarmy experience than a multiparty tradition. The year 1992 saw the armies of FRELIMO and Mozambique National Resistance (RENAMO, or MNR) edging their way toward each other for a reconciliation. Did they stand a better chance of success than Angola did? Let us hope so. The will to democracy is particularly weak in Lusophone Africa.

When I was at the Summit Meeting of the Organization of African Unity in Dakar, Senegal, in June 1992, I was privileged to be introduced to the new president of Zambia, Frederick Chiluba. Within a year he had learned a lot. One lesson for democracy was not only to be a good loser, but also to be a gracious winner. At first Chiluba's party was unable to grasp that point. The party seemed determined to humiliate former president Kenneth Kaunda. This seemed to be the surest way of sending a message to all presidential incumbents in the rest of Africa not to make "the same mistake as that made by Kenneth Kaunda"—that is, give in to democratic pressures!

It would be a disaster to send a message to all African presidential incumbents that humiliation awaits them if they cease to be heads of state. Chiluba had a special responsibility to Africa as a whole to avoid sending such a message. But thanks partly to Chiluba's own good sense, and partly to the advice of General Olusegun Obasanjo and other African elder statesmen, moves toward reconciliation between Chiluba and Kaunda were made. President Chiluba's highly publicized birthday greeting to former president Kaunda was particularly symbolic. But much of the goodwill evaporated when Kaunda declared his intention to run again for president. Harassment of him became recurrent.

More needs to be done, not only in Zambia but also in the rest of Africa, to make former presidents feel honored and respected even when they are defeated. In the United States all former presidents are politely addressed as "Mr. President."

The will to democratize is sometimes compromised by an unwillingness to accept the triumphant *ideology* in a contest. This was most dramatically illustrated in Algeria. The pluralistic experiment was not, in reality, ready to accept the triumph of the ideology of the Islamic Salvation Front (FIS). Elections were held, and then aborted when the winner was not acceptable to those who were able to command military support to frustrate the democratic process. Algeria is now plunged in a "no-win" situation, as the democratic secularists seek to neutralize the majoritarian Islamists.

One of the major dilemmas confronting the new African democracies is whether economic liberalization should have preceded political liberalization. Should Africa have reduced the role of the state in the economy before it increased the role of the people in the political process? Would that have strengthened Africa's *will* to democratize?

Experience in Asia seems to lend support to that strategy. South Korea embarked on vigorous capitalism before attempting liberal democratization. On the whole, this approach has also been true of Taiwan and of most members of the Association of South East Asian Nations (ASEAN). Successful Asian capitalist countries have pursued the legacy of Adam Smith before they have paid any attention to the legacy of either Thomas Jefferson or the Jacobins.

An even more dramatic case is that of the People's Republic of China since Mao Tse-tung's death. The giant of Asia has definitely been moving toward greater economic liberalization, while remaining impeccably opposed to political liberalization. The Tianenmen Square suppression of 1989 was a measure of opposition to political liberalization, but China's commitment to economic liberalization has remained unabated. The Chinese people have a *desire* for democracy but not yet the *will* to force the aging elite to provide it.

On the other hand, Mikhail Gorbachev attempted political liberalization (*glasnost*) before any systematic economic liberalization (*perestroika*). The result in the former Soviet Union was rapid political disintegration without meaningful economic transformation. It was not only the Soviet empire of Eastern Europe that disintegrated in the wake of *glasnost*. It was also the bicontinental body politic of the Soviet Union itself. The Chinese are justified in seeing Gorbachev as the man who destroyed the country that had made him leader—the former USSR.

In Africa, Ghana has from time to time explicitly faced the dilemma as to which should have first priority—political recovery or economic recovery. Ghana's founder-president, Kwame Nkrumah, opted for the primacy of politics. He declared in the 1950s, "Seek ye first the political kingdom and all else will be added unto you."[47]

Did Nkrumah mean that political independence for an African country would bring "all else added unto you"? Or did he mean the liberation of the whole of Africa (including the Republic of South Africa) was a precondition for Africa's "political kingdom"? Or was his concept of "political kingdom" a combination of both Africa's liberation and its unification into a united country on a continental scale?

Clearly, political independence for individual African countries has never "added all else unto you." For individual African nations Nkrumah's emphasis on the state as the primary actor in Africa's development has been invalidated.

Thirty years after Nkrumah's dictum of "seek ye first the political kingdom," another Ghanaian leader seemed to have drastically revised the dictum. Flight Lieutenant Jerry Rawlings's politics from the mid-1980s until

1992 seemed to be based on the dictum, "Seek ye first the *economic* kingdom and all else will be added unto you". Jerry Rawlings—in spite of left-wing rhetoric—submitted his Ghanaian government to the rigours of structural adjustment and related discipline of the World Bank and the International Monetary Fund (IMF).

It was not until 1992 that Jerry Rawlings's government—under both domestic and international pressures—at last conceded political democratization. A timetable was more firmly announced for multiparty elections. Political liberalization was at last catching up with economic liberalization in the new Ghana. Was "the economic kingdom" about to demonstrate that it would have "all else added unto you"? At least for Ghana, the question is still wide open. Will the new Jerry Rawlings, elected into power, still continue to put economic recovery first as a precondition for successful political reform? If he did, will he be as vindicated as have been South Korea, Taiwan, Southest Asia, and possibly the People's Republic of China? Will he be negating Nkrumah's premise of the primacy of African politics? Or is there a third dictum that demands to be explored: "Seek ye first the cultural kingdom and all else will be added unto you"?

The fate of both political and economic liberalization hinges on cultural variables which have too often been underestimated. We may need to grasp the cultural dimension before we can fully gauge the scale and durability of social change in Africa. Every constitution needs to be culturally viable. Every development project needs a cultural feasibility study.

But history does not wait for historians. History has its own momentum. In many African countries political liberalization has been taking place without either a cultural feasibility study or an economic stock-taking. Liberal democratic activism has been under way from Madagascar to Mali, from Marrakesh to Maputo, from Dar-es-Salaam to Dakar. The scale of activism has varied from country to country—but a liberal, pluralistic contagion has been spreading across the continent. Yet the question persists: Is it only a desire for democracy, or is there a real will and capacity to democratize?

We posed a wider scenario—"Seek ye first the cultural kingdom and all else will be added unto you." This third scenario requires understanding the cultural preconditions of both political will and economic competence. Africa needs planned democracy—preceded by a feasibility study to ascertain the cultural viability of any proposed economic or political system. Slogans like "privatization" and "democratization" need to be accompanied by a cultural manual specific to the society or to the region. Africa's desire for democracy has reached significant proportions. Devising a culturally inspirational agenda for the future may transform that democratic desire into a powerful democratic will.

CONCLUSION

Colonial rule enclosed together people who previously lived separately—and divided people who were once united. Ethnic tensions are conflicts of values. They have also become the greatest threat both to Africa's stability and to African democracy. The answer lies in purposeful national integration and a shared experience in ideas and values. Africa is in search of a creative ideology.

When multiple cultures confront each other within the same national boundaries, their relationship can be at varying degrees of social depth. The minimum stage of relationship is that of coexistence—when two cultural communities barely know about each other. Each may have its own conservative paradigm of thought grounded on ethnic exclusivity. Indigenous conservatism can reign supreme at this level.

The second degree of relationship is that of contact—when two groups either begin to trade with each other or participate jointly in the job market, or become members of the same political party, or listen to each other's music. Above all, the contact must include sharing ideas and evolving shared priorities. Traditions of the elder, the warrior, and the sage may interact between ethnic cultures.

The third degree of interethnic relationship is that of competition—when these contacts result in rivalry for resources, for power, or for social and economic opportunities. Debates about ideology and policy are part and parcel of this competitive stage of nation-building. Capitalism may conflict with socialism in the political arena.

The fourth relationship between two ethnic cultures is that of conquest—when one of the ideologies or cultures begins to get the upper hand. One ideology, for example, may become more influential than other(s). Or the newly dominant system of values may successfully claim a disproportionate share of power, resources, or socioeconomic opportunities. Nepotism could prevail even under socialism.

The fifth stage of relationship between cultures is that of *compromise*. This is a stage when the competing ideologies, political values, and traditions find a *modus vivendi*, an acceptable formula of conflict resolution and a viable basis of social partnership.

The sixth stage of relationship is that of *coalescence*—when the values and identities of the political groups begin to merge, and their boundaries become less and less distinct. The cultures, values, and ideologies, and even language intermingle, and a larger sense of identity starts to emerge. That enlarged identity could be national consciousness. A national ideology may be evolving.

In some African countries ideological divisions are also affected by *race relations* and by *economic factors*. But it should be borne in mind that race and economics are often integrative as well as divisive. The balance varies from society to society.

The struggle for national integration and state-building in Africa is still in its infancy. Ideological intercourse and cultural interaction are part and parcel of the evolution of dignitarianism, ethnicism, nationhood, and the consolidation of collective identity in the postcolonial era.

Normative Instability as Source of Africa's Political Disorder

I. A. Menkiti

The state is an artifact, a crafted institution designed with an end in view. Understood as an artificial construction geared toward an end, its robustness or ill health becomes then a function of how well, or to what extent, it manages to accomplish that which it was set up to accomplish. As we look through history, we will find that states have been geared toward a multiplicity of ends. Thus there has been talk of the warfare state, the theocratic state, the socialist or capitalistic state, and, most recently, the democratic state.

Keeping these preliminary observations in mind, it can be argued that the problem of political instability on the African continent is best approached through multiple analytical tracks. There is the popular approach often described as the developmental approach, which tries to explain things by reference to issues of economic poverty and inadequate infrastructure, whether these be traced to the residual effects of slavery and colonialism or to the fraudulent activities of Africa's new class of kleptocrats.

But there is also another approach that might be called the value or normative approach, in which the central explanation of Africa's current political problems is said to be discoverable in the consequences arising from the dissolution of Africa's ancestral values. The sense here is one of a tragic shifting away from a space of original dignities to a confused space of piddling activity, where role occupiers now enact roles without understanding their true meaning, so that when the rules say "jump," then jump is what all automatically have had to do. As to the true reason, the full meaning of the principles behind the rules in question, no one is quite sure, not even those who announce them most noisily. When this state of cognitive disarray is then added to the presence of raw centralized power that European statism introduced into Africa, we have on our hands, it is argued, a combustible mix.

Basil Davidson has written in regard to the problems in Liberia:

The ancestral culture of the peoples of Liberia as with those of neighbors near and far, knew plenty of abusive violence. But they possessed rules and regulations for the containment and repression of abusive violence; and these were the rules and regulations before the scourge of the slave trade and the colonialism that followed it, that enabled them to evolve their sense of the value of community.[1]

And to those who look askance at talk of the "value of community" he adds that:

they have yet to understand how communities anywhere and at any time, are able to emerge and grow strong in their rules and structural restraints, but are also able, if these should become lost or cast away, to fall into utter disarray or self destruction.[2]

But, Davidson aside, there is yet another aspect to this issue of a claimed relationship between normative failure and political instability. It has to do with a view made prominent by Theodore H. von Laue. In his book *The World Revolution of Westernization*, he argues that European institutions have so widely spread to the rest of the world that a failure on the part of Third World peoples to deal adequately with European values is at the core of their malaise. The rest of the world wants industrialization and an efficient economy, but that is not possible without a collateral absorption of the spiritual and moral values that made the West what it is today and which helped expand its hegemony around the globe. He writes:

Tragic indeed is the record of state building and development through the non-Western world, in the past and in the present; ominous are the prospects for the future.[3]

And the reason for this, in brief summary, is that "indigenous ways did not harmonize with imported modern ways,"[4] given the value resistance on the part of:

recalcitrant non-Western peoples—peoples gladly taking the latest fruits of modernity (including the pride of leadership in the world) yet unwilling or unable to submit to the demanding work routines and civic obligations which constitute the invisible aspects of effective power.[5]

This failure of value absorption is the chief culprit regarding why "the world revolution of Westernization, in short, has not created a peaceful world order guided by the ascetic and all inclusive rationalism, the best quality in Western civilization"[6]

A question that arises is how we are to assess this claim of von Laue—that an inability to put in place a new normative order, on the basis of which the project of a modern state could be accomplished, lies at the heart of Africa's problem, rather than the shattering of an ancient moral order, a shattering that was brought about by colonialism and its aftermath, neocolonialism. It is perhaps not necessary to settle this debate between von Laue and Davidson. Suffice it, perhaps, to note that, for both, values lie at the base of our problem, and this acknowledgment, despite their differing stances, is most likely enough for my purposes in this essay. The one observation I would like to make at this point, however, is that for all of us, European and African alike, a healthy dose of skepticism is necessary regarding the overall project of the modern state, since that project, as a matter of historical record, has turned out to be quite inimical to stable value systems.

Thus, as we look at Mengistu Haile Mariam in Ethiopia, or Jean Bedel Bokassa in the Central African Republic, or at Idi Amin in Uganda, not to mention, most recently, Sani Abacha in Nigeria, it is not clear how much of the respective debacles had to do with problems particular to Africa in its failure to absorb European norms of respect for the individual and how much had to do with the general wastage of modernity—a modernity that, with its vehicular twin, the centralized state, is not always what it is celebrated to be.

Often, we hear talk of "we the people." But what are we to make of this expression when it is seriously the case, in Africa as elsewhere, that the world's various peoples almost invariably fail to be properly enpeopled, insofar as the constituted state is concerned? The question, it seems, is what should count as the proper grounds for the people's enpeoplement, given the conditions of the modern world? Is it the mere fact of a standing army, or is it the strength of industrial organization spread over a landmass? Or the presence of a formally adopted document called a constitution? Or perhaps the sense of a shared community among a group of persons described as participating citizens?

No state today can avoid these questions, since each state continues the protracted messy business of making a nation out of itself, and this includes the United States, which von Laue often holds up as an example of what he means when he talks of the values that have propelled Western development. And even if we were to concentrate, say, on England, and not directly on America itself, it will be found that the business of nation making is still an ongoing process.

That the power of England as a state (as opposed to nation) should have been vested on the crowned head of him or her who occupies the English

throne and that this power came later to be balanced out by the powers allot-
ted to Parliament, and that Englishmen and -women, over time, were the
ones who brought these changes about because they were blessed with a
value disposition geared toward the protection of the dignity of Englishmen
and -women, and that this is what Africa and the rest of the world are lacking as they grapple with questions of state stability, is a proposition that may
or may not be true.

But whether von Laue is right that Africa's problem is a catching-up
problem in the area of values, or Davidson is right that Africa's problem is
one of a prior value system, dignified in its setting, but which has now been
emptied out as a result of alien intrusions, it is in my mind instructive that
for both authors values lie at the core of our problems. Put in the language
of "wholesomeness," which is often heard in these debates, we can say
that, for both authors, things are not whole because the values are not
whole and, furthermore, things cannot be made whole until, somehow, the
values are made whole and operational again.

Now, regardless of the path of causal attribution chosen by the interested
observer, it is my belief that this question of the relationship between values
and stability in the political order is an important one. Despite the possible
pitfalls involved in the raising of the question, African scholars, and non-
African scholars interested in Africa, ought to continue to raise it. The risk
that the debate might lapse into talk of racial or national essences, or into discussion of who is more value-civilized than his fellow man, is, in my mind,
a manageable risk. I do not, for my part, think that the debate would descend
to, or stay at, such a level.

The believer in racial or national essences would still have to prove his
case on grounds that are acceptable to the rest of the world. To take a light
example, if he were, for instance, to argue that the frequency of the utterance
of the word "incroyable" among the French is far greater than the frequency of the utterance of the word "unbelievable" among the English, and
from this go on to conclude that the French are genetically and culturally
programmed to a belief structure much more readily disposed to a recognition of new wonders, as opposed to the dour English who are programmed
not to be so easily excited, hence the attribution to them of a certain facil-
ity regarding the maintenance of a stiff upper lip—if this believer were to
argue such a thing, it is plain that we do not have to embrace his conclusion,
nor his manner of proceeding to that conclusion. All we would have to say
would be: so much for national essences.

Likewise for the other kinds of explanation pertaining to Africa in
which the explainer comes at things with an essentialist frame of mind,
either reasoning negatively that Africans lack moral and intellectual qualities, essentially, or reasoning positively that Africans possess deep feeling,

essentially (as opposed to Europeans whose own racial essence is supposedly to be found in cold logic and an unforgiving heart).[7]

I do not have to dwell on the futility involved in this manner of proceeding. Suffice it to note one thing, which is that in defending against the first sort of essentialist claim by lapsing into the second sort, the person of African descent is not likely to get very far, not even if he buttresses his view by noting that, after all, mankind began in Africa, and so claims of African inferiority cannot but be bizarre.

That it would be a bizarre proposition that Africa gave the world its body, but draws absolute zero on the scale of things when it comes to the mind, only forces the European denier of African worth to move to another level of denial—such as, for instance, that the body is one thing and the mind quite another; or that the body the bio-archeologist is talking about was an ancient body, and so has nothing to do with the body of Europe as presently constituted. The reader gets the gist that this sort of discourse, back and forth, can only get more and more bizarre. In the interest of avoiding such outcomes, we must move to questions whose practical bearing can be perceived by one and all. And this brings me back to von Laue and Davidson.

I mentioned earlier that I was somewhat skeptical about the overall project of the modern state and that, in any case, even the defenders of the mission of this state will have to concede that its movement around the globe has been disruptive to stable value systems. But having noted this, I must also admit that politics is a practical affair; that it deals with the art of the possible, or with what is already in place; so that in the light of the way things are right now in Africa, the continent must contend with the residue of its history, must play the hand it has been dealt, regardless of whether its problems arise from an inability to learn and sustain new values or stem, rather, from the fact that its ancestral value system had been destroyed by Europe's adventure.

With this in mind, I would like to explore, in what remains of this paper, the question of social justice in the present-day African state, keeping in mind the relationship between this justice and the vexing problem, currently before us, of political instability. This problem of political instability is an issue that affects everyone, not just the academic expert and policy maker, but also the man and woman on the street. Although some within the general population have said that Africa's concern, right now, should not be primarily one of social justice but of economic development, it is plain that we do not have to choose between the two. In any case, even if we were to make central the quest for economic empowerment, it still needs to be pointed out that unless Africa has social justice the fruits of economic development cannot be fully enjoyed. For social injustice breeds social resentment, and social resentment is a dangerous thing in the life of nations.

If significant numbers of individuals or groups of individuals feel deeply excluded or perhaps outright victimized, then they are not likely to be willing actors in the various activities that secure the stability of the state. On the contrary, they would be moved actively to resist or else to lose hope and switch off. And if they lose hope and switch off, it can be expected that negative economic consequences will also follow from *that*; for one must consider the cash value of hope. In this regard, then, as we scan the continent, these African states, what do they need to have in place before we are able to say of them that they possess the attribute of social justice, that they are, in simple words, socially just?

To begin our discussion, we may note that philosophers have generally approached the topic of justice by talking first of the circumstances of justice.[8] Of these circumstances, or conditions, three might be mentioned forthwith. These are the conditions that I see as having the most direct relevance to the African situation, and can be itemized thus: (1) the condition of moderate scarcity (partial resources, if you like); (2) the condition of limited or partial goodwill; and (3) the condition of approximate equality of strength. All three refer to certain salient considerations of common sense.

First, if we all lived in some sort of lush Edenic tropical paradise, then, strictly speaking, questions of justice would not arise. For, in that case, each and every single one of us could help himself or herself to the aggregate bounties of our paradise, and there would not be an issue of distributive fairness with which to contend. On the other hand, if instead of a lush paradise we only had one loaf of bread, say, for an entire population of 200 million, then it is obvious that there is no way to get a handle on the situation insofar as distributive fairness is concerned.

Secondly, in the matter of the condition of limited or partial goodwill, it is the case that a population is typically made up of men and women who are not entirely blessed with angelic dispositions nor entirely loaded with demonic ones. If everyone were a saint or an angel, then distributive rules would not be needed; for then each of us would be so overflowing with goodwill toward the other that each, without prompting, would want to say to the other, "What is mine I consider to be yours, and, truly, even though I give you what is mine, you need not consider what is yours mine." And again, on the other hand, if everyone were a devil through and through, then you would have to put a policeman on every street corner, and, of course, that would not be enough; for the policemen themselves would also be swimming in deviltry.

Thirdly, we can well see in the other condition having to do with approximate equality of strength something easily accessible to common sense. Typically, in a population, there is not one person, or one group of persons, so exclusively powerful that things would always go the way this powerful person, or group of persons, wants. The physically imposing individual who is said to be as tough as nails can always be done in by a bullet fired by a small-boned individual. And if things get bad enough, this small-boned individual can band together with others to scheme poison. In other words, the giant of a man does not have to fall in physical combat but can fall just as well through the equally effective intermediary agency of some well-chosen reactive chemical agents. Innocuous-looking intelligence agents are well aware of these matters. Here I do not mean to make light of a serious subject but only to underscore certain facts regarding our situation in the world—facts that have been described by reference to approximate equality of strength.

Now, how do these conditions attach themselves to the African situation? Of the three circumstances mentioned above, the one that seems the most pressing within the African context could be said to be that having to do with the limitation of resources. It would however be incorrect to so rank this factor in the scale of importance that we neglect the other two vis-à-vis their own relative standing within this order of importance. Surely, when Africa's critics push to dismiss the continent as some sort of unsalvageable basket case, and do this by pointing to such examples as Rwanda in 1994, Uganda in the days of Idi Amin, Zaire in the 1960s and 70s, Nigeria during the Biafran civil war, Sudan in its decades-old civil war between north and south, and so on, what these critics have in mind is not the issue of material or resource limitation but of assumed ill-will between the various African groups. Their negative and unwarranted view of Africa as suffering terminally from some sort of atavistic bloodlust is geared entirely toward the second condition, or circumstance, of justice. And if you point out to these critics the case of Mandela's achievements in South Africa, or of Nyerere earlier in Tanzania, they still show reluctance in revising their judgment, telling you that South Africa is, after all, a special case and that, in any event, it has too much of the labor of Europe to count as an African success story. In continuing with these basic negativities, they say, and say over again, that nothing will change, that the circumstances in Africa are fundamentally askew, irretrievably flawed.

But it is precisely here, at this level of talk, that those of us who are African, and that others who are not African but who retain some goodwill toward Africa, must stand fast and speak—speak indeed of basic enabling conditions, thereby taking on the critic in this matter of fundamental grounds. For, yes, it could be granted that, strictly speaking, the immediate questions we face in Africa today are not directly questions of social justice in its pure sense of distributive fairness, but rather questions of the fundamental conditions for a stable political order, conditions that need to be in place before social justice as a question can arise. But even granting all of this, it will not be enough for the critic to point to the killings and reprisal killings, or to the elite and the military siphoning off millions, perhaps billions, of dollars from state treasuries. These things, though bad enough in themselves, are not simply pointers to the absence of social conscience as the critic would have us believe. What we have in these examples is not straightforwardly a question of innate ill-will between Africa's various groups but, rather, is a question of the linked bases of stable political authority and what might go wrong once this linkage is ruptured. Therefore, if things seem to have gone wrong, we must be willing to stay away from facile generalizations.

I say this because I am convinced that once we look closely at the matter we will find that it is not the case that the conditions are completely hopeless for the emergence of just institutions. On the contrary, there are emerging factors, as well as older attitudes and sentiments, that can be made usable again despite the years of historical drift and social dislocation. I have in mind here the potential power of the sort of affective communities that thrived on the continent to move more rapidly toward the demands of social justice than is the case with other types of communities. Justice, it seems to me, is not something that can be achieved by default or by mere structure alone. It fundamentally arises in the desires and intentions of individuals and involves an attitude of connection regarding the human claims of others.

What I propose is that we turn the critic's approach on its head and argue instead that what he takes to be an obstacle, once it is properly understood, could be seen as a blessing in disguise. Recall that the complaint has been that Africans know how to take care of one another when they belong to the same tribe or ethnic group, but do not know how to play fair when it comes to members of other tribes or ethnic groups sharing citizenship with them within a common state. The orbit of Africans' loyalty, it is observed, is limited and is destined to be limited so long as the ethnic or tribal group is there to claim primary attention.

But the question one has to ask is: Why is it necessary to have this assumption that the order of affect brought in place by the tribe, or ethnic group, is necessarily and always mutually exclusive when matched with the requirements of loyalty to the state? For it seems to me that once we get beyond the simple case of marital or romantic fidelity, loyalties are not of their nature always mutually preemptive. It is not the case that once a slice of it is given to the one, then the other can never hope to get a slice. To believe in mutual exclusivity is to indulge in a very adversarial way of looking at the world. I mean by this statement the calculative, zero-sum, Hobbesian approach to matters of the social world, with its underlying assumption that the other is always the enemy, always separately situated, so that in the end human life on earth comes to be seen as nasty, brutish, and short. If we are interested in breaking away from the rigidities involved in this sort of understanding we would do well first to comprehend the cultural biases behind it. Even the European Marxist critic of industrial capitalistic society is himself still functioning under the spell of the Hobbesian understanding. How else to explain his rhetoric of justice by class, of conflict between the righteous workers of the world and the uncouth ruling classes? The image we have is still one of antagonistic exclusions, of us versus them.

My point in all of this is to argue that contrary to all the built-in expectations of conflict between loyalty to tribe or ethnic group and loyalty to state, there is no reason for us to accept the basic assumption of mutual exclusivity on which the expectation of a conflict of loyalties is based. I contend instead that once an order has been put in place by the tribe, or ethnic group, that order is potentially transportable. In fact, I would venture to say that so-called tribal life is a superior training ground for life in the aggregate community of the state. This may seem to fly in the face of evidence, but it must be remembered that the modern state, whether in Africa or elsewhere, is built on assumptions that are hard to square with the deeper sources of human loyalty. Its public avowals notwithstanding, the modern state's notion of loyalty to the public domain is at best superficial; it does not run deep. It is this superficial structure of loyalties that we have inherited from Europe; and the life it places before us is based on the commitments of unattached and separately situated individuals. In that life, politicians can run for office for whatever personal reasons they deem fit, and do not need to have been chosen by a tribal council of elders based on independent evidence of their normative standing within the community. And given the exclusionary notions of power that are part of the modern state, whoever controls the organs of state power, after having won an election, keeps the upper hand in running the show until voted out in the next campaign. Of course there are checks and balances, but the new leaders need not have undergone any elaborate or sustained training in public duty before assuming office. They can harbor all manner of ill-will toward the defeated opposition, and the opposition to them. As for the voters themselves, they could have all voted according to the dictates of their bellies or their special interest groups. Lacking training in public duty, and absent a sense of loyalty to a grounded social group, the desire to do justice or to respond to the human needs of others may run only as long as the next strategic alliance has to be formed.

The point here is that the civic spirit needs training in order to be adequately pointed outwards, and tribal society is an invaluable resource toward this end. It is an invaluable resource because its notion of group life is, for the most part, not an instrumental one. Human groups are expected to maintain their mandate and their dignity, and the idea of their resting their foundation on a sort of calculative rationality of "you scratch my back and I scratch your back," and "we'll make deals as we move along," and "as long as it suits us," since human society is merely a convenient fiction, is simply unacceptable. I hope I have not been too harsh on the presuppositions of the modern state. What I wanted to show, primarily, is that the order of affect put in place by traditional society is arguably a more dignified source of commitment to public duty. The ability to generate a noncalculative loyalty on the part of its component members in the domain of public life is a blessing, not a hindrance, to the solution of the problem of social justice within the modern African state.

Let me therefore return to the view of resource limitation as an impediment to the claims of justice. Recall that in that first condition discussed earlier, the issue of the availability of resources was very much a central part of the story of social justice. Focusing on this issue for a moment, we will find that Africa's situation is a somewhat complex one. On the one hand, there is the known fact of hunger, poverty, and ill health. On the other hand, there is also the known abundance of natural resources, albeit undeveloped natural ones.

In terms of landmass alone, the African continent is not what the Mercator projection shows it to be. In fact, it is one of the largest continents around. If you took the whole of China, the whole of India, Europe, the United States, and if to all of these you added the South American giant Argentina, you could fit all of them into the continent of Africa, and it would not necessarily be a tight squeeze.

And the type of landmass we are talking about here is not just uninhabitable desert and rugged mountain ranges. The percentage of arable land to total landmass is higher than in most parts of the world. Africa has roughly half of India's population, and yet its arable land is almost twice that of India. The same percentage regarding arability also holds true vis-à-vis Latin America and China, though the population variable is different. One also notes that the climate is ideal for crop growth, given its tropical nature. In addition, the rivers and lakes provide ample opportunity for fish protein, and the forests can supply timber. It is also the case that the continent provides one-seventh of the world's minerals, with new discoveries announced every now and then. Because of this fact, uninhabited places like the Sahara Desert cannot be counted out but are also part of the story of Africa's riches. The Sahara does not have the natural resource of water or of arable land, but it does have those of oil and other minerals.

But in spite of all of the above, the African people are still hungry, still poor and inadequately housed.[9] It is an ambiguous situation, and I believe that in the light of this ambiguity, the position taken by development theorists is not entirely misplaced. In pushing more vigorously on the front of economic self-sufficiency than on that of social justice, they are inspired by a vision of what is possible. For without development, food will continue to be scarce and disease prevalent. Observers of the continent know this to be the case and have drawn the conclusion all along regarding the need for increased industrial output. Irving L. Markovitz, following closely the views of Surendra Patel, writes:

> With oil and gas in the north, coal in the south, and hydropower in the center; with Africa's mighty rivers accounting for 40 percent of the world's potential hydroelectric power, the continent's energy potential appears unlimited. Nevertheless, with eight percent of the world population, the continent can only boast of two percent of world production, less than half of the United Kingdom.[10]

What we have in the above passage is a good statement of the complexity or ambiguity of the African situation—the tension between what is there in place right now and what is beckoning around the corner. Earlier I tried to show that in the matter of the dispositional attitudes argued to be part of the question of social justice, Africa, contrary to prevailing opinion, is actually in an advantageous position; that even though things may not always look right on the level of observed surfaces, yet we should make sure that what we see on the surface is not allowed to obscure the strengths within of the African continent. This cautionary remark should again be restated, this time in regard to that first condition of moderate resources (moderate scarcity, if you will).

The point of the restatement is to show that Africa's critics should not be allowed to have the final word regarding the assumed hopelessness of the continent's situation. Although there have been and continue to be bloody ethnic conflicts, and although the continent's poverty continues apace, if we dare to look beneath the surface we can see that the prospects for Africa's material development are bright, and also that the basic underlying attitudes of Africans toward one another, and toward the common spaces earlier inhabited by the tribal nation, speak to a resource that can still be made to do beneficial duty even in these disheveled modern times. I say this fully aware of the messiness of the present situation. But whether Africa is finished before it ever got started, or whether the prospects are good, as I have suggested, will obviously depend on the question of whether what we face arises from a deficiency of material structure, seen as reversible, or instead from a deficiency of material structure, seen as irreversible, and on top of which is added a fundamental deficiency of moral will on the part of those who operate the structure. Whereas the critic leans toward the latter interpretation, I myself lean toward the former.

And this brings me then to the issue of the grid on which the modern African state is situated. It is an issue that ties in directly with the third and final condition of justice, which, at the beginning, I staked out for discussion. This condition, you will recall, is the condition of approximate equality of strength. By way of entry into this segment of our discussion, let me make a few preliminary observations.

First, what are we to make of the fact that today many Africans are actually older than their own countries? Could one imagine an American older than America itself or a Frenchman older than France? And yet this sort of thing is not only imaginable but real in the case of Africa. When the critical observer notes the failure of loyalty and respect toward the modern African state, this matter of state infancy is important to keep in mind, especially since we are dealing here with an elder continent, a continent in which elderhood, on its own and for good reasons, carries the basis of respect.

The other observation I wish to make relates to the way and manner in which this modern African state was formed. This state, as we all know, is a product of colonial history. Whether this is a good or a bad thing overall is not my question at this stage. My interest, rather, is to explore the sources of certain structural deficiencies in the modern African state, the point being that whatever forces gave rise to the modern African state, as a matter of historical activity, are also bound to have significant effects on the present contours and the present internal dynamics of that same state.

In saying this, one is not necessarily engaged in the futile exercise of flogging a dead horse. For when, for example, in West Africa large segments of the Yoruba population are included in Nigeria, and significant other segments of the same Yoruba population are included in what is now the Republic of Benin, it does not take a genius to see that something is out of kilter, not quite right. In piling up into one unit of state administration unrelated groups of persons and splitting up organically related groups, the Berlin Conference left for Africa a wobbly inheritance.

The colonial state worked as an administrative unit because there was something else to back it up. Once the colonial era officially ended, the leftover colonial state needed a different sort of glue to hold it together. We in Africa are still struggling to find this glue, a glue that will bind together, perhaps in a different manner, that which earlier was bound together by European powers in their own way and for their own purposes. This task is very pressing, especially in light of the question of social justice. This is so because for the most part, at this point in our history, the question of social justice in Africa seems to be inextricably bound up with issues of group affiliation. The problem of justice in the state looms as a group-borne problem in need of group mediation.

For in nearly all of the documented cases of state abuse of citizens, persons, or rights, the violations in question have tended to involve an ethnic or tribal dimension. The belief is widespread that who gets in or gets out, is promoted or demoted, or loses life, that all of this, even the question of who is spared, is a matter determined by a prior fact—the unalterable prior fact of ethnic or tribal affiliation. For this very reason, the question of social justice in the modern African state constantly finds itself being enmeshed in the difficult question of ethnic and/or tribal affiliation. Thus our third condition of relative equality of strength, which can be put differently as the condition of equal vulnerability, takes on, and must of necessity take on, an urgent and complex function.

Since justice is concerned with the issue of what is a fair and equitable distribution of the burdens and advantages of social life, and since in Africa today, peoples' shares of these burdens and advantages are often seen as dependent on which tribe or ethnic group they belong to, then this condition of equal vulnerability must, it seems, be viewed through the additional lens of group filiation, not just through that of separately situated citizens most or all of whom are assumed to be ethnically or tribally unattached. I am moved to make the foregoing observation because one's vulnerability is a function of one's power to prevent abuse or injury to one's person, and that power, we have seen, is sadly, in the case of Africa, expanded or diminished depending on which group one belongs to and whether the group is holding on to power or is out of it. What, then, can the theorist of justice do, given this rather serious problem, interested as he or she is in the conditions marking the feasibility of just democratic governance?

Some have suggested redrawing the map of the African states so as to reflect better the ancient and ongoing realities of the continent. By proceeding this way, it is hoped that things could be brought closer in line with the moral authority of the tribal or ethnic group. We have seen how on occasion severe exclusions and persecutions have led to attempts by the persecuted groups to force the issue through outright secession or through violent guerrilla warfare in the bush. For the most part, the leaders of governments have tolerated discussion about the value, or lack thereof, of the redrawing of the colonial map. But as soon as actions follow and the leaders feel threatened, they resort to force, claiming the inviolability of inherited borders.

Now, it is no doubt understandable for the state, as is, to want to preserve its borders. But the conservation of borders can itself become an exercise in futility, a self-defeating project, if the citizens of the state, for whom the borders are being conserved, find that their very state not only is not able to empower them, but has become instead a killing field, with them as victims. This has happened already and far too many times in many of the African countries—as witness the examples of Sudan, Uganda, Nigeria, Rwanda, Burundi, to name just a few. And with Kenya tottering on the brink of disaster, with Zaire (now Democratic Republic of Congo) repeatedly described as a terminal case of corruption, it may not be enough to claim preservation of borders or to point to the successful example of South Africa where borders have been preserved despite severe racial exclusions and ethnic conflicts. So the problem of ethnic affiliation is a serious one and must be acknowledged. My own view is that although borders may eventually need to be redrawn, we do not have to do so right now. Social justice is still a powerful silent partner in the preservation of state boundaries. If the African state earns the respect of its citizens through the achievement of justice in the public domain, then it may not matter whether Africa remains as is, with its present boundaries, or is adjusted back to its earlier arrangements. What is important is that citizens feel secure in their persons and that they know their life prospects are not being dismantled by the very state that is supposed to be advancing them.

There is no doubt that we, as Africans, are at the present time caught between two dignities, one whose power is faded, the other whose power is yet to come. On the one hand, the old precolonial order had an organic elegance and an internal sense of purpose that are clearly lacking in the modern African state. On the other hand, if a regional or continentwide assemblage of African peoples were to be achieved, it would command a certain political majesty, a dignified presence married to effective political power. Our problem appears to be the in-between situation in which we find ourselves, a situation that leads us to accommodate ourselves to actions that are offensive to African dignity.

But as I have argued above, whether we remain with our present distributions, or revert to a distribution closer to the precolonial one, or perhaps move to a larger assemblage of African peoples, the question of social justice would still be a pressing issue. Even in the organic communities of old, questions of fairness did arise, though not to a destabilizing extent. How else to explain the force of that poignant Ibo expression, *Nna gbo ogwu* (as in the name Nnagbo). The expression, an injunction that the father settle with authoritative fairness any and all conflicts between the children, speaks to a recognition that in the normal course of events, even the offspring belonging to one and the same affective family unit will disagree, perhaps carry on a quarrel, but that it is left to the father, and also the mother, to keep the combatants at bay and to do so by appeal to principles of fair adjudication.

I believe I have said enough to show a recognition of the seriousness of the ethnic problems against which many African states are struggling. But having spent time recognizing the seriousness of the problem, I have nonetheless reasoned that we do not have to give up on the quest for social justice, even if it be within the disheveled frame of the modern African state. In my mind, the difficulties are not so final that we have a hopeless situation on our hands, so that, barring a violent rearranging revolution, all talk of justice remains misplaced. But if we are to continue to talk about social justice within the frame of the African state, we must also look for ways to shore up that third condition of justice under discussion, namely approximate equality of strength, or equal vulnerability. Although there are many imbalances of power as between the different African groups finding their political life within the bounds of a common state, yet the vulnerability of each group, vis-à-vis the other, may be more equal than we realize.

First, we must not underestimate the power of resentment, when focused and unabating, effectively to destabilize a polity. The more serious a group's injury from an injustice, the more sinister may be the resentment provoked. And the more sinister the resentment, the greater the likelihood of a form of responsive action that is bound to produce continuing instability even after the one group's victory is achieved. I mean here the sort of situation where both victor and vanquished are so thoroughly worn out that the victorious group, instead of enjoying its victory, finds the taste more akin to that of sawdust in the mouth. The point here is that power and its calibrations are constantly shifting, and numerical or material disadvantages may yet be compensated for by other things whose nature is less tangible. It is said, and correctly so, that in mortal danger one is infinitely sharp of hearing. Oppressed groups backed into an ultimate corner and fighting for raw survival have something that an oppressing group often does not have—volitional intensity. The oppressed can make up in obduracy of will or raw courage what they do not have by way of numbers. This equalizing phenomenon is also part of the story of the balancing out of vulnerabilities on which justice depends. Where numbers are not equal, it is still the case that fear of mutual assured destruction can be underwritten in some other way. Mao Tse-tung, the late Chinese leader, was used to saying that despite the material superiority of Western armaments, his troops knew who they were, had will and motivation on their side, and would, as a consequence, show up the West for what it really was: a paper tiger. Whether this is seen as a mere rhetorical flourish by an aging leader or as containing a sound insight of common sense, I leave it to the reader to decide.

Second, there is the possibility of effective alliances between various oppressed groups who share common resistance against a dominant majority. Groups knowing that they may be next in line may band together and resist while resistance is still possible. Such has been the case in the former Yugoslavia, where Catholic Croats and Bosnian Muslims joined together to resist the more powerful Serbian group, thus creating an ongoing stalemate. After the fall of Vukovar, the Croats knew what they had to do; the Muslims, too, after the laying waste of Mostar.

Likewise in the case of El Salvador, where an unchallenged army, counting on its cohesion as a fighting unit and liberally supplied with arms from abroad, over time became more and more recalcitrant, clamping down on weaker segments of the population—teachers, peasants, trade unionists, the Church, and various others. When the oppression finally became unbearable, the different dispossessed Salvadorean groups joined forces to fight the army to a stalemate, exposing its vulnerability even as it exposed theirs. Peace talks followed, made possible by mutual exhaustion and the rapidly changing military and political realities outside the borders of El Salvador, most notably the ending of the Cold War and the turning of attention elsewhere by both Washington and Moscow. These two external powers had supported the two sides of the conflict. But the real reason for the stalemate was the ultimate balance of internal forces and the realization by both sides that they had reached a mutual and equalizing vulnerability. It could be argued that the emergence of a legislative assembly, a civilian police force, and a supreme court in El Salvador would not have come about without the prior realization of equal vulnerability on the part of the combatants.

In addition to the two general considerations above, one having to do with the corrective power of resentment and the other with the equalizing possibility of alliances between dispossessed groups who then challenge the power of the dispossessing group, I mention a third and final general consideration: that the world situation is changing rapidly and in unexpected ways, and it is incumbent on Africa's leaders to be aware not only of these changes but also of their ramifications for Africa.

One important change is that the old accepted understandings about the inviolability of state boundaries are being increasingly questioned under the pressure of events. Once-powerful states are breaking up and national and/or ethnic identities are reasserting themselves. Witness the case of the once-powerful Soviet Union and of Yugoslavia earlier mentioned. Then there is Czechoslovakia, which has now been split up, although peacefully. Whether the Albanians of Kosovo and Macedonia succeed in establishing their own independent state, an outcome the Serbs have vowed to prevent, only time will tell. Meanwhile we have a multitude of examples of accomplished breakups (such as Pakistan from India, Eritrea from Ethiopia, and Nagorno-Karabakh from Azerbaijan) or threatened breakups (such as Quebec from Canada and Catalonia from Spain). All over the world many different groups are clamoring for self-expression through establishment of their own political state, and in many cases they are succeeding. It is against this background that Africa's quest for social justice within the state must be assessed. The fact is that the world is now thinking the unthinkable, or at least what was unthinkable just a few years ago. The consequences of this mental shift are profound for the African continent. If fundamental injustice is not removed from the life of the African state as presently constituted, then what is going on in other parts of the world will surely happen in Africa also.

If it does, it is likely to be a more messy affair, given the complications introduced by the continuing involvement of foreign interests in the present life of the continent. To see how messy it could all get, one only has to think of Rwanda in 1993–94, and also of Burundi. My point in this third general observation is that a very important global assumption that has helped the African state keep going, even in the midst of very serious acts of injustice, is now recognizably being dismantled. For if the Europeans acknowledge that their own states need not stay bound together, they can only come across as double-faced and duplicitous if they insist that the African state be kept together regardless of whether or not it has become a killing field. Thus African leaders who previously hid under the mantle (some would say mantra) of territorial integrity to commit injurious acts to citizens' persons cannot hope to do so much longer. In the end each territory's integrity will have to be secured.

I have tried to address certain salient considerations bearing on the question of social justice within the African state. I selected and discussed three conditions seen to be important to the disposition of the question, namely the condition having to do with resources, the condition having to do with relative goodwill, and the condition of equal or equalizable vulnerability. Regarding the first two conditions, Africa was seen to be well positioned even after we factored in all of its current difficulties. And regarding the third, considerable space was spent showing that despite the complication introduced into African political life by problems of ethnic identity and the subsequent tendency of political distributions to hang on matters of group or tribal affiliation, the disparities of power that exist between the different African groups sharing a common statehood need not be seen as presenting an insurmountable obstacle. These nativist groups, where they are not equal, can still be made more or less equally vulnerable, given the powers of brooding resentment to destabilize a polity, ultimately pulling down winner and loser alike. Secondly, the formation of countervailing alliances between various oppressed groups will often emerge as a governing majority becomes increasingly overbearing and resorts more and more to acts of fundamental injustice. Finally, we also argued that the old global assumptions regarding the sacrosanctity of state borders can no longer be relied upon by African leaders to help preserve the African state, regardless of the level of injustice found within it. Territorial integrity, if it is to be maintained, will have to be maintained based on the quality of justice in the land.

Good Government Is Accountability

Ajume H. Wingo

My argument will follow two main tracks: the structure of institutions, and the character dispositions of citizens that make possible good government. I must hasten to say that precolonial Africa displays a variety of ways of organizing human relations, maintaining order, and ensuring human flourishing. Some people had no centralized state, while others did. I will concentrate on those that had centralized authority exercised via the machinery of government. Examples of the latter are the Baganda of Uganda, the Akan of Ghana, the Zulu of South Africa, and the Fondom (or kingdoms) of the North West and Western Provinces of Cameroon. In most cases I will concentrate on the Nso Fondom in the North West Province of Cameroon for illustration, but similar structures and ethos can be found throughout Africa.[1]

I. MORAL FOUNDATION AND MORAL EDUCATION

Cultivating character disposition—virtues and the underlying morality that enabled people to lead their lives peaceably within the polity—in precolonial Africa was an integral aspect of the society and state. So connected was the social to the political life that hitherto anthropologists and historians of precolonial Africa have found it difficult specifically to identify and disentangle any separate sense of political education within precolonial African states.

Nowadays, education is often thought of *only* as something institutionalized and explicitly intended and planned—the ministry of education, school classrooms, a curriculum, teachers, students, and educators imparting knowledge. If one examines precolonial Africa in this light, there is not much one can explicitly connect with social and political education. I submit that there was and still is more to political and social education than institutionalized didactic learning. There were and are aspects of social education that resided outside school classrooms. I refer to these as the demonstrative aspects of education. They involve the inculcation and the introjection of moral and social values into a citizenry using as a medium aesthetic and everyday activities and phenomena, which in precolonial Africa included birth and death celebrations, architectural design, and social organizations. I choose these phenomena for two main reasons: first, they were both recognized and expected of people in precolonial Africa; and second, the activities were valorized.[2] That is, they were recognized as traditions and consciously and coercively perpetuated. My main aim is to show how these informal activities helped prepare the pedagogical ground for precolonial governance that was accountable even to the most remote of its citizenry and how the political structure was informed by these everyday activities. I also show that by means of such demonstrative education, the value of community and the public good in general were designed nonarbitrarily to take priority over individuals' self-interest while at the same time respecting their moral worth—human dignity (explained below). While these practices were not instituted as instruments for the protection of presocial or prepolitical rights, nonetheless, the recognition of human dignity did form the framework of human dealing with one another. I must add that the sacred dignity of a human being and community was paramount, and all other virtues were fashioned around this *summum bonum*. The dignified individuals collectively made up the community, and the community became the humus for meaningful life. This should not surprise us in a community like Nso, where the term for happiness is *viwiir*, derived from the word *wiir* meaning a person, and *viwiir*, bringing people together.

Moral and social education in Nso started from the time of birth and continued throughout adult life. The celebration of the birth of a child in Nso was once a lovely and lively grand occasion that brought people together. They ate, they drank, they sang, they bantered, and they danced to recognize the dignity of a human being—the baby. The celebration said, in effect, nonrationally (not irrationally)[3] or without any appeal to rational justification, that without any merit, language, shaped consciousness, achievement, desert, or culture, the newborn was a dignified being, deserving sacred respect, come what may. The respect for a bare innocent baby, a *tabula rasa*, a potential bearer of an identity and rationality (whatever that may turn out to be) was the first-order moral respect that every human being deserved by virtue just of being human. This was the sacred foundation of morality—the dignity of the human *qua* human. In virtue of this sacred human worth and irrespective of the political and social station that individuals occupied, everyone in Nso was a self-authenticating source and recipient of moral claims and justifications. The moral worth of an individual was at the foundation of morality. All the mantles of life, the garbs of our everyday language, the draperies of political and social life, the merits, the deserts, the honors, the status, the beauty, the emotions, the acquired virtues and vices, were important to the society but secondary, and constituted the second-order moral worth of persons. Yes, honor was important and played an identification role in the lives of people in Nso, but moral justification went beyond the draperies of life. (I will say more about the moral worth of humans below when I discuss burial ritual.)

The elders, the wise ones, carefully chose the names of the newly born babies. For instance, children were named after familial ancestors, significant events of the day, epoch, pathos, and ethos. This naming tradition is still alive in many parts of Africa. One of my uncles is named "Barah," or "Englishman," reflecting the visit of a group of Englishmen to our *nto'*, or palace, at the time of his birth.

An interesting event coincided with the birth of two children and informed their names. The Fon of Nso, along with others from then West Cameroon, were invited in a familial colonial ritual to meet and greet Queen Elizabeth in Nigeria. The Fon of Nso attended, but refused to greet the queen by shaking her hand on the grounds that the Fon of Nso does not shake hands with people. The authority reminded him that she was the queen, to which he replied that he had many in his Fondom. He left Nigeria under threats of punishment by the colonialists, and on his arrival in Nso two children were born. He named one of them "Kidze nwah" ("it is written in the book") and the other "Verr-sheye," or "we [Nso people] are waiting for the consequences." The echo of consequences was not surprising given the torture that the Nso endured in a war with the Germans in 1906 for refusing to supply able-bodied men as carriers and plantation workers.

At a naming ceremony the child in question was passed from hand to hand. For weeks people visited the compound. The aroma of fine cuisine wafted through the air. There was plenty to eat and drink and chat about. Like sharp scissors, the birth celebration began to prune children's identities as moral entities and as individuals within a community. From the outset children were enlivened by being passing from hand to hand not only by their parents but also by their kin, kith, kindred, and strangers who came to share in the joy of the child's birth. The choral laughter of women described in Nso as "falling laughter" gave the children their very first aural stimulation. The blessing of the house by sprinkling water from an ancestral calabash was its first tactile stimulation, and the aroma of the kitchen initiated the child's olfactory nerves. The conversations, singing, drumming, and dancing acted as aural stimulation as well. The birth celebration marked the beginning of the infusion of children's identity into that of the community. Young boys and girls rejoiced and were reminded of their own identities. They sang, drank, danced, and fetched water for cooking. These activities helped buttress and underscore the dignity of the community and its collective interests. For many, the presents given in birth celebrations were no doubt an opportunity cost. The celebrants were farmers, bricklayers, and so forth who surely had other things to do but forwent them for the occasion. Personal identity and community, never so articulated, were emergent effects of everyday activities and celebrations.

The deaths of members and the consequent rituals and celebrations were other occasions apart from birth to recognize the moral worth at the bedrock of morality in Nso, the dignity of the human being merely as human. In precolonial Nso, as in many places in Africa, the burial of a person was a community affair. The *bum-bum!* sound of gunshots was a voice of death. As if moved by a centripetal force, the community converged to bury the deceased. There was/is a saying in Nso that just as we all come the same way we all depart the same way. The phrase "the same way" refers to our bare humanity at the time of birth and death.

Titles were desserts accompanied by social recognition and honor. There were many, and most old people had them. Since titles were state concessions and tenures of good behavior, a misbehaving title holder could be stripped of it—but only his title, never his humanity. As a form of recognition and respect for their hard-earned titles, men and women must not be addressed by their proper names. However, prior to their burial, two unusual things were done to titled people: they were stripped of their titles and called by their proper names—names given at their birth. This was a way of tearing down the draperies of earthly life and uncovering and respecting the person's basic humanity. This was the way that we had, as we believed our ancestors had, of resorting to the sacred moral worth of individuals—their dignity as human. Even the Fon of Nso was called by his name before laying him to rest. Chem-Langhee, Verkijika FanNso, and E. M. Chilver emphasize:

> Before the Fon's body was propped upon the grave-stool made by *vibay ve kpu*, *Ndzeendzev* removes his cap, thus bringing his office to an end. When the body was seated held by camwood posts and hide thongs, when a creeper attached to his wrist is brought to the surface and the grave is about to be filled, Taawong addressed the Fon by name for the first and last time:
> *Kpu Binglo', bey bo fon yo' lay; fon ban moo shuuy*
> Binglo' dies, but the Fon does not pass away; the Fon shines like the sun.[4]

This ritual (that surely drowns out reason's quiet voice) was a way of resorting to the first-order moral dignity and recognition of a person *qua* person. This was, in effect, a recognition of our human equality irrespective of what else we might have been on earth. The moral worth of human beings was the basis of the utmost moral justification. The ritual was a nonrational (not irrational) pedagogical tool that taught people to see the moral worth of human beings beyond the acquisitions of life on our journey as "passengers to the grave."[5] Even manslaughter (not to mention murder) violated this dignity and involved prolonged purification rituals to wash the victims clean before they were normal human beings again and could rejoin the society. Warriors underwent special cleansing rituals after each war was over. The full thrust of the human worth forced Nso people to abandon capital punishment, preferring instead to exile those found guilty of capital crimes to a reservation called Kiyung Ndzen, literally translated as "over at fool's home." It was also called Kutupir ("stupid"). Geographically, Kutupir lies at the corridor of Nso territory just before our Bamoum neighbors.

Where is the place of African kings as mystified superhuman or gods? The force of superhuman appellation dissolves when one realizes that what some anthropologists refer to as magic was simply a way that the African people had of recognizing the wisdom of their leaders. In Nso the Fon was seen as "possessing *semvifone*," roughly translated as kingly psychic force, sometimes compared to a high wind at night. He was also seen as vulnerable. Former a'Fon were alluded to as *Kimforkir,* "ultimately destroyed or crushed."[6] They were ultimately equal to everyone else.

How did interaction facilitate a sense of community? Familial interaction was facilitated by the architectural design of living spaces. Part of social learning accrued to people as supervening effects of the designs of living spaces. It would not have taken an architect to observe that living spaces were purposefully designed to socialize the dwellers. Precolonial Nso people lived in compounds. They still do. A compound was a combination of houses with a common playground in the middle. It was a home to many related small families forming a bigger one. A typical compound had a lineage head, or *Taa-lah,* with his wife or wives, two or three elders, uncles who may be married or unmarried, aunts, children of distant relatives or friends as well as ones born and raised in the compound, or "children of the compound." The community house was usually located next to the lineage head's lodge. Personal houses were constructed close to one another to facilitate interaction. Greeting in the morning was a custom, and one's misfortune in the course of the day was often attributed to a person who failed to greet one in the morning and vice versa. Visits to partake in meals were quotidian activities among dwellers. Children were free to wander from one house to another within the compound. The point that I am making here is simple: the architectural design facilitated interaction among the dwellers, thus creating a community in which the individual identities were nested within the fabric of the community's. According to Kwasi Wiredu:

> So strong, in fact, is the sense of communal belonging in the traditional setting that an individual's very sense of self is contextualized not only to the fact of community but also to its values; so that a person, for all concerned, is not just an individual born of human parentage, but also an individual of that description whose settled habits evince sensitivity to the basic values of the community.[7]

The community house served as a place for the gathering of men and women for communal meetings and weekly social organizations. When their interests clashed, people talked for hours and hours to arrive at consensual agreement. (I will elaborate on consensus below.)

Interfamily social organizations (about which more below) were primarily concerned with socialization as an end. The organizations were of two varieties, defined by membership. Membership was inscriptive when the organization involved family rituals, and was voluntary and open to non–family members when it was secular. Most importantly, members of these social organizations were regarded as equal irrespective of their social, political, and moral standing. The member, for example, had the right to his opinion, a right freely exercised. There were constitutions detailing the times of the meetings, the duties of the leaders, the fines for transgression of the rules, and so forth. Most of the social organizations involved pecuniary transactions in the form of save and thrift, rotating credit, and mutual help. Whatever transaction took place, socializing—bantering, merrymaking, dancing, singing, drinking, eating—was an essential core of these organizations. So important were these organizations that Kwame Anthony Appiah observes:

> if the state is ever to reverse recent history and expand the role it plays in the lives of its subjects, it will have to learn something about the surprising persistence of these "premodern" affiliations [social organizations], the cultural and political fretwork of relations through which our very identity is conferred.[8]

The organizations were arenas for the exercise of virtue and for young people to learn such virtues as discipline—when to talk, when not to talk, what to say, and what not to say in the public. New members were expected to spend time learning behavior befitting the organizations. Cohesion and solidarity were often the supervening effects of such gatherings. Individuals also learned to net their self-identity within the larger fabric of members'.

The recognition of human worth played a crucial rule in their everyday lives. I use the phrase "everyday life" cautiously to denote the nonpublicly recognized aspects of interpersonal, interfamilial affairs. How did the people of Nso in their everyday life deal with the human conditions that give rise to morality and justice?[9]

If and when conflicts of interest emerged among individuals, it was resolved by deliberation. Families and friends who experienced conflicts of interest mostly engaged in face-to-face deliberation and dialogue until they arrived at a common understanding or consensus, if at all.

Rarely did friends and/or family members settle their differences of interest by voting. Precolonial Africans elevated consensus as an avenue for settling conflicts of interest in private clubs—social organizations described above. Of course, consensual arrangements required of individuals certain virtues—imagination, discipline, courage, toleration, and listening.

What I have shown here is the quotidian life of precolonial Africa with a built-in practical moral and virtue education. In the section that follows, I will argue that political institutions were constructed around the moral value track that inhered in African societies. The priority of values over the institutional structure defies a long tradition of Mandevillian argument to the effect that social and political institutions can be arranged so as to render the desired collective outcome independent of individual character and belief. In short, good institutions render political education useless.[10] I opine that pure political processes and structures without the desired values can be dangerous for a society. They can thwart good government and human flourishing, as is clear in the United States where "pure procedural" criminal justice has seen a particular section of its citizenry—African-American men—disproportionately represented in the criminal justice system. A procedural structure of justice constructed on moral grounds is bound to be sensitive to such outcomes.

II. THE INSTITUTIONAL TRACK: POLITICAL EDUCATION AND THE NSO STATE

How did the precolonial political arrangements and processes enable people to deliberate or in general deal with the sticky, vexing, and divisive issues that raise questions about what is fair, what is just, and what is good? Assuming that there was such a thing as the common good, we may have a general idea about it but know not exactly what it is and therefore have to seek for it using our imagination via public deliberation. Figuring out what was publicly just, good, and fair was what public palaver or talk was all about in Nso. Palaver denotes deliberation mixed with emotion and some form of order. Palaver was a significant aspect of life in Nso. Individuals derived intrinsic pleasure from figuring out the public good.

The intrinsic pleasure I refer to is epitomized by an Akan gold weight, a genre piece representing two crocodiles with a shared stomach evoking the proverb, *à la* Kwame Anthony Appiah: "Stomachs mixed up, crocodiles' stomachs mixed up, they both have one stomach but when they eat they fight because of the sweetness of the swallowing." Appiah explains that "the meaning of the proverb, which expresses one of the dilemmas of family life, is that while the acquisition of each family member benefits the whole family (there is only one stomach), the pleasure of enjoyment is an individual thing."[11] Proverbs could be accommodating. It could also mean that while we are looking for the just, the good, and the fair, let us enjoy the search. To deprive individuals in Nso of the search for a common answer would not have been regarded as a relief from doing unsavory and a sticky work but as a deprivation of a fine pleasure. For as I maintained, deliberation was not only a matter of looking for common answers to common problems, it was also a matter of the pleasure of searching, and people took delight in palavers. We should bear in mind that palaver was also an inroads search for answers to real disputes, real conflict of interests, real public problems. Using the proverb above, Wiredu insists that "if they [crocodiles] could but see that the food is, in any case, destined for the same stomach, the irrationality of the conflict would be manifest to each."[12] While people enjoyed palaver, fighting and family division did ensue very often. The question is: What happened when people as deliberators failed to see eye to eye or, like rams, when they locked horns, because as the saying goes, "two rams cannot drink from the same bowl at the same time, in time they will lock horns"? The answer to this question about conflict of interests lies in the constitution of Nso government.

The institutions were designed to lubricate the avenue for consensual government. I must indicate that government by consensus was hardly limited to precolonial Africa. Jane Mansbridge, a leading contemporary theorist in grassroots democracy, has identified government by consensus as another legitimate form of democracy, referring to it as "unitary" democracy.[13] I will not belabor the definition of government by consensus because she has done an exhaustive job of defining and giving an account of it. Kwasi Wiredu has also shown that consensus was indigenous to precolonial African political arrangements and processes.[14] My main task is to show what happened from the point of view of the institutions in Nso when people palavering and deliberating could not arrive at a consensus. How were Nso institutions designed to handle the task?

The institutional framework was constructed on the moral bedrock of human dignity as well as community regarded as a value. Human dignity and community were prepolitical values, and the Nso constitution was designed around them. Taking heed of preexisting customs and values was hardly new or limited to Nso. John Stuart Mill, an uncompromising liberal philosopher, insists:

> When an institution, or a set of institutions, has the way prepared for it by the opinions, tastes, and habits of the people, they are more easily induced to accept it, but will more easily learn, and will be, from the beginning, better disposed, to do what is required of them both for the preservation of the institutions, and for bringing them into such action as enable them to produce their best results.

It would be a great mistake in any legislator not to shape his measures so as to take advantage of such pre-existing habits and feelings when available.[15]

I cannot here give a panoramic map nor describe details of the complex constitution of Nso government, with its networks of checks and balances. What I say here is skeletal.

Certainly, Nso has changed since precolonial times, but her political institutions are still very much alive and in fact flourishing. This is partly to do with the weak Cameroon state as well as the Nso people's ability to dance to the tune of our changing political world—they adapt, they compromise, and they preserve most of what they have.

I classify the Nso political system into four main categories: the basic political constituencies; the office of the Fon, or *fonship;* the *Nwerong* regulatory society; and the *Manjong,* or warrior society. Built into the constitution was political education, which must be explored to get the feel of the constitutional framework. I must again restate that the first section of this paper dealt with the informal moral education and structure, while this section will deal with formal political pedagogy underwritten by collective or expert judgments about the good, the fair, and just.

Descent in Nso was and still is patrilineal. The family lineage was the basic political constituency. It was physically embodied and expressed by a compound called *Lah,* and these were (still are) ubiquitous, headed by family heads called *a'Taa-lah* or *a'faay* or *a'Shufaay* ("*a*" stands for plural). The lineage head was the political and spiritual leader of a group of five generations in depth.[16] If a lineage grew too big, a sublineage was formed headed by *a'Sheey*—a sub-*a'Faay.* Individuals belonged to these constituencies whether they were alive and lived in or out of Nso, or were ancestors, or were still to be born. The lineage heads who were descendants of the first settler in the villages in which the constituencies of the *a'Faay, a'Shu-faay,* and *a'Sheey* were physically located bore the title of *a'Taanteh,* or elders of the village. In addition to their official duties as lineage heads was duty to seal consensus among other lineage heads in their jurisdictions regarding matters that required the intervention of outsiders to the lineage—for instance, land disputes and witchcraft accusations. Family heads were officially responsible for maintaining order, arbitrating minor cases, transmitting palace instructions, representing their lineages in the palace and elsewhere, and making reports to the palace as occasion demanded.[17]

The fonship was an office headed by a Fon, who upon election moved to live in the palace. "The palace is the political center of *Nsaw* [Nso]; it belongs to the people of *Nsaw* not to the Fon."[18] A stool, called *kava',* signified the fonship, which was an embodiment of the Nso past, present, and future generations. In the absence of the Fon, people greeted the stool. The Fon was the paramount political leader and intermediary between the living and the ancestors. As spiritual leader he appointed a male deputy priest, called *Taawong,* and a female priestess, called *Yeewong.* Their functions were purely spiritual, centered on the honoring of ancestors.[19]

Most significantly, the Fon was also a *symbol* of the unity of the Nso people. He had seven councillors, called *vibai* (*kibai* is singular). The *vibai* were lineage heads as well, titled *Shu-faay.* But as *vibai* they were officers of state, and their appointment was a matter that primarily affected the state as a whole, rather than just members of their respective lineages, to whom they were also lineage heads.[20] A *kibai* was first and foremost an officer of the state; his primary duties were those connected with state affairs; his consultants in state matters were his fellow councillors, not the elders of his lineage. The offices of *vibai* were tenures of good behavior and conduct.[21] The Fon presided over the council of state and formerly made final decisions in matters of peace and war. He was *ex officio* head of all clubs in Nso. He alone ratified appointment to all offices, including lineage heads, and he reserved the right to remove any officer from office.[22] He was the commander in chief of the armed forces or warrior society.

Part of the palace was occupied by the *Nwerong* regulatory society. It was referred to as a palace in its own right—a judiciary branch of the Nso government responsible for interpreting and enforcing the law. The decisions of *Nwerong* were impersonal, unlike those of the Fon, his councillors, and the lineage heads. Unlike the Fon, *vibai,* and lineage heads, who could be called upon by the people to account personally and publicly for their actions and behavior, *Nwerong* could not. The *Nwerong* palace was headed by *a'Taa-ntoh* (elders of the palace). These men were truly elders, clairvoyants, well-educated (of which more below), and reputed for their impartiality and strictness in enforcing the law. Like the councillors, they lived close to the palace. The *Nwerong* was one of the main checks and balances to the power of the Fon and his councillors. The members if the Nwerong restrained the Fon and obviated his monopoly over the exercise of political power. Like the Fon councillors, the *a'Taa-ntoh* met formally once a week (in the Nso eight-day week) and responded at short notice to situations regarding the state. Again, they were family heads as well. *A'Taa-ntoh* were first and foremost officers of the state, and their education and election was a state-regarding affair, not just a family one.

Another important institution was the militia—the *Manjong,* or warrior society. *Manjong* was divided into two branches—*Mfu-gham* in charge of defense, and *Mfuh bah,* offense. They had sub-branches all over Nso fondom and even in areas with heavy Nso population. They were headed by two military generals: *Mforme Ngham* and *Mforme Baa,* positions that were for life unless a serious transgression occurred—that is, they were tenures of good behavior.

Royal daughters were eligible for marriages that created and reproduced political alliances and social networks between the Fon of Nso and other nations in the region. Once married to another Fon, they served as Nso ambassadors—they negotiated peace and reported to the (Nso) capital, Kimbo.[23]

To understand the function of these institutions, it is necessary first to understand political education in Nso. Two forms of education could be identified: the first was a broad demonstrative political education for members of the polity at large, and the second was a special training accorded to the would-be *a'Taa-ntoh* officers at the *Nwerong* palace. The general political education was nondidactic, or demonstrative. It involved inculcating the character disposition that enabled the citizenry to live tolerantly within and support the Fondom. Respect for the dignity of the human being and the community's values was important. So part of the education was to harness individual desiderata with the core values of the community.

General political education was discharged demonstratively via entertainment from various official quarters of the palace. The first was the *Ngiri* society, composed of male descendants of the Fon, called *wanntoh*. The second was from the *Cong, Corr, Laa-lir,* and *Chong* women's organizations. Men were not admitted or allowed to see the inner circle of the *Cong, Laa-lir,* and *Chong*. In procession women ululated, directing to men: *ulu lului e 'lumina kibaa ndzee eee!! elu lului e 'limina kibaa ndzee eee!!* ("Men, there is madness outside, men, there is madness outside.") It was believed that men who saw the *Cong* would go mad. There was also *lafoo-lir,* or nowhere to hide, which has an inner circle opened only to the initiated women and a secular outer circle to everyone.

The *Manjong,* or warrior society, pedagogy was formal. Hunting expeditions were used as a training ground for young fighters, a tradition that is still alive today. Virtues such as courage, obeying commands, and working as groups were imparted to young warriors during hunting expeditions. Besides, the *Manjong* houses were lively places for talks and palavers.

The training of future *a'Taa-ntoh* officers of the *Nwerong* palace was less informal. The pedagogy for palace stewardship, pageship, and a potential *a'Taa-nto* was a lengthy one. Formal leadership education started at the *Nwerong* regulatory society and continued via initiation for those who aspired to rise to the highest echelon in the palace. Two young men were recruited in their youth for a pedagogical process that went on for nine years. They were in charge of the lower *Nwerong* palace; the *a'Taa-ntoh* were in charge of the higher one, *Yee-nwerong,* literally translated as the "mother of *Nwerong.*" During their long pedagogical process, they were prohibited from leaving the *Nwerong* palace unmasked. Other boys were recruited to undergo the same education for potential official state positions. This description of the training deserves to be quoted at length:

> … the two houses each held about 30 boys, in addition to those who slept in the palace. They first slept on *kiba'*, a board of raffia stems, laid on the ground, which was liable to be confiscated as firewood unless it was stored away. They were later allowed to *tang kiba'*, pay for the bed, by feasting those ahead of them and thus allowed to raise their beds from the floor and tied them to the walls. The discipline visited on them—hard beds, sparse food and regular small beating to toughen them—was strict. After completing their service the youths were graduated in batches according to years of entry, first given their [symbolic] building pole and told to *tang nto'*—offer to the palace—and then to partake in a feast to which their parents contributed. Such young men referred to themselves, with pride to their toughness, *asnshiyse lav se kiba'*. They were obliged to report each *Ntangrin*, the seventh day of the Nso week at *nwerong la'*, to receive instructions from the palace stewards, and supply firewood once a year to the palace. At this point they could enter *ngwerong nsaasa'*, associated with the lowest grade of masks worn to accompany a feather-cloaked *shigwala* mutuary masker, or allowed to hold the rope restraining the fearsome *kibarangko*. When fully adults they could be allowed to seek membership in one of the mask-lodges cum drinking clubs.[26]

The graduates of this training played very important roles in the fondom as the Fon's official eyes and ears. They were also spokespersons for the Fon and in charge of the complex palace bureaucracy and protocol. Once these graduates were old enough (about 65 years), they were eligible through complex initiation and oath taking to be members of the *Yee-nwerong*, the highest level of the *Nwerong*. Members of this *Yee-nwerong* were the most trusted of all in Nso. They were home to impartiality, courage, equanimity, and wisdom. Apart from justice and fairness, they had no ax to grind and nothing to prove. They were gracious people and hardly seen in public drinking places. They were the real lawkeepers and interpreters and the last connection between the ancestors and the living. Even the Fon had to be initiated to be a member. This initiation was necessary not because the Fon partook in their judgments but because when called upon to answer questions regarding his office he was obliged to step into that space, the *Nwerong* sanctum sanctorum, or *lav Yee-nwerong*. And that required initiation.

The bulk of character education happened in the countless Nso social organizations. Members of the organizations pride themselves on their goodness and fairness to one another. Sections of the *Nwerong* and *Ngiri* regulatory societies were social organizations. Pecuniary transactions were involved—save and thrifts and rotating credits. Accountability of leaders to members was primed. The map of organization would be very dense. The

Fon belonged to one society called *ngwah kibu,* which took place in the Fon's palace. The Fon was also a member of another one known as *ngwah mengang.* Members of this rotating credit contracted to contribute to their pot. Failure to do so was met by a group of masqueraders called *mengang* who went into the defaulter's residence and literally excreted all over—living room, bed, under the bed, dishes, attic, roof. Members of this organization were the most financially trusted. Their social capital was grand.[25]

The reason I bring in these organizations as avenues for political education is because they were publicly recognized in Nso. In the event of the death of a neighboring Fon, they were delegated by Nso officials to represent them. These organizations were unlike the lineage voluntary organizations, which I identified above with moral education. Those were publicly recognized as well but enforced mainly by customs and mores.

III. ACCOUNTABILITY, CONSENSUS, AND PARTICIPATION

Nso political arrangement was an integrated system designed to connect and harmonize individual and group into the power structure. As such, Nso polity was highly federated.[26] E. M. Chilver and P. M. Kaberry observe that:

> Unlike the conquered chiefdoms absorbed into Bamum (Mvem), the sub-chiefdoms of Nso, recognizing the paramountcy of the Fon of Nso remained on their original sites, retained their hereditary dynasties, and were allowed autonomy in the management of local affairs except in the matter of war and capital punishment.... Thus the lineage in Nso functions as a political, economic and religious corporation under a head who, if he is accountable to living members and ancestors, is also directly responsible to the Fon. To the best of our knowledge, nowhere else in the Bamenda grassfields do lineage heads enjoy such extensive authority: but nowhere else does a ruler exercise such influence on their appointment.[27]

The Fon symbolized the unity of Nso above all else. He was like a thread that ran through the entire decentralized and federated system. Thus, the Nso proverb: *Nso dze Nsobi' Fon, a Fon dze Fon bi' Nso* ("the Nso are the Nso on account of the Fon, and the Fon is the Fon on account of the Nso").[28] This proverb emphasized the accountability of the governing officials to the people. Thus Kaberry, an authority on Nso history, observes:

> The Nsaw [Nso] system, like most centralized systems, is one of checks and balances, but the sanctions against an abuse of privilege are not merely negative. The relationship between the Fon and his people is a moral one. The Fon himself says: "What is a Fon without people? I am in the hands of my people." And

the Nsaw have two sayings which epitomize their conceptions of chieftainship: "The Fon has everything; the Fon is a poor man," and "The Fon rules the people, but the people hold the Fon."[29]

Tyranny and despotism were not in the vocabulary of these precolonial political arrangements. First, the state agents came from among ordinary folks. They lived with them. The Fon himself was an ordinary citizen, most often a farmer, an occupation he kept alongside the state function. The state agents kept their occupations as farmers, carpenters, and so on. Only happy people were elected as state agents. This should not be surprising because as I pointed out earlier, the word for happiness in Nso language (Lamnso) is *viwiir,* derived from one's ability to bring people together. Only a people's magnets were elected to state offices.

The *Nwerong* palace, nestled within the fabric of the political arrangement, enjoyed a great degree of autonomy in its judgments. As such it counterpoised the Fon, the councillors, the family representatives, and, as the custodian and interpreter of the laws, the warrior society. Concerning the power of Fon Nso, Kaberry insists:

> But the chieftainship [fonship] is not a despotism. Though the Fon is paramount and has the right to initiate and to make the final decision in all matters affecting the country, he is also responsible for and accountable to his people. He is a source of welfare and well-being; and when he acts in a way to threaten the welfare of the country *he may be called to account as a person, for his authority is not of an impersonal kind,* as is that of *Nwerong.* Both *Ngwerong* and *manjong* may fine him if he acts in a way contrary to the ideals of chieftainship or to the interest of the country; His Queen Mothers and councilors should advise and restrain him; and his commoner lords, when all these agencies have failed in time of adversity or crisis, have the right to intervene and give advice, admonish, instruct or, if necessary, support him.[30]

The *Nwerong* would punish a wayward Fon. As I maintained earlier, the Nso political arrangement as well as others in the region are still alive and flourishing. As recently as April 26, 1999, thirty *a'Fon* of the North West Province of Cameroon were sanctioned by the *Nwerong* for attending the funeral of an elder, John Ngu Foncha, who is known as the father of the Reunification of Cameroon. "According to a spokesman for the Kwifons' [*a'Nwerong*], the Fons [a'Fon] led by [Fon] John Ambi II of Bafut and S.A.N Agwafor of Mankon, were against the tradition which forbids them from attending funeral ceremonies and seeing corpses and as such will pay 30 goats, two cows, 50 bags of salt, 20 tins of oil, 100 fowls and undergo traditional cleansing."[31] (See footnote for the full quotation.) On a similar note, Nso *Nwerong* suspended Mforme Gham (remember that he is officially

appointed by the Fon) from his office for ten years for conspiring to intervene in the *Nwerong* judgment. The newspaper, *Nso Voice* (one of three Nso
local newspapers), reads, "Mforme Gham, of the two Generals, has been
slammed a ten year suspension. The suspension orders issued on the 2nd of
November [1998] followed his attempts to house and protect one Mathias
a soya seller exiled by Nwerong for being the brain behind the rampant goat
theft in town."[32] (See footnote for continuation of the report.) Herein lies the
accountability of the rulers to the ruled. In a similar situation, one Fon of
Nso sold property to the Catholic mission without the consent of the people. According to report from the *Nso Voice:*

> Addressing the mammoth crowd that formed a large circle under a sacred tree
> in Mbve, Shey Wo Bamfem, one of the sub-Chiefs, speaking on behalf of
> Nwerong Society, declared to the population that the Fon's vast farm land in
> Shisong, once sold to the Reverend Sisters by the Late Fon, Ngah Bifon II, had
> been unconditionally taken back.
>   The Nwerong Society noted that both the Fon and the Reverend were
> wrong to carry such transactions for it said, it is not embedded in the tradition
> of a people that land be sold out "by the tribe."
>   The Fon is the people and the people the Fon, Nwerong ruled, "anything
> done between the two is done in the name of the tribe and the protection of
> posterity."[33]

As I maintained, Nso government was depended neither on the tallying
of individuals' mere preference—cesarean utilitarianism—nor on the coerced
substitution of individuals' assessment of their interests for a collective or
expert judgment—paternalism, or what Bernard Williams has referred to as
"government house Utilitarianism." Yes, the people chose their leaders, but
the Fon in formal consultation with state's councilor ratified the leader and
reserved the right to reject the candidacy, a right that he rarely exercised.
Normally full weight was given to the wishes of the groups most closely concerned by the appointment to ensure success through the support and
cooperation of the governed. Kaberry points out that in the case of *Manjong,*
the opinion of the clubhouse concerned was sounded out by the Fon's delegates or the members themselves submitted a name or names to the Fon for
approval. In the case of a lineage leadership, the Fon's delegates made dis-
creet inquiries of the members of the lineage involved, of other lineage heads
within the same clan, and of influential and trusted neighbors who spoke
from knowledge about the character of possible candidates. They reported
back to the Fon, who either ratified or vetoed the candidates. In all these
instances, the Fon do not rule singlehandedly.[34]
    Nso was and still is truly a mixed bag of various groups of people with
diverse cultures unified by a common political culture symbolized by the

Fon. Refugees from neighboring fondoms further mongrelized Nso. E. M. Chilver and P. M. Kaberry recorded oral tradition to the effect that the population of the Nso Fondom was "enlarged by the arrival of settlers. The majority of them originated from the north, north-west and west."[35] Kishani detailed lineage and fondom like those of the Do', Ndzeendzev, Tang from the north, the Ki', Nkim, Mbite'ey, and so on.[36] Nso was and is composed of other sub-fondoms such as Nkar, Mbiame, Nzerem, Nseh, Kilun, Din Viku (Oku), and Djottin Noni. These fondoms exercised a great deal of autonomy. Some of the fondoms kept their languages, for example, Oku and Djottin Noni. Members of these sub-fondoms were free to migrate to Kimbo, the capital of Nso, and many did.

The mosaic composition of Nso can begin to tell us something about the shape that political arrangements, processes, palaver, and deliberation took. The Nso political structure was framed on the assumption of a dissensus and apparent disagreement of interests among its citizenry, not the other way around. Conflicts of interests were various and ranged from the lineage level of government to the top of the political arrangements. Again, at this point I will not belabor nor rehearse Mansbridge's seminal work on deliberation and consensus. Rather, I will attempt here to show what happened in Nso when the people could not arrive at a consensus. It is worth keeping in mind that the complex political structure of Nso was designed to entice the citizenry into a participatory spirit, ensure accountability, and solve the problems of conflict of public interests.

Some of the issues at the center of Nso talk (palaver) and deliberative forums included the following: selection and impeachment of leaders, witchcraft accusations, land disputes, ostracizing people on capital crimes, declaring war and signing treaties, reprimanding leaders, taxation, budget, and legislation—interpreting and amending laws and criminal justice.

The networks of social organizations prevalent in Nso were the combustion points for most matters of public concern because most public discussions began within these social organizations. There, imagination ran wild. No voice was privileged. Everyone spoke, producing the aura of a "Portuguese parliament." Like the "Chinese whisper," people added their own spices to the talks, making them more engaging and accessible to all. That was how imagination was left unfettered. That was generally where and how some of the vexing public-regarding issues of the day were formulated. Part of the respect and tolerance members displayed toward one another had their roots in the moral worth of individuals as free and equal. The call for individual political equality would have sounded redundant to them. The free-for-all talks were a forum for rehearsing and sorting out what issue belonged where—public or private or both. Matters regarding the organization were discussed after the free-for-all talk in a more controlled fashion.

Since these were not cesarean utilitarian forums, there was time (as I have maintained) for more controlled talks. People spoke in turn. Members would signal one another by tapping them on the shoulder, then they would walk quietly outside to consult with one another, and when it was their turn they spoke to a listening audience. Discussions went to and fro until some form of consensus was reached. When a consensus wasn't reached, the matter was postponed for the subsequent meetings. Kishani said of the warrior society:

> In this *lave Mfu'* [*Lave* is a meeting house], the best minds among the Nso usually expounded the fruits of their meditations on political questions and issues for others to accept and promote by first critically debating and practically approving their transmission for final approval by two *Amforme* [two appointed generals of the warrior societies] and eventually by the Fon.[37]

Witchcraft accusations were common within family lineages. For example, Z, a family member, died, and Y, another family member, accused another X of having "a hand" in Z's death. Obviously, not everyone would have seen eye to eye in this form of accusation that generally lacked objective justification. Some would claim that the cause of Z's death was his perpetual drunkenness. The family split into factions. The lineage head summoned the family. Discussion began. People fought with crude evidence. Point: "Why wasn't X sad when Z's death was announced; X's sadness wasn't real." Counterpoint: "Z had been ill for all I can remember; he was an old man and it was time for him to join the ancestors." These accusations were charged with emotion. Normally, problems like these were solved at the family level.

Others, like land tenure, were hot as well—who gets what piece of land, where, and when. During the interfamilial claims about which interests clashed, an appointed person, called *Ngwaan* (chief of protocol at the family lineage level), acted like a listener. He was a man with photographic memory, who spoke little and listened a lot. If talks stalled or no consensus was reached, *Ngwaan* briefed and (in time) advised the elders of the family (who rarely sat in palaver sessions) regarding the conflict. The elders would intervene with their wisdom. They consulted with the ancestors. Consulting the ancestors was (at this level) a metaphor for consulting the past wisdom and precedence housed in our traditions and customs. If a consensus was reached, it ended there; if not, it was taken one step further. *Ngwaan* consulted the neighboring lineage heads, *a'Faay,* who gave their opinion to the family members. If no agreement was reached, *Ngwaan* consulted with the elders from the surrounding compounds, who spoke with their voice of ancestral wisdom. If a consensus was arrived, then *Taa-ngwenn,* or *Taa-nte',* an officer appointed by the family lineages and ratified by the Fon to seal consensus, was then called upon to pour libation and perform rituals to ancestors. The ritual sealed and legitimized the consensus. Sealing the consensus was a very expensive procedure because all the inhabitants of the jurisdiction or constituency in question were invited to an expensive feast and ritual performance. The lineage head and members provide all the palm wine and food. Any family disagreements that transcended the lineage corridor were sealed in this fashion—by a sumptuous feast and ritual performance. Family members did not want their palaver to go this far. They tried to reach consensus before outsiders came in to sap their resources.

If it happened that a consensus was not arrived at, then the matter went to the palace. The Fon and his counselors, *vibai* (*vibai* also act as judges at the weekly court sessions in the palace) consulted and deliberated on it and came to an agreement. If no agreement was reached, then it was either reformulated and sent back to the source or was taken to the level of the *Nwerong*, the highest compartment—the supreme house where the clairvoyants, the impartial judges, consulted with one another and ancestors to make their judgment. This was always the last stop. The problem could still be reintroduced but in a different guise. A judgment at this level involved the Fon, the family representatives, *vibai*, and, above all, the chief priest and priestess.

I would like to note that the present political arrangements in Nso is very much the same as described above. Describing the precolonial political arrangement does not tell us anything about what we should do with our present state of political affairs in most African countries. Before I say anything about it I would like to point out the following crucial point about Nso polity. First, Nso has never been a homogeneous society. In fact, Nso is neither an ethnic group nor a homogeneous culture apart from its political culture. Any type of cooperation one finds in Nso today was proactively forged by the ingenuity of our ancestors, who never assumed that people will always agree. They integrated diverse groups of people into a lively Nso polity. Miriam insists that, "The social categories of Nso are neither exclusive nor endogamous. The various groups have certain rights and certain responsibilities vis-à-vis each other and the *fon,* and are actually significant, but they are not in fact hierarchical in any measurable sense."[38] As recently as circa 1960, Nso integrated a constituency composed of the Mbororo with their first family lineage head, Fon Juli. Now settled in Nso, the Mbororo were nomadic cattle raisers. Second, the Nso ancestors divided the citizenry into different groups of *wirfon,* or the people of the Fon, further divided into two groups, the *wanto',* or royals, the *njiyslavsi,* or retainers, and the *mtaarNso,* or free commoners. The purpose was arguably to politically mobilize and enliven the members into an enthusiastic orderly political participation, much like intercollegiate soccer competition. Third, politics was and is an affair of the day (not draped). The constitution is transparent, and via political education people are equipped as it were with checklists of the dos and the don'ts of their public officials that enable them to hold them accountable for their behavior, actions, and conduct. To highlight this, I would like to point out that today Nso boasts three local newspapers, two in English and one in Lamnso (Nso language), and an academic journal. Fifth, Nso and many of the fondoms in Cameroon had a flourishing non-partisan politics before the physical arrival of the Germans in the region in circa 1900.

IV. CONCLUSION: CONTEMPORARY AFRICAN NATIONS AND ACCOUNTABILITY

Nowadays in most of Africa it is nearly impossible to hold government agents (from the level of the police up to the head of state) accountable. First, no one (except perhaps government officials) knows what the state agents are supposed to be doing in the first place. There is no checklist that I or anybody is aware of that tells the citizens the dos and don'ts of government officials. As such, corruption is the order of the day. Second, government-house utilitarianism is in operation. Colonial legacy looms. The colonial officers answered to their home government, never to the African people, and since independence, the new African elite have failed to reverse that form of accountability. Colonialists attempted to destroy all of the African past, a legacy taken over by an African elite who failed to look into their unwritten past. Good legislators never destroy old institutions, no matter how bad they may be; they only change, transform, or transfer the energy to good institutional arrangements.

I would like to note that Africans are not brand new people, nor is politics a brand new activity in Africa. In fact, Africans are far older than the various recognizable nation-states one finds nested on the continent today. African intellectuals have failed to analyze the African unwritten political past. Yes, the Western political tradition is now an inextricable part of the African political tradition. But African political theorists tend to treat Western political arrangements as the only paradigm of good government, as if one good afternoon these arrangements sprung up like mushrooms from the earth. This unnecessary and blind adherence to partisan politics has helped to divide the already divided people. Some may claim that adversary democracy is necessary because we hold fundamentally different conceptions of the good. They may point to the wars of religion following the Reformation in the West as an example of conflict of the good. I contend that African religion, for example, was and is not an institutionalized one. It was a personal affair and remains so today—there was neither evangelization nor proselytization of African religion that I know of. So most of Africa was relieved of this religious baggage.

Analyzing African political arrangements from the inside out, rather than from the perspective of the foreigner looking in, can yield great benefits. Political institutions based on an adversarial conception of politics have their places; but as Jane Mansbridge has demonstrated, the unitary or consensual form can also generate good government. Like anywhere else, Africa's past includes war and personal and social conflict. But it also includes valuable social protocols, political arrangements, and values that have been obscured by colonial and neocolonial thinking, and that merit reconsideration and revival.

Society and Democracy in Africa

Kwasi Wiredu

I. CIVIL SOCIETY, COMMUNALISM, AND CONSENSUS

One way in which colonialism injured Africa was through the rupture it caused in the integration of the civil with the political aspect of her social life. That integration was one of the strong points of traditional society. Indeed, in traditional life the distinction between the state and civil society was largely irrelevant. This seamlessness was, however, not complete, for it was still possible in traditional times to distinguish between societies that were organized as states and those that had no state apparatus. The Zulu of South Africa are an example of the first class of societies, while the Tallensi of Ghana exemplify the second.

One thing that can be learned from nonstatal societies is that political organization is not inevitable for all human communities. On the other hand, there has to be a certain minimum of order in any human community. That order has to be, at least, because communication is the most basic characteristic of a normal person. And it has to be moral, because there cannot be an order of human relations without some principles for harmonizing human interests. Of all such principles, those of pure morality—that is, those requiring of the individual an impartial regard for the interests of others motivated by a certain minimum of altruism—are the most indispensable. Without a modicum of morality one could not have any modicum of civility.

But morality and communication provide only a framework for a social order. Traditional societies, like modern ones, featured a variety of forms of association—occupational, recreational, and, in most cases, political. But from the point of view of the manner in which these forms of civil relations were connected with the political, there is a very significant contrast between the traditional and modern eras, a contrast that holds serious challenges to contemporary African thinkers. Many, possibly all, traditional African societies were communalistic, but in the contemporary world they are all visibly under the impact of social processes, such as industrialization, that are individualistic in tendency.

A communalistic society is one in which extended kinship linkages play a dominant role in social relations. The smallest kinship setup to which any young adult belongs with a lively sense of belonging is already a significant society. To take a matrilineal case—the patrilineal alternative being derivable by appropriate modifications—it would consist of one's mother and one's siblings, one's mother's siblings and the children of their daughters, and, at the top, a grandmother. If this immediate matriarch has been moderately fertile, this provides a broad domain of human relations in which a sense of obligations and rights and of reciprocity is developed on the basis of natural feelings of sympathy and solidarity. This unit—still pursuing the matrilineal angle—links up, through the siblings of the grandmother and the children of their daughters, with an extensive network of analogous kinship units which, in a given town, constitutes a lineage. By a kind of natural spillover, the sense of sympathy and solidarity easily acquires a community-wide scope. At this scale of extension there is inevitably a certain diminution in the sense of belonging and solidarity, but it is strong enough to give the individual a solid sense of security. As anyone can verify, this sense of security is easily lost in the relatively noncommunalistic setting of a modern city, with destabilizing consequences for individual psyches and for social equilibrium. Measured against the emotionally desiccated conditions of much city life, it becomes easy to perceive the role of kinship solidarity in the maintenance of morale in traditional rural life. So strong, in fact, is the sense of communal belonging in the traditional setting that an individual's very sense of self is contextualized not only to the fact of community but also to its values; so that a person, for all concerned, is not just an individual born of human parentage but also an individual of that description whose settled habits evince sensitivity to the basic values of the community.

The ethos of a communalistic society bears an important relation to the ethics of human community as such. The fundamental imperative of ethics is: adjust your interests to the interests of others even at the possible cost of some self-denial. The principle of adjustment is a similar principle to the golden rule, provided it is formulated with much more rigor than is customarily devoted to it. But such a principle of pure morality, though indispensable, is inadequate for the regulation of all aspects of human relations. How shall we arrange the perpetuation of the species, the restoration of cheer in the face of adversity, the utilization of human resources in production, the construction of public projects, or the particulars of recreational respite from toil? In the best formulation, the golden rule still does not proffer any guiding precepts here. It is a fact of simple observation that the cultures of the world display a great diversity of choices in all these matters, all compatible with the golden rule.

The principle underlying the choices of a communalistic culture, however, is not only compatible with the golden rule but also analogous to it. Individuals in such cultures are enjoined to think in terms of not what they can gain from their society but what the society can gain from them, so, however, that all can prosper. In other words, the individual's interests are to be adjusted to those of society, not vice versa. We find exactly the same outlook in the motto of the moral motivation: be ready to abridge your interests so that they can harmonize with the common interest. This is not a principle of the abnegation of individual interests, because it applies to all individuals, and in the upshot any one individual should be more frequently a beneficiary of the forbearance of others than a sacrificer of self-interest. Exactly the same is true of the communalistic imperative.

Consider the practice of mutual aid in traditional agriculture. It is not dictated by the golden rule. Societies that do not have such a practice are not immoral on that account. But the principle underlying the practice is in pursuit of the harmony of human interests to the advantage of society in general. A great many practices of a communalistic society are of such civil motivation and have no necessary connection with state regulation. The interesting point for us here, however, is that in the traditional milieu the state itself can be seen as a special organization for the pursuit of mutual aid, and its underlying principle bears the same analogy to moral principles as those of the civil institutions and practices of traditional communalism. But there is another reason for the apparent naturalness of the state in the traditional context: government was formed on the basis of kinship representation. Ruling councils consisted of lineage heads and a "natural" ruler selected from a royal lineage. The continuity of the affairs of the state with the workings of the other sectors of the traditional culture was well-nigh complete.

There is, connected with the continuity of the civil with the political in traditional life, a consideration very crucial for our discussion. It concerns the pervasiveness of consensus as a mode of group decision-making. It is well known that traditional Africans generally, if perhaps not universally, placed such a high value on consensus in deliberations regarding interpersonal projects that their elders would "sit under the big trees and talk until they agree." Agreement here need not be construed as unanimity concerning what is true or false or even about what ought or ought not *to be done.* It only needs to be about what is to be done. People disagreeing about the first two kinds of issues can still agree as to what is to be done by virtue of compromise. There is no such thing as compromising about what is or ought to be. But reasonable people of divergent beliefs about such matters, needing nevertheless to act together, can mutually prune down their reservations so that they can avoid immobilization. We notice at work here the same phenomenon of the adjustment of interests that we have commented on above, interests here, however, being both practical and possibly intellectual. Consensus, short of the limiting case of total unanimity, is an affair of compromise, and compromise is a certain adjustment of the interests of individuals (in the form of disparate convictions as to what is to be done) to the common necessity for something to be done.

Since some commentators are apt to perceive the advocacy of consensus as a kind of demand for conformity, it might be useful to emphasize that the suggestion is not that anyone has a right to demand consensus of anyone else. Such a demand would contradict the very essence of the quest for consensus. One may hold forth, in a forum of rational discussion, on the advantages of consensus as a mode of decision-making. But that case is simply submitted to the free evaluation of others, as in any genuine dialogue. Moreover, it probably bears repetition that consensus, as a factor of decision-making in social action, does not entail unanimity or conformity in intellectual or ethical belief. The idea is simply that, in spite of any diversity of such belief, a willingness to compromise in order to reach an understanding regarding what is to be done would facilitate harmony in group action. It is suggested, beyond this, that in the political sphere such a spirit of compromise can be expressed in institutions that are different from those familiar in some of the most glorified democracies in the world today.

One might venture to speculate that the quest for consensus must come easily to the communalistic consciousness, for what is involved is the same adjustment of the interests of the individual to those of the community to which that consciousness is attuned as a matter of culture. It might be speculated further that in such a culture faith in consensus would be carried over to the realm of political decision-making. In fact, reality coincides with speculation in the case of many historical African states. This, however, seems to have been a contingent rather than a necessary harmony, for some despotic African states as communalistic as any are also known. But this should not surprise excessively, for human cultures are known to display inconsistencies of tendency almost as much as consistencies.

In any case, since it is rational to learn from better examples, we will, in what follows, focus on the model of government by consensus in our heritage. My argument will be that consensual governance in our tradition was essentially democratic; that the majoritarian form of democracy seen in the multiparty systems in Britain and the United States is drastically antithetic to both our own traditions of democracy and the complexities of our contemporary situation; and that, although the kinship basis of our political systems of old cannot be reinvoked in this day and age, it is still a practical proposition to try to fashion out a contemporary nonparty form of government based on the principle of consensus. In this way perhaps we can hope to restore the lost continuity between the state and civil society in Africa.

II. DEMOCRACY, CONSENSUS, AND CIVIL SOCIETY

Democracy is government by consent. But consent can be obtained in various ways. You can get the consent of people for something by drugging, deceiving, hypnotizing, bribing, brainwashing, or persuading them. I take it that the last is the only legitimate technique for obtaining consent. Therefore, the cryptic assertion that democracy is government by consent is to be understood as envisaging only consent by legitimate means. The modern procedures of general elections in the multiparty forms associated with existing democracies are widely regarded not only as legitimate ways of seeking the consent of the governed but also as the only legitimate ones. The second part of this claim is, of course, false. By and large, it defines the end by the means. To see its falsity, remember that a direct democracy, for example, is, by definition, one in which there are no elections. Of the first, more moderate part, namely the claim that multiparty general elections are legitimate ways of seeking consent, what needs to be said is not so straightforward, but let us for the time being accept it as correct. Even so, given what has just been said, this gives no support to the tendency to suppose that if a system of governance, such those of certain traditional African societies, does not use such an electoral arrangement, then it is necessarily undemocratic.

Beyond all this, however, it must be noted that even the most virtuously secured representation is only half the battle of democracy won. The best-conducted elections only get you the personnel of representation. But the point of the exercise is to link the governed with the deliberations and decisions of the governing body. Representatives, then, are instruments of mediation. They must discover the wishes of their constituencies, and they must bring these to bear in an effective way upon the deliberations of the governing body. Effectiveness here is to be judged by the degree to which the wishes concerned are taken account of in decisions. On both sides of the linkage there are great practical and, indeed, also theoretical complications. If representatives are to be chosen by some voting system, there are both mathematical and ethical problems to be considered. Is a simple majority a legitimizing quantity? In any case, how are the units of representation to be mapped out? It cannot be pretended that the democracies of Britain and the United States, for example, have achieved any perfection in these matters, though those of Europe, especially Belgium and Switzerland, have more evidently taken these problems to heart because of the greater prevalence of religious and ideological factionalism.

Suppose these problems are to be solved in some tolerable manner. How do representatives keep in touch with the views and wishes of their constituencies as they evolve in relation to the flow of events? And how do they render account regarding the fate of those views in the process of decision-making? Besides, the desirability of a mechanism for the evaluation of the performance and the review of the status of representatives cannot be ignored. It is not clear to what extent modern multiparty democracies have solved or addressed or even acknowledged these problems.

Nor do these democracies inspire confidence by the manner in which different views are treated in the decision-making and policy implementing processes. Different views are, indeed, not ignored. In the United States, for example, there is a system of committees in which opposition party representatives play very substantial roles in the formation of policies. Moreover, there is a system of "checks and balances" that constrain the executive activities of the president. The "checks," in fact, can sometimes become unbalanced, as when the presidency is in the hands of one party and the Senate and the House of Representatives are in the hands of another party whose desire or, at least designation, is to oppose. Not infrequently, opposition becomes obstruction, giving rise to a phenomenon called gridlock, in which the government is unable to carry through any meaningful policies. In modern African democracies, opposition even more frequently means obstruction, though governments are able to act to the good or often to the ill since they are not either temperamentally or constitutionally given to paying attention to the opposition.

To return to the United States, her democracy can be rightly called majoritarian. The president is elected, barring an improbable Electoral College complication, by a simple majority, and the formation of an administration, together with enormous powers, lies in his hands. To the extent to which the direction in which these powers are exercised is contrary to the will of those belonging to or sympathizing with the opposition party, who are often as numerous as those on the side of the government, to that extent there is a relative disenfranchisement of a section of the population. Government now becomes, in immediate reality, government with the consent only of the majority. Granted, this disenfranchisement is the result of a generally accepted constitutional provision, so that what we have here is a preestablished disharmony. But this does nothing to assuage the frustrations of the opposition, which are given vent to in all kinds of antiadministration schemes, only falling short, mercifully, of a coup. Needless to say, these activities are countered in kind from the other side.

Some, not steeped in a culture of conflict, may well think that it should be possible for human beings to arrange the business of governance in a more humane and rational way. They are certainly unlikely to be impressed by the hackneyed wisecrack that the virtues of multiparty democracy are easy to deprecate but difficult to duplicate in any alternative system. However, if such critics are Africans, they face an obvious embarrassment, for in Africa party-political dissensions have been known to lead to coups. Even in coupless times, such conflicts have led or contributed to death and destruction on an unspeakable scale. Still, such an African critic can reflect that party-political conflict is historically foreign to Africa. The claim is not that political conflict is foreign to Africa, which would be absurdly false, but only that conflict emanating from the activities of those special forms of organization called political parties is not indigenous to Africa. It is an epiphenomenon of colonialism, which accounts in part for the discontinuity between the state and civil society in today's Africa.

In precolonial African politics of the consensual kind, there were various loci of disagreement and conflict. Royal families could harbor serious rivalries in the quest for succession. The populace could react adversely to the policies of a council of state and manifest their animadversions quite demonstratively. What is more, the council itself could be a theater of sharp disagreement. But such circumstances are what consensus is made of. If all concerned were permanently of one mind, there would actually be no need for a council, and no need for a quest for consensus. Thus consensus, incidentally, proves to be a confirming instance of the adage that too much of everything is bad.

Of course, not all disagreements can be resolved into a consensus in all circumstances. There has to be a will to consensus in the first place. The African elders who would sit under a tree and talk till an agreement was reached as to what was to be done undoubtedly had that kind of a will. But it is a precious disposition and is often lacking in the human heart or located in only half of it. It is, most certainly, absent or only half-existent in the motivation underlying a political party, which is the attainment of governmental power. To be sure, this is only possible under a constitution with the provision that the party that, within a specified definition, wins a general election is entitled to form the government.

Now, winning an election under multiparty conditions means winning *against* other parties. Unless the multiplicity of parties splinters the allegiances of the voters to such a degree that results are inconclusive—a situation that, paradoxically, can induce a limited will to consensus—when a party wins and gets into power, other parties lose and get out of power or stay out of it. But think what being outside of power means. Barring the case in which the ideas of the losing party are only trivially different from those of the winning one, this means that, for the relevant duration, they will not receive the consideration due to them in the formation of government policy. That, indeed, would not be a secret to them, since all this is constitutionally prearranged. But the reader might like to recall the psychological infelicities that this situation brings to the losers and their consequences commented on previously. Here let us note the victors' psychology too. They are known not to hide their joy at the opportunity to implement their whims or programs, if they have any, to the exclusion, as much as possible, of those of the losers.

But such an attitude is the quintessence of uncooperativeness, leading to an adversarial approach to politics with its manifold severities. It is also quintessentially antithetical to the spirit of communalism, whose principle, as suggested earlier, is the adjustment of the interests of the individual to the interests of others in society. In political terms this means adjusting one's interests in the implementation of certain programs to the interests of others in the implementation of other programs. Given that all these cannot be implemented at one and the same time, a cooperative spirit would logically call, at the very minimum, for compromise, which is the beginning of consensus and also, perhaps, of wisdom.

It should be noted that fashioning out a compromise is not a mechanical process; it takes deliberation, that is, rational discussion. We see here the great importance of deliberation in a consensual system, which certain of our elders of old realized more clearly and practiced more steadfastly than we have seemed to do. Deliberation need not always lead only to compromise. Remember, compromise presupposes the survival of disagreements concerning what is or ought to be the case. Thus consensus need not necessarily be an end of all debate. Since debate on one issue can engulf all kinds of other issues, matters settled by previous compromise are fair game to the debating consciousness. But this means only that the quest for consensus in social action is an ongoing affair. Still, if discussion is serious and rational, it can sometimes lead to persuasion, so that there is not only agreement as to what is to be done but also about what is or ought to the case. In either case, the result is cooperation rather than competition of the adversarial kind.

As we have seen, cooperation does not come easily to political parties. A political association, however, need not have such a resistance. An association of this kind is simply a group of people of a like mind as to what is best for their country coming together to explore ideas and set up a mechanism of persuasion to attract as many people as possible to their point of view. Objective? To find ways, electorally and otherwise, to influence the composition of government and the direction of its decisions. If political bodies of such a description operate under a constitution in which winning a certain number of seats or votes in a general election does not entitle a group to form a government to the exclusion of other groups, then conditions conducive to cooperation, compromise, and, consequently, consensus should be at hand. Under such a dispensation elections need not even be officially contested by associations, their presence in an elected assembly being felt only by the persuasions of the elected. It can be rationally expected that in an assembly composed in this way, deliberations would be, in a deep sense, nonpartisan.

A system of the sort just barely broached may rightly be called a non-party system, not because it proscribes political parties, but because such parties do not form the basis of government. They cease, in fact and even in logic, to have any relevance in a consensual milieu. In this respect such a system bears an important analogy to a traditional African system of the consensual type. In that tradition the basis of government was not parties but lineages. Local and, at a second remove, national councils consisted mainly of heads of lineages. In a somewhat mild sense, these lineage heads may be said to have been elected, in that an unpopular character stood little chance of becoming a lineage head. But if a person was the most senior in age and was strong in wisdom, eloquence, and practical logic, consultations encountered little delay, and the status was conferred. These criteria were clear and generally acknowledged. To all intents and purposes, a lineage head was leader and representative for his lineage by common consent.

It is probably needless at this stage to stress that in council, decisions were taken by consensus. In this way, the various lineages may be said to have been linked to governmental decisions by a chain of consent. But someone speaking from the standpoint of modern democracy might question whether the system is genuinely democratic. From that point of view, it might seem that the way of selecting lineage heads fell grievously short of a real election, vitiating the entire system as far as democracy is concerned. If offense is at least sometimes the best defense, one might return the question to the asker and request proof of the genuineness of modern elections as indicators of the will of the electorate. This immediately brings us back to a question earlier considered but not answered, namely, whether modern multiparty elections are a legitimate way of seeking the consent of the governed. The answer is that they can be, but in many well-known cases it is questionable that they are. The only legitimate way of seeking the consent of an adult in political matters is by rational persuasion. This thought alone must cause one to take an extremely dim view of electioneering campaigns as they have been known in, for example, the United States, a star democracy in the eyes of many. First of all, the process is so expensive that only groups with the command of enormous funds can be in a position to present seriously an option to the people. Second, much of the expenditure goes into a kind of advertising that spurns all the canons of rational persuasion. If we nevertheless grant that, for example, the president of the United States is a democratically elected president, then it is obvious that we are being content, in this characterization, with quite rough approximations of the relevant criteria. This consideration goes without saying in many parts of Africa, where bribery and deception are only the kinder and gentler alternatives in the array of well-known methods of acquiring votes. If we now come back to the question of whether the traditional African mechanism of representation was democratic in the same spirit of approximation, there should be little to discourage one from suggesting that it indeed was so in its own historical context and in a quite robust sense. This conclusion is reinforced by the fact that traditional decision-making by consensus brings us nearer to rule by the consent of the people than does decision by the majority, which secures, at best, only rule by the consent of the majority.

A greater apparent cause of skepticism regarding the democratic pretensions of the traditional system in question derives from the position of chiefs in that form of statecraft: chiefship is hereditary and, in principle, lifelong. It is true that a wayward chief can be dismissed, but the scope of selection is limited to one lineage, a severe limitation. Besides, the position of a chief seems to be enveloped in an aura of sanctity that makes him inaccessible to criticism, which is a first prerequisite of a democratic polity. The force of this objection, however, disappears almost completely when it is realized that in the consensual system a chief is more a symbol than a ruler: he is a symbol of the unity of the state. He is also regarded as the link between the people and their ancestors. This latter, however, says more about traditional metaphysics than about traditional politics. As far as politics go, what is represented in official communiqués as the decision of the chief is, in fact, not his personal will but rather the decision of the council of which he is just the chairman.

Given the fluidity of traditional constitutional arrangements, it must be admitted that a chief of unusual charisma could conceivably stamp his authority on a council beyond the prerogatives of a mere chairman. But this is not an instance that determines the rule, for too overbearing a charisma soon invites impeachment and dethronement. Needing some explanation also is the fact that the position of a lineage head is lifelong. First, the duration of the office was not usually overlong since incumbents were, as a rule, quite advanced in years. But, second, it lasted only so long as the elder remained acceptable to the given lineage.

Why, however, may not the office be held by a young person in preference to an older one? This question brings us to a great difference between our times and olden times. In bygone days it was reasonable to assume that the older person was a more knowledgeable and competent person and the more appropriate representative. In our time that assumption does not hold. Here, then, is an aspect of the traditional system that we cannot now rationally imitate. There are other, even more important, ones. Amidst the cosmopolitanism of the urbanization that has resulted from industrialization in our societies, even such as it has been, hardly any argument is needed to show that the lineage basis of political representation would be neither practical nor appropriate, at least at the national level. At the levels of the villages and small towns, chiefs do still have considerable political sway in Africa, but now only jointly or in parallel with nontraditional local and regional councils.

By and large, what we can learn from the traditional system concerned are two things; namely, the nonparty basis of representation and the reliance on consensus in decision-making. Actually, the two amount to one, for a thoroughgoing adherence to consensus implies a nonparty approach to government. If every decision is to be by consensus, then the formation of government must follow suit. But once government is no longer formed on the basis of parties, such organizations will lose their most distinctive character as mechanisms for the conquest of state power. With this must disappear other negative characteristics, such as their adversarial and aggressive attitude to other such organizations, their financial acquisitiveness, since their mission requires a lot of money, and their tendency toward internal power struggles. A democracy involving political organizations free of such traits will be both conceptually and pragmatically different from multiparty democracy. It would, in the truest sense, be democracy with a truly human face. Such a democracy is, I think, what a careful study of some of the antecedents in our traditions promises.

In these reflections I have been thinking most particularly of traditional governance among the Buganda of Uganda, the Zulu of South Africa, and the Akan of Ghana, but exemplars can be multiplied. Actually, outside Africa too, in, for example, continental Europe—Switzerland and Belgium come to mind again—there are constitutional arrangements that have pointed away enough from majoritarianism to attract the designation "consensual." These, however, still remain party-based, and the consensus aimed at is limited, being a kind of understanding among parties. The polity we have in mind, on the other hand, is completely partyless and is motivated by a quite radical commitment to consensus.

Quite apart from the moral excellence of consensus as an ideal, the need for it is a life-and-death matter in Africa. In the postcolonial period our experiments in democracy have been imitations of Western multiparty majoritarianism. But this has politicized and exacerbated preexisting dissensions and created new ones with deadly consequences. It should have been clear on only a little reflection that, in view of the ethnic configurations and other divisions in many African countries, such a system bore nothing but danger for us. Frequently, small ethnic groups have been politically marginalized in the face of the dominance of larger ones. Sometimes, historical grounds of division, not necessarily ethnic, have operated to produce the same results. In either case disaffection has tended to find nonconstitutional manifestations, to the doom of peace and stability and the loss of countless lives.

There in no reason why peoples who in the not very distant past managed a political system based on consensus cannot work out an analogous one in present conditions. A question sometimes asked is how the people can be mobilized in the absence of political parties. But mobilized for what? To pay their taxes? Political parties are not known to be devoted to such crusades. To cast their vote in the first place? Nonparty state information services can do part of the job. The rest can be done by voluntary political associations. Where the objective is to disseminate genuine information or to engage the people in rational discussion, what is needed, on either side, is not emotional intensity but an honest and coherent message and a curious and critical audience. The terminology of mobilization is in fact a hangover from the anticolonial struggle. In the days of that struggle it was necessary to fire the people by means of mass rallies with enthusiasms for various demonstrative acts of opposition to colonial authorities. (One is here, of course, talking of the relatively bloodless forms of struggle. The armed struggle called for different strategies.) It was necessary, in other words, to *mobilize* the people to oppose colonialism. Ironically, those were the days when political parties, as distinct from national movements, made the least sense in Africa. Be that as it may, the language of mobilization is decidedly anachronistic in our present circumstances.

At this historical juncture, there is an urgent need for African intellectuals, including historians, philosophers, political scientists, economists, anthropologists, sociologists, linguists, constitutional scholars, jurists, journalists, and other leaders of opinion to put their heads together to explore the history, rationale, conceptual basis, and constitutional framework for a nonparty system of politics based on consensus. From the multiplicity of the disciplines just mentioned, it can be inferred that the issues surrounding this idea are legion. Only some have been touched upon in an introductory way in this discussion. In approaching my conclusion I would like to stress the importance of issues related to representation by elections. Electing a representative by a simple constituency vote is a majoritarian procedure, unless there is a score of a hundred percent. Any element of majoritarianism is a loss of consensus. It seems unlikely, however, that such elections can be altogether obviated in the setting up of any modern representative government. But supplementary bases of representation with relatively flexible mechanisms of election can be considered. Occupational groups, for example, could select supplementary representatives by some agreed procedure that minimizes adversarial competition as much as possible. One significance of this example for our present discussion is that it would be a way of linking civil society with the state in a manner reminiscent of the continuity that existed between these two levels of social existence in traditional society.

In concluding this advocacy of a nonparty system of politics, I would like to dissociate myself from any concealed hankering after a one-party system. This is especially necessary since some politicians in power wishing to create a one-party situation without a one-party designation have been known to use the banner of the nonparty idea. The fundamental difference between a nonparty system and a one-party one is that the former embraces the freedom of political association while the latter execrates it. The one-party system is, in fact, not only incompatible with freedom of political association but also with the freedom of expression, for the expression of ideas among persons is already a kind of association. It is obvious, then, that those who use the name of the nonparty system but look unkindly upon political associations do take that name in vain. Political associations in a nonparty polity would, in fact, be an exceedingly important point of mediation between civil society and the state, because, as a forum of discourse, they would belong to civil society just like literary societies, while, as vehicles of political education and representation, they would be directly connected with the state.

A further significance of such political associations is that they could be training grounds for the enlargement of political orientations beyond ethnic concerns, which would be a boon to African politics. When ideological or specific policy considerations motivate political associations, tribal antagonisms are likely to be greatly reduced or altogether overcome. In the absence of the quest for state power, such motivations are the likeliest basis of political associations. Examples of analogous associations already abound in civil society in Africa as elsewhere. There are any number of religious, recreational, and occupational associations, especially cooperatives and mutual aid societies, in which tribal or ethnic considerations play hardly any role in their formation or operation.

Civil society, furthermore, can offer to the state extremely important models, or at least illustrations, of the possibility of nonparty government and, in some cases, of government by consensus. Consider, for example, the way a university is governed. In places where the process is democratic, representation at various levels is by a combination of election and appointment. As a rule, elections are not contested by any groupings bearing any serious analogy to political parties. Any analogies in the modes of association would gravitate in the direction of the more ordinary forms of political association that are not oriented toward the automatic conquest of power, though, in comparison with even these, associations for university elections are informal and quite ephemeral. Thus there are no parties in the relevant sense in university politics. Yet university governance does involve quite serious tasks in the administration of persons and resources. University politics can, of course, be vitiated by factionalism, even without any analogue of political parties. All persons possessed of a sense of objectivity and moderation must regret such proofs of poor habits among an academic community. But they will thank their stars for the absence of the party analogue, since its presence would aggravate the situation out of all recognition. It is known also that other components of civil society, such as mutual aid societies, operate by means of not only governance devoid of "parties" but also decision informed by consensus.

These last considerations and the previous ones, together with the non-party and consensual suggestiveness of certain of our traditions of governance, would seem to show that those who dismiss out of hand the plea for a nonparty polity based on consensus as utopian or worse may not be totally infallible. But in any case, the dialogue must continue. That is the only rational option. It is also the option born of the quest for consensus.

Notes ◄

Introduction

1. Teodros Kiros; *Moral Philosophy and Development* (Athens: Ohio University Press, 1992), p. 176.
2. See Teodros Kiros, *Self-Construction and the Formation of Human Values* (Westport, CT: Greenwood Press, 1998).

Chapter 1

1. Both thinkers have also said some encouraging words about the sage philosophy project, as well as offering their criticism. For Hountondji, the charge of "reaction to Western skeptics" was made as recently as during the last World Congress of Philosophy, Boston, August 1998. At the same time, he asserted he had always been supportive of the project.
2. H. Odera Oruka, *Sage Philosophy: Indigenous Thinkers and Modern Debate on African Philosophy* (Nairobi: ACTS Press, 1991), pp. 17, 34.
3. John Kekes, *Moral Wisdom and Good Lives* (Ithaca, NY: Cornell University Press, 1995), p. 4.
4. H. Odera Oruka, Jesse Mugambi, and Jackton B. Ojwang, *The Rational Path: A Dialogue on Philosophy, Law, and Religion* (Nairobi: Standard Textbooks Graphics and Publishing, 1989), p. 2.
5. Brand Blanshard, "Wisdom," in *Encyclopedia of Philosophy*, vol. 8 (New York: Macmillan, 1967), pp. 322–24, quote p. 323.
6. Odera Oruka, H. *Sage Philosophy*, pp. 9, 10.
7. Blanshard, "Wisdom," p. 323.
8. Ibid., p. 324.
9. Gerald Wanjohi, *The Wisdom and Philosophy of the Gikuyu Proverbs: The Kihooto World View* (Nairobi: Paulines Publications Africa, 1997), pp. 42–44.
10. Kekes, *Moral Wisdom and Good Lives*, pp. 16–17. Richard McKeon, *Introduction to Aristotle* (New York: Modern Library, 1974), pp. 428–9; 1140a, 26–29.
11. Kwame Gyekye, *Tradition and Modernity* (Philadelphia: Temple University Press, 1997), p. 3.
12. Ibid., p. 13.
13. Jay van Hook, "African Philosophy and the Universalist Thesis," *Metaphilosophy* 28:4 (1997), pp. 385–96, quote p. 390.
14. D. A. Masolo, *African Philosophy in Search of Identity* (Indianapolis: Indiana University Press, 1994), pp. 59–65.
15. Ibid., pp. 63–65.
16. Ibid., p. 241.
17. Kwame Gyekye, *An Essay on African Philosophical Thought: The Akan Conceptual Scheme* (London: Cambridge University Press, 1987), pp. 24–29; Segun Gbadegesin,

African Philosophy: Traditional Yoruba Conceptions and Contemporary African Reali-
ties (Frankfurt: Peter Lang, 1991), pp. 8–11.

18. W. T. Jones, *A History of Western Philosophy,* vol. 1 (New York: Harcourt, Brace and World, 1952), pp. xi–xii.

19. Gyekye, *Tradition and Modernity,* p. 11.

20. Ibid., pp. 236–38; F. Ochieng-Odhiambo, "Some Basic Issues about Philosophic Sagacity: Twenty Years Later." Paper presented at the Pan-African Symposium on "Problematics of an African Philosophy: Twenty Years Later," Addis Ababa, December 1–4, 1997.

21. Jones Lozenja Makindu, interview with the author, in Maragoli, Western Province, Kenya, on May 12, 1996. Assistance in interview and translation by Chaungo Barasa.

22. Wanyonyi Manguliechi, interview with the author, October 7, 1995; translated from Bukusu to English on site in Western Province, Kenya, by Chaungo Barasa, later transcribed by Shadrack Wanjala Nasong'o. The interview exists on tape, and both tape and transcript are in possession of the author.

23. Odera Oruka, *Sage Philosophy,* p. 92.

24. Ali Mwitani Masero, interview with the author, October 6, 1995, in Western Province, Kenya; translated from Bukusu to English on site by Chaungo Barasa, later translated and transcribed by Shadrack Wanjala Nasong'o. This interview exists on tape, in possession of the author.

25. Nyando Ayoo, interview with the author, in Sega, Nyanza Province, Kenya. Testimony corroborated by interviews with Martine Outa, Barasa Nyango, and Dorka Nyando, all from Sega, on November 19, 1995. Translated on site by H. Odera Oruka, later translated and transcribed by Oriare Nyarwath. Tape and transcript in possession of the author.

   This article contains only brief accounts of the sages. For fuller accounts, especially one which goes into detail on the sages' role in conflict resolution, please see another article by the author, "Contemporary African Sages and Queen Mothers: Their Leadership Role in Conflict Resolution," in Judith Presler and Sally Scholz, eds., *Peacemaking: Lessons from the Past, Visions for the Future* (Amsterdam: Rodopi, forthcoming).

26. Kekes, *Moral Wisdom,* pp. 4–5.

27. Ibid., p. 9.

28. Ibid., pp. 10–11.

29. Henrietta Moore, ed., *The Future of Anthropological Knowledge* (London: Routledge, 1997), pp. 2–3.

30. Ibid., p. 2.

31. Ibid., p. 7.

32. Dismas Masolo, "Decentering the Academy," in Kai Kresse and Anke Graness, eds., *Sagacious Reasoning: Henry Odera Oruka in Memoriam* (Frankfurt am Main: Peter Lang, 1997), pp. 237–38.

33. Christopher Lasch, *The True and Only Heaven: Progress and Its Critics.* (New York: W.W. Norton & Co., 1991), p. 522.

34. Andrew Dalbanco, "Consuming Passions," in *New York Times Book Review,* January 19, 1997, p. 8.

35. Haig Khatchadourian, "Philosophy and the Future, in a Global Context," in *Metaphilosophy* vol. 23: 1–2 (January/April 1992), pp. 25–33, quote p. 25.

36. Ibid., p. 27.
37. Ibid., pp. 26, 32.
38. See also Irene De Puit, "Beyond Knowledge, Wisdom: A Revindication of the Practical Character of Philosophy," in *Thinking* 11:2 (1994), pp. 22–24; and James R. Watson, "In the Monstrous Shadow of a Worldly Wisdom," in *History of European Ideas,* 18:4 (1994), pp. 525–38.
39. Kai Nielsen, "Philosophy and the Search for Wisdom," in *Teaching Philosophy* 16:1 (1993), pp. 5–20, quotes pp. 8, 10.
40. Ibid., p. 13.
41. Ibid., p. 9.
42. Ibid., p. 16.
43. Stanley Godlovitch, "On Wisdom," *Canadian Journal of Philosophy* 11:1 (1981), pp. 137–55, quote pp. 148–49.

Chapter 2
1. Claude Sumner, "Ethiopia: Land of Diverse Expressions of Philosophy, Birthplace of Modern Thought." *Proceedings of the Seminar on African Philosophy, Addis Ababa, 1–3 December 1976. (Actes du séminaire sur la philosophie africaine, Addis-Abéba, 1–3 décembre 1976),* ed. Claude Sumner, Ph.D., p. 394. Printed for Addis Ababa University by Chamber Printing House, Addis Ababa, 1980.
2. See Jean Cauvin, *L'Image, la langue et la pensée,* vol. I, *L'Exemple des proverbes (Mali),* Collectanea Instituti Anthropos, no. 23 (St. Augustin: Anthropos-Institut Haus Völker und Kulturen, 1980), pp. 21–22. I am here following the thought of this author in his chapter 1 of part 1, "Proverbes et société orale," pp. 21–50. Of course, mine is the selection from this chapter of the sections I consider relevant to the specific objective of the present essay, the English translation of these, their illustration with Oromo proverbs, and the comparison with Ethiopian written sapiential and philosophical literature. But the main argument of this chapter is Cauvin's, with whom I am in complete agreement (except for the profile of images in the transmitted content which he has not given for Minyanka proverbs). I wish to express my deepest gratitude for letting me thus make use of his printed book.
3. Proverb 791. The proverb number corresponds to the "Classified Proverbs" in my book *Oromo Wisdom Literature,* vol. I, *Proverbs: Collection and Analysis* (Addis Ababa: Gudina Tumsa Foundation, 1995), pp. 72–240.
4. See J. Cauvin, op. cit., pp. 22–23.
5. Proverb 22.
6. Proverb 297.
7. J. Cauvin, op. cit., pp. 23–25.
8. Proverb 101-a. Ibid., pp. 25–26.
9. See Claude Sumner, *Ethiopian Philosophy,* vol. I, *The Book of the Wise Philosophers* (Addis Ababa: Central Printing Press, 1974), pp. 118–19.
10. Proverb 743.
11. Proverb 113-a.
12. Proverb 109.
13. Proverb 747.
14. Proverb 41.
15. J. Cauvin, op. cit., pp. 26–32.
16. Ibid., p. 32.

17. *The Life of Skəndəs* 32 a 12–14. See C. Sumner, *Ethiopian Philosophy*, vol. IV, *The Life and Maxims of Skəndəs*, p. 35. Printed for the Ministry of Culture and Sports by Commercial Printing Press, Addis Ababa, 1981.
18. *The Life of Skəndəs* 49 b 10; see Ibid., p. 41.
19. *The Life of Skəndəs* 50 b 1.
20. *The Life of Skəndəs* 55 a 2; see Ibid., p. 65.
21. *The Second Series of Maxims* 120 a 6; see Ibid., p. 65.
22. See C. Sumner, *The Source of African Philosophy: The Ethiopian Philosophy of Man.* Volume 20 of *Aethiopistische Forschungen* (Stuttgart: Franz Steiner, 1986), pp. 63–65.
23. J. Cauvin, op. cit., pp. 33–34.
24. Proverb 481.
25. See Proverb 39-a.
26. See Proverb 39-b.
27. See Proverb 8.
28. See Proverb 254.
29. See Proverb 32.
30. See Proverb 3.
31. See Proverb 58.
32. See Proverb 27.
33. See Proverb 28.
34. See Proverb 61.
35. See Proverb 23.
36. See Proverb 184.
37. See Proverb 1006.
38. See Proverb 628.
39. See Proverb 270.
40. See Proverb 755.
41. Proverb 281.
42. See Proverb 705. See also J. Cauvin, op. cit., pp. 34–37.
43. Proverb 624-a.
44. Proverb 624-b.
45. Proverb 624-c.
46. See J. Cauvin, op. cit., pp. 37–39; 95–96.
47. Proverb 326.
48. Proverb 326.
49. Eugenio Cerulli. "The Folk-literature of the Galla of Southern Abyssinia," *Harvard African Studies*, vol. 3, *Varia Africana* 3 (1923), p. 193, no. 20. See Proverb 854, with its references to *Kana beketa?* (in Oromo). Lesson II, no. 2 (30 Furma/Tahesas 1962 E.C.; 8 January 1970), p. 3, no. 37; Onesimus Nesib, *The Galla Spelling Book* (in Oromo) Moncullo, near Massowah: Swedish Mission Press, 1894), p. 67, no. 28.
50. E. Cerulli, op. cit., p. 135, no. 133, verses 94–98.
51. See J. Cauvin, op. cit., pp. 39–42.
52. Ibid., pp. 43–44.
53. Ibid., pp. 44–45.
54. Proverb 172.
55. J. Cauvin, op. cit., pp. 47–50.

Chapter 3

1. As he would be the first to acknowledge, this insight is already present in what sociologists call "labeling theory." See Mary McIntosh "The Homosexual Role," in *Forms of Desire: Sexual Orientation and the Social Constructionist Controversy,* Edward Stein, ed. (New York: Routledge, 1998), pp. 25–42.
2. Hacking, "Making Up People," in *Forms of Desire,* op. cit., p. 87.
3. Cited in Hacking, "Making Up People," in *Forms of Desire,* op. cit., p. 81.
4. Appiah, in *Color Conscious: The Political Morality of Race,* K. Anthony Appiah and Amy Guttman (Princeton: Princeton University Press, 1997).

Chapter 4

This is a revised version of a paper presented at the Pan-African Conference on Philosophy in Addis Ababa, Ethiopia, in December 1996. In its original form, it appeared in *Perspectives in African Philosophy,* Claude Sumner and Samuel Yohannes, eds. (Addis Ababa: Rodopi Publishers, 1997). I wish to thank Eliza Dame, May Farhat, David Gullette, Teodros Kiros, and participants at the Pan-African Conference on Philosophy for their helpful comments on earlier drafts of this manuscript.

1. Ibn Khaldun, *The Muqaddimah: An Introduction to History,* translated from the Arabic by Franz Rosenthal, 3 vol. (London: Routledge and Kegan Paul, 1986) 1:195. Hereafter, citations from the *Muqaddimah* are abbreviated and listed as volume number:page number.
2. 1:303.
3. Muhsin Mahdi, *Ibn Khaldun's Philosophy of History* (London: Allen and Unwin, 1957). Explication of his sociological system also can be found in Amal Almawi, "Ibn Khaldun: A Pioneer Sociologist," master's dissertation, Boston University, Department of Sociology, 1988.
4. M. A. Enan, *Ibn Khaldun: His Life and Work* (Lahore, India: 1975), pp. 51–52.
5. See his essay, "Ibn Khaldun and his Time," in *Ibn Khaldun and Islamic Ideology,* ed. Bruce B. Lawrence (Leiden: E. J. Brill, 1984), p. 15.
6. Toynbee, *A Study of History: The Growth of Civilizations* (New York: Oxford University Press, 1962), vol. 3, p. 322.
7. See Muhsin Mahdi, op. cit., p. 33.
8. Continuity—not interruption as in western Europe—marked the character of the Arab and Islamic intellectual traditions. For discussion of some of the sources used by Ibn Khaldun, see 2:157, 187–188; Enan, op. cit., pp. 123–29, 148, 155, 164, 172, 180. Ibn Khaldun's student Taqi al-Din al-Makrizi adopted the methods of Ibn Khaldun in his own treatment of the history of Egypt. See Enan, op. cit., p. 98–100.
9. R. W. Southern, *Western Views of Islam in the Middle Ages* (Cambridge, MA.: Harvard University Press, 1962), p. 88.
10. Quoted from Bruce Lawrence's essay "Ibn Khaldun and Islamic Reform," on p. 69 of *Ibn Khaldun and Islamic Ideology.*
11. Enan, op. cit., p. 150.
12. Enan refers to the Austrian Von Hammer-Purgstall's *Über den Verfall des Islams nach den ersten drei Jahrhunderten der Hidschrat* (1812), in which Ibn Khaldun was called the "Montesquieu of the Arabs."
13. Among others, Hodgson is quite critical of Rosenthal's translation.

14. See H. Simon, *Ibn Khaldun's Science of Human Culture,* trans. by F. Baali (Lahore, India: 1978), pp. 92–93.
15. Enan, op. cit., p. 158. Also see Barbara Stowasser, "Religion and Political Development: Some Comparative Ideas on Ibn Khaldun and Machiavelli" (Washington, DC: Center for Contemporary Arab Studies, 1983).
16. Hegel, *Lectures on the History of Philosophy* (Englewood Cliffs, NJ: Humanities Press, 1983), vol. 3, p. 25. Hegel's remarks on Islamic thinkers are minimal and can be found on pp. 27–29.
17. Hodgson thereby is able to avoid understanding Islamic history from the point of view of the West, as well as to avert the more common view today that Islam represents something completely new rather than transforming an existent civilization and taking it in a new direction. See Marshall Hodgson, *The Venture of Islam: Conscience and History in a World Civilization* (Chicago: University of Chicago Press, 1974), vol. 1, p. 50. For an appreciative reading of Hodgson's concept of Oikoumene, see Albert Hourani, *Islam in European Thought* (Cambridge, UK: Cambridge University Press, 1991), p. 79.
18. Mahdi, op. cit., p. 104.
19. 2:52.
20. 3:89; 3:253–54.
21. 3:253.
22. 1:195.
23. 1:214.
24. See 1:202–39.
25. 1:215, 266.
26. 1:92.
27. Mahdi, op. cit., p. 178.
28. See 1:84.
29. 1:216.
30. 1:196–97.
31. 1:197–99.
32. 1:203–4; 217–18.
33. Jon W. Anderson, "Conjuring with Ibn Khaldun," in Lawrence, op. cit., p. 119.
34. 3:72.
35. 3:73.
36. 1:197.
37. 1:72.
38. 1:72.
39. 2:275–76.
40. Charles Issawi, *An Arab Philosophy of History: Selections from the Prolegomena of Ibn Khaldun of Tunis (1332–1406)* (London: Darwin Press, 1987), p. 7.
41. 2:213.
42. There is some doubt exactly whom Ibn Khaldun meant to refer to in his use of the terms translated by Rosenthal as "Arab." Some maintain he meant Bedouins, while others insist he means Arabs as they existed before the rise of Islam.
43. 1:305.
44. 1:458.
45. 1:174.
46. 3:31–32.

47. G. W. F. Hegel, *Philosophy of Mind* (London: Oxford University Press, 1971), p. 42. In fairness, Hegel's preceding page contains the following: "Man is implicitly rational; herein lies the possibility of equal justice for all men and the futility of a rigid distinction between races which have rights and those which have none."

48. Hegel, *Philosophy of Mind*, p. 45.

49. Hegel, *Lectures on the History of Philosophy*, op. cit., vol. 2, p. 24.

50. Hegel, *Philosophy of Mind*, p. 44.

51. Rosenthal, in Lawrence, op. cit., p. 19.

52. Hodgson, op. cit., vol. 2, p. 303 (quoted in Hourani, op. cit., p. 75).

53. Bernard Lewis, *The Arabs in History* (New York: Harper and Row, 1966), p. 142.

54. 3:392, 395.

55. Herder (as quoted by Hourani, op. cit., p. 25).

56. Southern, op. cit., p. 17.

57. See the discussion of nature and history in my book *The Imagination of the New Left: A Global Analysis of 1968* (Boston: South End Press, 1987).

58. My own particular concern with revitalizing imagination and the individual has been to decipher the meaning of revolts like May 1968 in France, to uncover the latent aspirations and imaginations of millions of people. In such moments of crisis, what I call the "eros effect" occurs, fusing individuals and groups together, and their individual imaginations become the basis for a new "group feeling" that is not tribal or national—but a newly emergent species self-consciousness. In this context, the subversive irony of Hegel's immanent dialectic finds expression in the fact that identity politics contains within itself a new concrete universal. See my book *The Subversion of Politics: European Autonomous Movements and the Decolonization of Everyday Life* (Englewood Cliffs, NJ: Humanities Press, 1997).

Chapter 5

1. Claude Sumner, "The Treatise of Zara Yaquob," in *Ethiopian Philosophy*, vol. II (Addis Ababa: Commercial Printing Press, 1976), p. 1.

2. Ibid., ff. See as well the summary of the debate in Sumner, *The Source of African Philosophy: The Ethiopian Philosophy of Man* (Stuttgart: Franz Steiner Verlag, 1986), pp. 41–42.

3. Sumner, *The Source of African Philosophy*, p. 42.

4. V. Y. Mudimbe, *The Invention of Africa* (Bloomington: Indiana University Press, 1988).

5. Descartes, *Meditations* (New York: Bobbs-Merrill Co., 1960), p. 34.

6. Sumner, "Treatise of Zara Yaquob," p. 9.

7. Ibid., p. 9.

8. Ibid., p. 10.

9. Ibid., p. 11.

10. Ibid., p. 11. For a remarkably similar argument but without the explicit religious bent, see Aristotle's *Nicomachean Ethics* (Cambridge, MA: Harvard University Press, 1982). See the discussions of moral evil in Book III.

11. Ibid., p. 13.

12. Ibid., p. 13.

13. Ibid., p. 13.

14. Ibid., p. 15.

15. Ibid., p. 16.

16. Ibid., p. 17.

17. Ibid., p. 19.
18. Zara Yacob does not directly mention Christ himself but is severe in his criticism of the European and Ethiopian Christians of his time, as is clearly stated in various passages such as the following: "the Frang tell us: God's doctrine is not with you, but with us" (p. 12), and "However to say the truth, the Christian faith as was founded in the days of the Gospel was not evil, since it invites all men to love one another and to practice mercy towards all. But today my countrymen have set aside the love recommended by the Gospel [and turned away towards] hatred, violence" (pp. 12–13). Zara Yacob would have few disagreements with the interpretations of Christianity in the able hands of the distinguished political philosopher Glenn Tinder. In his highly acclaimed book *The Political Meaning of Christianity* (New York: HarperCollins paperback edition, 1991), Professor Tinder has introduced the notion that Christianity is guided by the vision of the prophetic stance, which is based "on two basic Christian tenets, the selfish nature of humans, and the hope that is present in Christ" (p. 13).

Chapter 6
1. David E. Apter, *Rethinking Development: Modernization, Dependency, and Postmodern Politics* (London: Sage, 1987), p. 20.
2. V. Y. Mudimbe, *Les Corps glorieux des mots et des êtres: Esquisse d'un jardin africain à la bénédictine* (Montreal: Humanitas, and Paris: Présence Africaine, 1995).
3. Samuel Onyango Ayany, *Kar Chakruok mar Luo* (Kisumu: Equatorial Publishers, 1952).
4. Pierre F. Bourdieu, *Outline of a Theory of Practice* (Cambridge, UK: Cambridge University Press, 1977); *Distinction* (Cambridge, MA: Harvard University Press, 1984); Charles Taylor, *Human Agency and Language: Philosophical Papers 1* (Cambridge, UK: Cambridge University Press, 1985); Ernest Gellner, *Reason and Culture* (Oxford: Blackwell, 1992); Charles Taylor, *The Ethics of Authenticity* (Cambridge, MA: Harvard University Press, 1992).
5. Charles Taylor, *The Ethics of Authenticity*, p. 5.
6. Ernest Gellner, *Reason and Culture*, p. 2.
7. Robin Horton,"African Traditional Thought and Western Science," *Africa* 37:1–2.
8. Ernest Gellner, *Reason and Culture*, p. 2.
9. Ibid.
10. John A. Hall and I. C. Jarvie, introduction to Hall and Jarvie, eds., *Transition to Modernity: Essays on Power, Wealth and Belief* (Cambridge, UK: Cambridge University Press, 1992), p. 5.
11. Michel Foucault, *The Archeology of Knowledge* (New York: Pantheon, 1972); *The Order of Things* (New York: Pantheon, 1973).
12. Claude Lévi-Strauss, *Structural Anthropology* (New York: Basic Books, 1963); *The Savage Mind* (Chicago: University of Chicago Press, 1966).
13. Gellner, *Reason and Culture*, p. 19.
14. I owe this insight to the late Airo Akodhe, first my student and later a colleague at the University of Nairobi and Egerton University. In "The Concept of Fallibility in the Thought of Kwasi Wiredu" (1990), his thesis for the M.A. degree in philosophy which I supervised, Mr. Akodhe interprets Wiredu's views on knowledge in a historical perspective as constituting a fallibilist thesis and argues that this is either coincidentally akin to or derived from Popper's fallibilism.

15. Kwasi Wiredu, *Philosophy and an African Culture* (Cambridge, UK: Cambridge University Press, 1980), pp. 1–25.

16. Kwasi Wiredu and Kwame Gyekye, eds., *Person and Community: Ghanaian Philosophical Studies, 1* (Washington, DC: Council for Research in Values and Philosophy, 1992).

17. Karl R. Popper, *Conjectures and Refutations: The Growth of Scientific Knowledge* (5th ed. revised) (London: Routledge, 1989), p. 122.

18. *Collected Papers of Charles Sanders Peirce,* C. Hartshorne and P. Weiss, eds. (Cambridge, MA: Harvard University Press, 1934), pp. 569, 396–97.

19. Frederick Copleston, *A History of Philosophy,* vol. VIII (New York: Image Books, Doubleday), p. 306.

20. Giovanna Borradori, *The American Philosopher* (Chicago: University of Chicago Press, 1994); Karl. R. Popper, "Prediction and Prophecy in Social Sciences," in Patrick Gardiner, ed., *Theories of History* (New York: Free Press, 1959), pp. 285–86.

21. Popper, "Prediction and Prophecy," p. 283.

22. Karl. R. Popper, *The Myth of the Framework: In Defense of Science and Rationality* (London: Routledge, 1994), p. 69.

23. Karl R. Popper, *The Myth of the Framework,* p. 142.

24. I. C. Jarvie, "Gellner's Positivism," in Hall and Jarvie, eds., *Transition to Modernity,* p. 255.

25. Karl. R. Popper, *The Myth of the Framework;* Kwasi Wiredu, *Philosophy and an African Culture.*

26. Karl R. Popper, *Conjectures and Refutations,* p. 22.

Chapter 7

This paper is greatly indebted to previous joint work and consultations with the late Omari H. Kokole from Uganda, who died in 1996. This paper is dedicated to his memory.

1. Indeed, the ethnoreligious wars in the Balkans, racial unrest in the United States and Europe, and religious and ethnic conflict in Africa and South Asia are testimony to the enduring nature of primordial cultural allegiances. On cultural factors' role in world politics, see, for instance, Morris Dickstein, "After the Cold War: Culture as Politics, Politics as Culture," *Social Research* 60 (Fall 1993), pp. 531–44; Kay B. Warren, ed., *The Violence Within: Cultural and Political Opposition in Divided Nations* (Boulder, CO: Westview Press, 1993); Ali A. Mazrui, *Cultural Forces in World Politics* (London and Portsmouth, NH: J. Currey and Heinemann, 1990); and Emile Sahliye, ed., *Religious Resurgence and Politics in the Contemporary* World (Albany, NY: SUNY Press, 1990).

2. Ancestor worship is practiced in several different parts of the world—from Asia to South and Central America—not just in Africa; consult, for instance, Kris Jeter, "Ancestor Worship as an Intergenerational Linkage in Perpetuity," *Marriage & Family Review* 16:1–2 (1991), pp. 195–217, for a cross-cultural study of ancestor worship.

3. See Kofi A. Busia, *The Position of the Chief in the Modern Political System of Ashanti: A Study of the Influence of Contemporary Social Changes on Ashanti Political Institutions* (London: Frank Cass & Co. Ltd., 1968); and Jomo Kenyatta, *Facing Mount Kenya: The Tribal Life of the Kikuyu* (London: Books, 1938). See also Josiah Mwangi Kariuki, *"Mau Mau" Detainee* (Oxford: Oxford University Press, 1963).

4. Conservatism's meaning, like all ideologies, appears to be different across time and space; consult, for instance, Brian Girvin, ed., *The Transformation of Contemporary Conservatism* (London and Newbury Park, CA: Sage, 1988)—although it is confined to Europe and North American conservatism—and Roger Scruton, *The Meaning of Conservatism,* 2nd ed. (London: Macmillan, 1984).

5. Consult, for Burkean views on the American Revolution, Edmund Burke, *Speeches on the American War, and Letter to the Sheriffs of Bristol* (Boston: Gregg Press, 1972 [c. 1891]).

6. On this kind of governance in Africa, consult A. E. Afigbo, *The Warrant Chiefs: Indirect Rule in Southeastern Nigeria, 1891–1929* (London: Longman, 1972); H. F. Morris, *Indirect Rule and the Search for Justice: Essays in East African Legal History* (Oxford: Clarendon Press, 1972); and Ntieyong Akpan, *Epitaph to Indirect Rule: A Discourse on Local Government in Africa* (London: Cass, 1967).

7. See David Harrison, *The White Tribe of Africa: South Africa in Perspective* (Berkeley and Los Angeles: University of California Press, 1981), esp. pp. 84–102.

8. See, for instance, Randall Collins, "Liberals and Conservatives, Religious and Political: A Conjuncture of Modern History," *Sociology of Religion* 54 (Summer 1993), pp. 127–46.

9. See John Middleton, *Lugbara Religion* (London: Oxford University Press, 1969).

10. John S. Mbiti, *African Religions and Philosophy* (New York and London: Doubleday and Heinemann, 1970).

11. For a collection of essays on Awolowo, see Olosope O. Oyelaran, ed., *Obafemi Awolowo: The End of an Era?* (Ile-Ife, Nigeria: Obafemi Awolowo University Press Ltd., 1988).

12. For a biography of Odinga, see the series of interviews between him and H. Odera Oruka in H. Odera Oruka, *Oginga Odinga: His Philosophy and Beliefs* (Nairobi: Initiative Publishers, 1992).

13. On the influence of ethnicity on modern African politics, see, for instance, Henry Bienen, Nicolas Van de Walle, and John Londregan, "Ethnicity and Leadership Succession in Africa," *International Studies Quarterly* 39 (March 1995), pp. 1–25; Julius O. Ihonvbere, "The 'Irrelevant' State, Ethnicity, and the Quest for Nationhood in Africa," *Ethnic and Racial Studies* 17 (January 1994), pp. 42–60; and Kenneth Ingham, *Politics in Modern Africa: The Uneven Tribal Dimension* (London and New York: Routledge, 1990).

14. For one report on an instance of conservatism in African politics, see Athumani J. Liviga and Jan Kees van Donge, "The 1985 Tanzanian Parliamentary Elections: A Conservative Election," *African Affairs* 88 (January 1989), pp. 47–62.

15. See, for example, Kwasi Wiredu, *Philosophy and an African Culture* (Cambridge, London, New York, et al: Cambridge University Press, 1980) pp. 8, 24.

16. For a cross-cultural analysis of the links between age and leadership, consult Angus McIntyre, ed., *Aging and Political Leadership* (Albany, NY: SUNY Press, 1988); for a specific study see Paul Spencer, *The Samburu: A Study of Gerontocracy in a Nomadic Tribe* (Berkeley, CA: University of California Press, 1965).

17. For this brief definition we are indebted to the *Dictionary of Anthropology,* ed. Charles Winick (Totavia, NJ: Littlefield, Adams and Co., 1966), p. 230.

18. For one of the rare English-language works on Bourguiba, consult Norma Salem, *Habib Bourguiba, Islam and the Creation of Tunisia* (London & Dover, NH: C. Croom Helm, 1984).

19. This formulation is often attributed to Julius K. Nyerere.

20. Consult, on the warrior tradition, Ali A. Mazrui, "The Warrior Tradition and the Masculinity of War," *Journal of Asian and African Studies* 12:1–4 (Jan.–Oct. 1977), pp. 69–81; and Ali A. Mazrui ed., *The Warrior Tradition in Modern Africa* (The Hague and Leiden, Netherlands: E. J. Brill, 1978).

21. For those who are interested in reading more about Uganda under Idi Amin, a useful guide may be Martin Jamison, *Idi Amin and Uganda: An Annotated Bibliography* (Westport, CT: Greenwood Press, 1992); for an early treatment, see James H. Mittelan, *Ideology and Politics in Uganda: From Obote to Amin* (Ithaca, NY: Cornell University Press, 1975).

22. One of the foremost experts on China and Mao is the Australian Ross Terrill; for an accessible account of the "Great Helmsman," see Terrill, *Mao: A Biography* (New York: Harper & Row, 1980).

23. See the periodical published by the Eastern African Centre for Research on Oral Traditions and African National Languages and the International Fund for the Promotion

24. For a recent biography of Nasser, consult Peter Woodward (London and New York: Longman, 1992); generally, on Nasser and Egypt, see P. J. Vatikiotis, *Nasser and His Generation* (New York: St. Martin's Press, 1978); and R. Hrair Dekmejian, *Egypt Under Nasir: A Study in Political Dynamics* (Albany, NY: SUNY Press, 1971).

25. Consult, on this subject, James S. Coleman, *Political Parties and National Integration in Tropical Africa* (Berkeley, CA: University of California Press, 1964).

26. Information on these parties in Tanzania, and other political parties in Africa, may be obtained from Roger East and Tanya Joseph, eds., *Political Parties of Africa and the Middle East: A Reference Guide* (Harlow, UK, and Detroit, MI: Longman and Gale Research, 1993).

27. On the spread of corruption, see, for instance, Robert Williams, *Political Corruption in Africa* (Aldershot, UK, and Brookfield, VT: Gower Pub., 1987).

28. His Excellency, Al-Hajj, Dr. Field Marshal Idi Amin Dada, VC, DSO, MC, and Conqueror of the British Empire.

29. For an earlier treatment of this royal theme, consult Ali A. Mazrui, "The Monarchical Tendency in African Political Culture," *British Journal of Sociology* vol. XVIII, no. 3, (Sept. 1967). Reprinted as chapter 10 in Mazrui, *Violence and Thought: Essays on Social Tensions in Africa* (London and Harlow: Longmans, 1969), pp. 206–30.

30. These frequently quoted remarks were made in a broadcast on British television in 1968. They were part of the first lecture in a series on *The Rise of Christian Europe* by Sir High Trevor-Roper reprinted in *The Listener* (London), November 28, 1968, p. 811.

31. See Guy Martin, "Francophone Africa in the Context of Franco-American Relations," in John W. Harbeson and Donald Rothchild, eds. *Africa in World Politics: Post–Cold War Challenges* (Boulder, CO, and Oxford: Westview Press, 1995), pp. 163–88.

32. Some of the earlier discussions of nationalism as a theoretical concept may be found in Louis Leo Snyder, *The Meaning of Nationalism* (New York: Greenwood Press, 1968), and Hans Kohn, *Nationalism, Its Meaning and History* (Princeton, NJ: Van Nostrand, 1965); for recent treatments, see, for instance, Ernest Gellner, *Encounters with Nationalism* (Oxford, UK, and Cambridge, MA: Blackwell, 1994); John Breuilly, *Nationalism and the State,* rev. ed. (Chicago: University of Chicago Press, 1994); Liah Greenfeld, *Nationalism: Five Roads to Modernity* (Cambridge, MA:

Harvard University Press, 1992); and Anthony H. Birch, *Nationalism and National Integration* (London and Boston: Unwin Hyman, 1989); and for a postmodern view, see Lewis D. Wurgraft, "Identity in World History: A Postmodern Perspective," *History and Theory* 34:2 (1995), pp. 67–85.

33. On these connections, see, for example, Colin H. Williams, *Called Unto Liberty! On Language and Nationalism* (Clevedon and Philadelphia: Multilingual Matters, 1994).

34. A recent historical treatment of Quebec's separatist movements is Guy Laforest, *Trudeau and the End of a Canadian Dream* (Montreal: McGill-Queen's University Press, 1995). In October 1995, the Quebec separatists were narrowly defeated in a referendum.

35. Relatedly, consult Mark Juergensmyer, *The New Cold War? Religious Nationalism Confronts the Secular State* (Berkeley, CA: University of California Press, 1993); and John Langan, "Notes on Moral Theology, 1994: Nationalism, Ethnic Conflict, and Religion," *Theological Studies* 56 (March 1995), pp. 122–36.

36. Consult Michael Barthrop, *War on the Nile: Britain, Egypt and the Sudan, 1882–1898* (Poole, UK: Blandford Press, 1984).

37. Belief in specially sanctified water is by no means peculiar to indigenous African religions. In Islam there is the Zam water of the well of Medina. In Christianity there is the holy water of Lourdes and the legacy of Saint Bernadette in France. This is quite apart from the Christian doctrine of sanctified or baptismal water at christening.

38. Readers interested in Pan-Africanism's history might find the following useful: P. O. Esedebe, *Pan-Africanism: The Idea and Movement, 1776-1991* (Washington, DC: Howard University Press, 1994); Imanuel Geiss, *The Pan-African Movement: A History of Pan-Africanism in America, Europe, and Africa* (New York: Africana Pub. Co., 1974); and Adekunle Ajala, *Pan-Africanism: Evolution, Progress, and Prospects* (New York: St. Martin's Press, 1973).

39. This inevitably has its effect on internal and external politics; see Tukumbi Lumumba-Kasongo, *Political Re-mapping of Africa: Transnational Ideology and the Redefinition of Africa in World Politics* (Lanham, MD: University Press of America, 1994), and *Nationalistic Ideologies: Their Policy Implications and the Struggle for Democracy in African Politics* (Lewiston, NY: E. Mellen Press, 1991).

40. The following may be consulted on the Mau Mau revolt: Wunyabari O. Maloba, *Mau Mau and Kenya: An Analysis of a Peasant Revolt* (Bloomington: Indiana University Press, 1993); Robert B. Edgerton, *Mau Mau: An African Crucible* (New York and London: Free Press and Collier Macmillan, 1989); and David Throup, *Economic & Social Origins of Mau Mau, 1945–53* (London and Athens, OH: J. Currey and Ohio University Press, 1987).

41. This has of course led to a lasting problem in modern African nations' political integration. Consult, for instance, Kenneth Ingham, *Politics in Africa: The Uneven Tribal Dimension* (London and New York: Routledge, 1990); Donald Rothchild and Victor A. Olorunsola, *State Versus Ethnic Claims: African Policy Dilemmas* (Boulder, CO: Westview Press, 1983); and John N. Paden, ed., *Values, Identities, and National Integration: Empirical Research in Africa* (Evanston, IL: Northwestern University Press, 1980).

42. Some alternatives to structural adjustment have been explored; see, for example, Kidane Mengisteab and B. Ikubolajeh Logan, *Beyond Economic Liberalization in Africa: Structural Adjustment and the Alternatives* (London; Atlantic Highlands, NJ, and Cape Town: Zed Books and Southern African Political Economic Series, 1995);

for a World Bank view on adjustment, see its *Adjustment in Africa: Reform, Results, and the Road Ahead* (Washington, DC: World Bank, 1994).

43. See Kwame Nkrumah, *Neo-Colonialism: The Last Stage of Imperialism* (London et al.: Heinemann, 1968).

44. See, for instance, Julius K. Nyerere, *Ujaama—Essays on Socialism* (Dar es Salaam, Tanzania: Oxford University Press, 1968); and L. S. Senghor, *On African Socialism*, trans. and introduced by Mercer Cook (New York: Praeger, 1964).

45. See for example, A. LeRoy Bennett, *International Organizations: Principles and Issues* (Englewood Cliffs, NJ: Prentice Hall, 1991), 5th ed.

46. See, for example, Naomi Chazan, et al., *Politics and Society in Contemporary Africa* (Boulder, CO: Lynne Rienner, 1988), esp. pp. 101–25.

47. See Kwame Nkrumah, *Ghana: The Autobiography of Kwame Nkrumah* (New York: International Publishers, 1957), p. 164.

Chapter 8

1. Basil Davidson, *The Black Man's Burden: Africa and the Curse of the Nation State* (London: James Currey, 1992), p. 247.

2. Ibid.

3. Theodore von Laue, *The World Revolution of Westernization* (New York: Oxford University Press, 1987), p. 6.

4. Ibid.

5. Ibid, p. 7.

6. Ibid.

7. On this matter of essences of nations and races, one has in mind certain views expressed by such writers as Lucien Levy-Bruhl; see, for example, his *Les Fonctions mentales dans les sociétés inférieures,* translated as *How Natives Think,* by L. A. Care (London, 1926). And on the positive valorizing side of the debate, see Léopold Sédar Senghor, especially his *On African Socialism* (London: Paul Mall Press, 1964), p. 74.

8. See John Rawls, *A Theory of Justice* (Cambridge, MA: Harvard University Press, 1971), ch. 3, section 22, pp. 126–30; Rawls bases his account of what he calls "the circumstance of justice" on David Hume's *A Treatise on Human Nature,* bk.111, pt. 11; also on Hume's *An Inquiry Concerning the Principles of Morals,* sec. 111, pt. 1, see also H-L-A. Hart, *The Concept of Law* (Oxford: Clarendon Press, 1961) pp. 189–95.

9. See in this regard Teodros Kiros, *Moral Philosophy and Development: The Human Condition in Africa* (Athens, OH: Ohio University Center for International Studies, Africa Monograph series no. 61, 1992), see ch. 2, pp. 38–88, and chs. 5–6, pp. 136–78.

10. See Irving L. Markovitz, *Power and Class in Africa* (Englewood Cliffs, NJ: Prentice Hall, 1977), p. 329.

Chapter 9

I am grateful to Kwame Anthony Appiah and Jane Mansbridge, Harvard University, for the discussions on the role of legitimacy in democratic philosophy as it relates to African states, new and old.

1. Most important to note is the fact that colonial activities were felt in many parts of Africa at different times depending on areas that immediately represented the colonialists' interests. Of course, colonialism was not a total system. The heavy physical presence of the colonialists was first felt in Nso circa 1906 when the Germans

with the aid of our Bamoum neighbors challenged Nso to a disastrous war. It is reasonable to view the German invasion of Nso as marking the beginning of the physical presence of the colonialists.

2. For more on values and norms, see Teodros Kiros, *Self-Construction and the Formation of Human Values* (Westport, CT: Greenwood Press, 1998), pp. 53–54.

3. By nonrationality, I mean aspects of our lives in which the dichotomy between rationality and irrationality are neither applicable nor useful, e.g., the love of one's parents and children.

4. The full citation reads: "Kaberry's 1945 notes placed the *faay Kibve* on the West of the *Shuufaay ntari*. It was here that the body of the dead Fon was washed, shaved, oiled and calmwooded by the *ayeewong*, wrapped in royal cloth supplied by *Ndzeendzev* and supplied with a new *ngwerong* cap. The dead body was carried head-first through the cleared forecourt to the *fem*, where a grave, marked out with a hoe by *Yeewong*, had been dug by *duy* and *won jemer fon*. It was carried in a sling of royal cloth by the seven *vibay vekpu*. The procession was led by *Taawong* striking the state double bell, followed by *Ndzeendzev* and by *Yeewong* carrying the bag of orange royal calmwood. Before the Fon's body was propped up on the grave-stool made by *vibay vekpu*, *Ndzeendzev* removes his cap, thus bringing his office to an end. When the body was seated held by camwood posts and hide thongs, when a creeper attached to his wrist is brought to the surface and the grave is about to be filled, *Taawong* addressed the Fon by name for the first and last time:

      Kpu Binglo', bey bo fon yo' lay; fon ban moo shuuy.

      Binglo' dies, but the Fon does not pass away; the Fon shines like the sun.
   The grave, a stepped shaft and chamber grave, is likened to the palace. The two steps leading down the chamber are, Mzeka tells us, alluded to as *Maandze nggay* and *taakibu'* respectively; the chamber, the line with raffia poles and royal cloth, and carpeted with leopard skins, as *faay kishiiy.*" B. Chem-Langhee, Verkijika G. FanNso, and E. M. Chilver, "Nto'Nso and Its Occupants," *Paideuma* 31 (1985) pp. 174–75.

5. The human worth posited above is different from Immanuel Kant's. His view on human equality was grounded on human potential for rationality. This should not surprise us given the obsession of philosophers with rationality at his time. The view of human worth posited here takes account of our ancestors and human with or without the potential for rationality.

      Liberals would do well to take heed of human dignity as the basis of morality, which I believe, provides for the ultimate justification of our equality. Abraham Lincoln, a great moralist, arguably went beyond the politics of human equality to free the slaves by appealing to our human dignity that lay at the penumbra of politics.

6. Chem-Langhee, FanNso, Chilver, op. cit. 5, p. 176.

7. Kwasi Wiredu, "Society and Democracy in Africa," *New Political Science*, 21:1 (1999), p. 34.

8. Kwame Anthony Appiah, *In My Father's House* (Oxford: Oxford University Press, 1992), p. 171.

9. For details, see Ifeanyi A. Menkiti, "Normative Instability and Political Disorder in Africa," *New Political Science* 21:1 (March 1999), pp. 73–87.

10. See, for example, William A. Galston, *Liberal Purposes* (Cambridge, UK: Cambridge University Press, 1991), p. 244.

11. "This figure evoked a proverb 'Funtumfunafu ne Denkyemfunafu baanu yafunu ye yafunkoro; naso woredidi a naworeko no, na firi atwimenemude ntira.' It means

roughly: Stomachs mixed up, crocodiles' stomachs mixed up, they both have one stomach but when they eat they fight because of the sweetness of the swallowing. The meaning of the proverb, which expresses one of the dilemmas of family life, is that while the acquisition of each family member benefits the whole family (there is only one stomach), the pleasure of enjoyment is an individual thing (the food has to get into the stomach through one of the mouths)." K. Anthony Appiah, *New York Review of Books*, vol. XLIV, no. 7 (April 24, 1997) p. 46.

12. The whole citation reads thus:
"Now, this adherence to the principle of consensus was a premeditated option. It was based on the belief that ultimately the interests of all members of society are the same, although their immediate perception of those interests may be different. This thought is given expression in an art motif depicting a crocodile with stomach and two heads locked in struggle over food. If they could but see that the food is, in any case, destined for the same stomach, the irrationality of the conflict would be manifest to each. But could such a perception arise? The Ashanti answer is, 'Yes, human beings have the ability eventually to cut through their differences to the rock bottom identity of interests.'" "Democracy and Consensus in African Traditional Society," *The African Philosophy Reader,* ed. P. H. Coetzee and A. P. Roux (London: Routledge, 1998), p. 377.

13. For details, see especially Jane J. Mansbridge, *Beyond Adversary Democracy* (Chicago: University of Chicago Press, 1980).

14. Kwasi Wiredu, "Democracy and Consensus in African Traditional Politics."

15. John Stuart Mill, *Utilitarianism, Liberty and Representative Government* (London: Everyman's Library, 1910), 180–81.

16. I benefited from an original description by Goheen Miriam, *Men Own the Fields and Women Own the Crops* (Madison: University of Wisconsin Press, 1998), chap. 2.

17. Phyllis M. Kaberry, "Traditional Politics in Nso," *Africa* 29:4 (1959), p. 372.

18. The citation continue: "Failure to attend the palace without adequate excuse, the bringing of private dispute into *takibu* [a literally public space where matters of public concern were discussed], refusal to drink the wine of the Fon in the company of others—all signify disregard for the affairs of the country and a disrespect for the people of Nsaw [Nso] who are symbolized in the person of the Fon himself." Phyllis M. Kaberry, "Traditional Politics in Nso," *Africa* 29:4 (1959), p. 371.

19. The phenomenon of ancestors in Africa is a very important one. It can be universalized. Each and every one of us has ancestors. Appealing to ancestors can enlarge our political obligations not only to the present generation but also to the future. Saving for the future could be justified by the institution of ancestors. Thomas Jefferson thought that the social contract was binding only to the actual contractors, not the future generations. John Adams insisted that "the earth belongs in usufruct to the living; 'that the dead has neither powers nor rights over it.'" Recently, this sort of belief haunted Americans in an attempt to justify morally the preservation of the environment for future generation beyond their foreseeable children, grand- and great-grandchildren. Confronted by this challenge, Amy Gutmann and Dennis Thompson argued: "Bestowing public honors and in other ways giving more recognition to citizens and public officials whose actions shows exceptional concern for future generations could shift the perspective of public debate in a small but significant ways. Exploiting the 'love of fame after death'—a motive that even Hobbes thought influenced political leaders—could extend the temporal horizons of the

democratic process." Amy Gutmann and Dennis Thompson, *Democracy and Disagreement* (Cambridge, MA: Harvard University Press, 1996), p. 162.

20. Kaberry, op. cit., p. 373.
21. I have benefited from Phyllis Kaberry's earlier descriptions of Nso government. Kaberry, op. cit.
22. Kaberry, op. cit., p. 373.
23. Goheen Miriam, op. cit., p. 33.
24. Chem-Langhee, Fanso, Chilver, op. cit., p. 167.
25. For details on social capital, see Glenn Loury, "A Dynamic Theory of Racial Income Differences," in *Women, Minorities, and Employment Discrimination*, ed. P. A. Wallace and A. M. La Mond (Lexington, MA: Health), pp. 153–86. Alejandro Portes, "Social Capital: Its Origin and Application in Modern Sociology," *Ann. Rev. Sociol.* 24 (1988), pp. 1-24.
26. Bongasu Tanla Kishani, "Philosophical Trends as a Cultural Wealth among the Nso of Cameroon," École Normal Supérieure, Université de Yaoundé, ENS Yaoundé, Série Lettre et Sciences Humaine, 1998, p. 152. The whole citation reads: "Nso as a federating polity seems to confirm that NgonNso ambition was to found a polity based on pluralism." Kishani, p. 152.
27. E. M. Chilver and P. M. Kaberry, *Traditional Bamenda: The Pre-colonial History and Ethnography of the Bamenda Grassfields* (Buea Government Printers, 1967) pp. 97 and 99.
28. Kishani, op. cit., p. 156.
29. Kaberry, op. cit., p. 373.
30. Kaberry, op. cit., p. 373, my emphasis.
31. The full report reads:
    "Some 30 North West Fons (traditional monarchs) have been fined by their 'kwifons' (traditional secret societies) for attending the burial of Dr. John Ngu Foncha on April 24th [1999] contrary to their tradition.

    According to a spokesman for the Kwifons' [a'Nwerong], the Fons [a'Fon] led by [Fon] John Abumbi II of Bafut and S.A.N Agwafor of Mankon, were against tradition which forbids them from attending funeral ceremonies and seeing corpses and as such will pay 30 goats, two cows, 50 bags of salt, 20 tins of oil, 100 fowls and undergo traditional cleansing.

    The spokesman said they were shocked when they heard an announcement repeatedly broadcast over Radio Bamenda, calling on the Fons to 'massively attend the state burial of our illustrious son and father of reunification, Dr. John Ngu Foncha' and signed by Fon Abumbi, President of the North West Fons' Union (NOWEFU).

    In reaction to the accusations, Fon Abumbi is reported to have pleaded for leniency arguing that 'we have neither seen the coffin nor have we passed by the burial ground. So we plead to our kwifons to be lenient on the fine imposed on us. We shall be cleansed as said by our kwifons'.

    According to Fon Abumbi II, they were forced into the situation by the fact that Dr. Foncha created the Southern Cameroon House of Chiefs and therefore deserved their presence and also because the various traditional delegations from all over the country expressed their wish to meet with them while in Bamenda."

    Isaha'a Boh, "North West Fons to Pay Fine for Attending Dr. Foncha's Funeral." *Cameroon-Bulletin* 469, Monday, April 26, 1999.

32. The report continues:
"Speaking to the [Nso] Voice [newspaper], TavNwerong—Shey woo Sar Wai, revealed that after his [Mathias] conviction and exile, Mathias immediately contacted Mforme Gham and his butcher colleague, Shey William Bafut for help. Being one of their strongest customer, they assured him that they will do what is humanly possible to reverse the decision. Mathias, Shey went on, was then asked to wait while Mforme makes the necessary connections with the palace. However, the Fon whom they have wish to contact was not in seat. It therefore entailed consulting the elaborate palace hierarchy. While this went on, the eviction automation expired and Nwerong was accordingly informed. Investigation and intelligence immediately went to work resulting in Mathias being discovered at Mforme's residence one morning, two months after being served. [M]forme at such betrayal from one of her pillars, Nwerong consequently slammed a ten-year suspension on Mforme Gham. He now steps down from one of the most prestigious posts in Nso hierarchy, leaving only Mforme Bah to assume absolute control for the meantime. He is banned from the Nwerong circles and from entering any 'Nfu' or 'Manjong' house in Nso. Shey William Bafut is equally banned from all Nwerong activities. Meanwhile Shey Saghen Peter is expected to be sanctioned for having knowledge but refusing to disclose the deal. As a man of title he acted simple mindedly. While Mathias actually left on November 15, heads has continued to roll as Mforme Gham's supporters are being singled out and dealt with accordingly.
    When approached by the [Nso] Voice, Mforme Gham preferred to remain silent.
    Mforme Gham is not however the first high ranking Ruler to be punitively disciplined since the accession of HRH [His Royal Highness] Fon Sehm Mbinglo I. Some high ranking traditional rulers have as a result of misconduct been severely sanctioned. As Nwerong fights hard to enhance its image—the take over of the Royal Farm of Shisong [by the Catholic Reverence Sisters] let us watch out for the next head to fall." *Nso Voice* 002, Monday, November 23, 1998.
33 . The full report reads:
"Nwerong Announces Regain of Nso Fon's Farm From Catholic
The long silent march that took a number of sub-chiefs toeing the line, some 12 Secret Police Forces and a plethora of the local population from the Nso Palace through the Squares and round the Mbve market on Oct. 26th, a market day, was one of the rare kind, quite unprecedented and albeit mysterious.
    The population quivered in fear of the unknown as the judicial body staged its walk through the town. At Mbve, some market women packed [their] bag[s] and baggage and were already poised to flee, but when it became clear that the march was a 'Peaceful' one, all surged towards the park to hear the new decree.
    Addressing the mammoth crowd that formed a large circle under a sacred tree in Mbve, Shey Wo Bamfem, one of the sub-Chiefs, speaking on behalf of Nwerong Society, declared to the population that the Fon's vast farm land in Shisong, once sold to the Reverend Sisters by the Late Fon, Ngah Bifon II, had been unconditionally taken back.
    The Nwerong Society noted that both the Fon and the Reverend were wrong to carry such transactions for it said, it is not embedded in the tradition of a people that land be sold out 'by the tribe.' The Fon is the people and the people the Fon, Nwerong ruled, 'anything done between the two is done in the name of the tribe and the protection of posterity.'

Reference was made to other pieces of land today hosting the Banso Baptist Hospital, the Catholic Church and the Shisong General Hospital that were given out by the Nso people, and no amount of money was paid by those very occupants in return. To talk of selling just one out of many pieces of land, it was decreed, is not routine.

The population was told that attempts has been made three times to dialogue with the Reverends and get back that piece of land without any use of force, but the later had been uncompromising.

Following the deadlock, Nwerong, the previous night resorted to traditional order maintaining that 'there is never one earth with two heavens.' It has decreed that it is the supreme administrator of Nso land and that no other authority is to infringe on its rules.

That very night a strong delegation headed by Nwerong groped to said piece of land at Shisong and traditionally fortified it. Growing crops especially beans were destroyed, a demonstration that showed confiscation and banning any other activity in the area.

All men and women have been called upon to be ready to answer the call to work on the Fon's farm whenever it is warranted.

Other issues were also addressed during the phenomenal outing. Nwerong vehemently warned that it was aware of the coming back of one Mr. Mathias who was exiled recently from Nso land due to business malpractices. 'Anyone, who shall be bold enough to host him this night will have Nwerong visiting him, and with very damaging repercussions' it warned.

Nwerong again spoke bitterly about the wanton selling of food items especially corn and beans by Nso women. It regretted that it was not the first time it was prophesying imminent hunger in the community in the nearest future, maintaining that a word to the wise is enough.

It also spoke detestably about the increasing high death tolls which plagued young people especially. It said the cross was all theirs to bear, warning them to stop pointing accusing fingers at the innocent parents but desist from the renewed atrocities of the time to save the lives and bring peace to their families and the society in question.

Nonetheless, the current surge of what was referred to, as 'quack doctors' was not left in the lurch. Nwerong called on those people to stop misleading the public and creating unnecessary divisive situations. 'No one can claim ability to diagnose all the illness of the world,' it said, 'do just that which is at your realm and stop poisoning people's morality by pointing accusing fingers at their uncles, grandfathers. . . .'

As Nwerong reiterated these points; it warned against rumor mongering which it said had seriously depraved the society. 'Say it as you heard here, don't add or subtract any substance,' it cautioned. The secret police force threatened that anyone who misrepresented facts and mislead the population, would pay dearly for the act.

As of press time, Nwerong has made public another decree suspending Nformi Gham and others from their sacred duties. The full story in subsequent issue of N. V. [*Nso Voice*]." *Nso Voice,* 001, Monday, November 5, 1998.
34. Kaberry, op. cit., p. 373.
35. Chilver and Kaberry, op. cit., p. 23.
36 Kishani, op. cit., p. 154.

37. The citation continues: "In fact, by this means, not only was political philosophical conceptualization well-advanced among the Nso, but also old and new political philosophies were evaluated, and *'news and calls for public work were transmitted within the capital* [Kimbo] *and from the capital to the village,* italics in original,' " Kishani, op. cit., p. 158.
38. Miriam, op. cit., p. 29.

K. Anthony Appiah is a Professor of Afro-American Studies and Philosophy at Harvard University. His many books include *Assertion and Conditionals, For Truth in Semantics, Necessary Questions,* and *In My Father's House.* Appiah's scholarly interests range from African and African-American intellectual history and literary studies to ethics and the philosophy of mind and language; he has also taught regularly on philosophical problems in the study of African traditional religions. He has been chairman of the Joint Committee of African Studies of the Social Science Research Council and the American Council of Learned Societies, and president of the Society for African Philosophy in North America. He is an editor of *Transition* magazine.

George Katsiaficas is a Professor of Humanities and Social Sciences at Wentworth Institute of Technology in Boston. Among his books are *The Imagination of the New Left: A Global Analysis of 1968* and *The Subversion of Politics: European Autonomous Social Movements and the Decolonization of Everyday Life* (winner of the 1998 Michael Harrington Book Award). Together with Kathleen Cleaver, he has edited the forthcoming book *Liberation, Imagination and the Black Panther Party.* He is editor of *New Political Science* and is currently researching Korean social movements since World War II.

Teodros Kiros is an Assistant Professor of Philosophy at Emerson College, and an Associate-in-Residence in the department of Afro-American studies, Harvard University. He is the author of *Toward the Construction of a Theory of Political Action* (1985), *Moral Philosophy and Development: The Human Condition in Africa* (1992), and *Self-Construction and the Formation of Human Values* (winner of the 1999 Michael Harrington Book Award). He is coeditor of *The Promise of Multiculturalism* (1998). His articles have appeared in numerous journals, including the *Journal of Social Philosophy* and *Quest.* He is associate editor of *New Political Science.*

D. A. Masolo teaches philosophy at the University of Louisville in Louisville, Kentucky. He is a well-known African philosopher. His publications include *Africa in Search of Identity.*

K. Anthony Appiah is a Professor of Afro-American Studies and Philosophy at Harvard University. His many books include *Assertion and Conditionals, For Truth in Semantics, Necessary Questions,* and *In My Father's House.* Appiah's scholarly interests range from African and African-American intellectual history and literary studies to ethics and the philosophy of mind and language; he has also taught regularly on philosophical problems in the study of African traditional religions. He has been chairman of the Joint Committee of African Studies of the Social Science Research Council and the American Council of Learned Societies, and president of the Society for African Philosophy in North America. He is an editor of *Transition* magazine.

George Katsiaficas is a Professor of Humanities and Social Sciences at Wentworth Institute of Technology in Boston. Among his books are *The Imagination of the New Left: A Global Analysis of 1968* and *The Subversion of Politics: European Autonomous Social Movements and the Decolonization of Everyday Life* (winner of the 1998 Michael Harrington Book Award). Together with Kathleen Cleaver, he has edited the forthcoming book *Liberation, Imagination and the Black Panther Party.* He is editor of *New Political Science* and is currently researching Korean social movements since World War II.

Teodros Kiros is an Assistant Professor of Philosophy at Emerson College, and an Associate-in-Residence in the department of Afro-American studies, Harvard University. He is the author of *Toward the Construction of a Theory of Political Action* (1985), *Moral Philosophy and Development: The Human Condition in Africa* (1992), and *Self-Construction and the Formation of Human Values* (winner of the 1999 Michael Harrington Book Award). He is coeditor of *The Promise of Multiculturalism* (1998). His articles have appeared in numerous journals, including the *Journal of Social Philosophy* and *Quest.* He is associate editor of *New Political Science.*

D. A. Masolo teaches philosophy at the University of Louisville in Louisville, Kentucky. He is a well-known African philosopher. His publications include *Africa in Search of Identity.*